PENGUIN BOOKS

ON THE PSYCHOLOGY OF MEDITATION

Claudio Naranjo was born in Valparaiso, Chile, in 1932. He studied at the University of Chile Medical School and at the National Conservatory of Music and, after winning a Fulbright Scholarship, at Harvard and at the University of Illinois. He was Professor of the Psychology of Art at Catholic University in Chile and research psychiatrist at the University of Chile Medical School until 1966, when he went to the University of California at Berkeley as a Guggenheim Fellow. Dr. Naranjo is also the author of *The One Quest*, as well as of monographs in experimental psychology published in Chile and of an Esalen monograph entitled *I and Thou, Here and Now*.

Robert E. Ornstein is a graduate of Queens College of the City University of New York and of Stanford University. He now teaches at the University of California Medical Center in San Francisco and is a research psychologist at The Langley-Porter Neuropsychiatric Institute. In 1969 he received the American Institutes of Research Creative Talent Award. Professor Ornstein is also the author of *The Psychology of Consciousness*, *On the Experience of Time*, and *The Mind Field* and editor of *The Nature of Human Consciousness* and *Common Knowledge*.

ESALEN BOOKS

*Available in paperback.

AN ESALEN BOOK

On the Psychology
of Meditation

CLAUDIO NARANJO
AND
ROBERT E. ORNSTEIN

PENGUIN BOOKS

Penguin Books Ltd, Harmondsworth, Middlesex, England
Penguin Books, 625 Madison Avenue, New York, New York 10022, U.S.A.
Penguin Books Australia Ltd, Ringwood, Victoria, Australia
Penguin Books Canada Ltd, 2801 John Street, Markham, Ontario, Canada L3R 1B4
Penguin Books (N.Z.) Ltd, 182–190 Wairau Road, Auckland 10, New Zealand

First published in the United States of America by The Viking Press 1971
Viking Compass Edition published 1972
Reprinted 1972, 1973 (three times), 1974, 1976
Published in Penguin Books 1976
Reprinted 1977

LIBRARY OF CONGRESS CATALOGING IN PUBLICATION DATA
Naranjo, Claudio.
On the psychology of meditation.
Bibliography: p.
1. Meditation—Psychology. I. Ornstein, Robert Evans, joint author.
II. Title.
[BL627.N37 1976]   291.4'3   76–149270
ISBN 0 14 00.4420 5

Printed in the United States of America by
Offset Paperback Mfrs., Inc., Dallas, Pennsylvania
Set in Linotype Janson

ACKNOWLEDGMENTS
Grove Press, Inc., Walpola Rahula, and Gordon Fraser Gallery: From *What the Buddha Taught*. Copyright © 1959 by W. Rahula. Reprinted by permission.

Harper & Row, Publishers: From *The Doors of Perception* and *Heaven and Hell* by Aldous Huxley. Reprinted by permission.

Hoopoe Ltd: From O. M. Burke: in R. W. Davidson (editor), *Documents on Contemporary Dervish Communities*, London, 1967.

Maclen Music, Inc., and Northern Songs Ltd: From *Tomorrow Never Knows*. Copyright © 1966 Northern Songs Ltd. All rights reserved. Used by permission.

Princeton University Press: From *Shamanism: Archaic Techniques of Ecstasy*, by Mircea Eliade, translated by Willard R. Trask, Bollingen Series LXXVI (copyright © 1964 by Princeton University Press): pp. 38–42. Reprinted by permission.

Princeton University Press and Routledge and Kegan Paul: From *Papers from the Eranos Yearbooks*, edited by Joseph Campbell, Bollingen Series XXX, Vol. 4, *Spiritual Disciplines* (copyright © 1960 by Princeton University Press): in Heinrich Zimmer, "On the Significance of the Indian Tantric Yoga." Reprinted by permission.

John Weatherill, Inc.: From *The Three Pillars of Zen, Teaching, Practice & Enlightenment*, edited by Philip Kapleau.

CONTENTS

PART I

Meditation: Its Spirit and Techniques

CLAUDIO NARANJO

PART II

*The Techniques of Meditation and
Their Implications for Modern Psychology*

ROBERT E. ORNSTEIN

PART I

Meditation: Its Spirit and Techniques

CLAUDIO NARANJO

Introduction

The time when East and West meet, our time, is one of meeting between religions, philosophies, and psychological schools that had hitherto ignored one another or looked upon one another with fanatical disdain. Furthermore, it is a time of meeting between science and religion, psychotherapy and education, a time when we envision the rise of the discipline of integral growth.

Increased ease in communication and cultural openness coincide with awakening of spiritual thirst. Perhaps because of dissatisfaction with and detachment from cultural forms that answered to man's yearning in the past, perhaps because of a measure of disappointment in the ultimate fruits of scientific and technological progress, an increasing number of people are becoming concerned with the question of personal development. An age of self-satisfaction is over, and we have entered an age of seeking.

In our search we look for new answers, but we also turn a respectful gaze to the wisdom of the remote past and to the wisdom of the East that we once thought obsolete and superseded. The extent of generalized interest in the spiritual traditions of Asia may be appreciated in the numerous books in the field that are published month after month, and in the establishment in Europe and in America of Eastern schools—Lamaist monasteries, Zendos, yogi ashramas, Sufi circles.

One particular and concrete instance of the newly awakened search is the rediscovery of meditation. According to an estimate of 1968, more than two thousand students were involved in meditation on the Berkeley campus alone, at the University of California. Numerous seminars or courses in meditation are being offered in the main cultural centers of the United States, mostly by yogis and Zen or Ch'an masters, and by persons like myself who are attempting to pour old wine in new bottles.

In spite of the wealth of information now available to the interested individual, one thing is lacking: a spirit of synthesis. The would-be meditator reads or hears about Zen meditation, about Christian meditation, about yogic practices, and feels that at some level all these are interrelated; but he cannot articulate what it is that these ways have in common, and he may be perplexed or disoriented by the discrepancies. Each way or tradition often claims to be the true one or the most effective. Even the worthiest representatives of a particular school do not generally go beyond a tolerant regard for other schools; they are too steeped in their own traditions to grasp the common root of all systems. Therefore, in this book I have pursued a threefold goal:

1. To explore the unity of spirit or attitude in the multiplicity of ways of meditation—*i.e.*, what meditation is *beyond* its forms.

2. To attempt a general classification of meditation techniques, not in terms of their cultural origin but in terms of their psychological nature.

3. To underline the nature of the psychological processes involved in meditation—processes that constitute the essence and goal of the practice and yet are not evident from the descriptions of the techniques.

The process of trying to understand the common denominator of meditation beyond seemingly different techniques results, I think, in the realization that meditation itself is not something separate or even different from other things. Perhaps this happens with every great idea: once we delve into its substance, we find that it is but one more name of a unity of which it is but one aspect or name. My own exploration of meditation shows me that the essence of meditation is also the essence of art, the essence of religion, the essence of true magic, the essence of psychotherapy, the essence of doing anything in the right attitude. I believe that to a meditator with the right understanding all life is meditation, and meditation is living.

I have not attempted to show in detail the relationships between meditation and other relevant practices, such as movement disciplines[1]* or some forms of psychotherapy,[2] but have indicated enough of the connections between the different ways of meditation and other activities to show that there is a common psychological ground in such seemingly disparate cultural manifestations as shamanism, the rise of moral injunctions, artistic vocation, prophecy, ritual—and meditation. Many fingers pointing at the same target from different directions will designate their object better than one or two.

My essay responds to the general title of the book, *On The Psychology of Meditation*, in the broad sense that it shows some psychological processes (such as "attending" or "letting go") that lie at the heart of the various techniques of meditation. Dr. Ornstein's essay deals with the psychology of meditation in a more specific sense: it brings together information stemming from contemporary psychology that is relevant to the understanding of these processes. Because of this, both essays may be considered as a unit. Dr. Ornstein's begins where mine ends: I am extracting psychological common denominators from a multiplicity of techniques; he is speaking of what experimental psychology has to say of such common denominators as attention, concentration, openness, repetition. In addition to this, he summarizes the information available to date on the matter of voluntary control of brain waves, an application of physiological feedback that appears, up to a point, to mimic meditation.

* Numbered reference notes begin on page 235.

1 / The Domain of Meditation

The word "meditation" has been used to designate a variety of practices that differ enough from one another so that we may find trouble in defining what *meditation* is.

Is there a commonality among the diverse disciplines alluded to by this same word? Something that makes them only different forms of a common endeavor? Or are these various practices only superficially related by their being individual spiritual exercises? The latter, apparently, is the point of view of those who have chosen to equate meditation with only a certain type of practice, ignoring all the others that do not fit their description or definition. It is thus that in the Christian tradition meditation is most often understood as a dwelling upon certain *ideas*, or engaging in a directed intellectual course of activity; while some of those who are more familiar with Eastern methods of meditation equate the matter with a dwelling on anything *but* ideas, and with the attainment of an aconceptual state of mind that excludes intellectual activity. Richard of St. Victor, the influential theorist of meditation of the Christian Middle Ages, drew a distinction between meditation and contemplation according to purposefulness and the part played by reason:

Meditation with great mental industry plods along the steep and laborious road keeping the end in view. Contemplation on a free wing circles around with great nimbleness wherever the impulse takes it. . . . Meditation investigates, contemplation wonders.[1]

Other authors distinguish concentration from meditation, regarding the former as a mere drill for the latter. An interesting case of restriction of the term appears in Kapleau's *The Three Pillars of Zen*.[2] He insists that Za-Zen is not to be confused with meditation. This is a paradoxical proposition, since the very word *zen*, from the Chinese *ch'an*, ultimately derives from the concept of dhyana, meditation. Zen Buddhism is, therefore, meditation Buddhism in a real and practical sense. Yet the distinction is understandable in view of the apparent diversity of forms that meditation has taken, even within Buddhism.

The distinction between ideational versus non-ideational is only one of the many contrasting interpretations of the practices called meditation. Thus, while certain techniques (like those in the Tibetan Tantra) emphasize mental images, others discourage paying attention to any imagery; some involve sense organs and use visual forms (mandalas) or music, and others emphasize a complete withdrawal from the senses; some call for complete inaction, and others involve action (mantra), gestures (mudra), walking, or other activities. Again, some forms of meditation require the summoning up of specific feeling states, while others encourage an indifference beyond the identification with any particular illusion.

The very diversity of practices given the name of "meditation" by the followers of this or that particular approach is an invitation to search for the answer of what meditation is *beyond its forms*. And if we are not content just to trace the boundaries of a particular group of related techniques, but instead search for a unity within the diversity, we may indeed recognize such a unity in an *attitude*. We may find that, *regardless of the medium* in which meditation is carried out—whether images, physical experiences, verbal utterances, etc.—the task of the meditator is essentially the same, as if the many forms of practice were nothing more than different occasions for the same basic exercise.

If we take this step beyond a behavioral definition of meditation in terms of a *procedure*, external or even internal, we may be able to see that meditation cannot be equated with thinking or non-thinking, with sitting still or dancing, with withdrawing from the senses or waking up the senses: meditation is concerned with the development of a *presence*, a modality of being, which may be expressed or developed in whatever situation the individual may be involved.

This presence or mode of being transforms whatever it touches. If its medium is movement, it will turn into dance; if stillness, into living sculpture; if thinking, into the higher reaches of intuition; if sensing, into a merging with the miracle of being; if feeling, into love; if singing, into sacred utterance; if speaking, into prayer or poetry; if doing the things of ordinary life, into a ritual in the name of God or a celebration of existence. Just as the spirit of our times is technique-oriented in its dealings with the external world, it is technique-oriented in its approach to psychological or spiritual reality. Yet, while numerous schools propound this or that method as a solution of human problems, we know that it is not merely the method but *the way in which it is employed* that determines its effectiveness, whether in psychotherapy, art, or education. The application of techniques or tools in an interpersonal situation depends upon an almost intangible "human factor" in the teacher, guide, or psychotherapist. When the case is that of the intrapersonal method of meditation, the human factor beyond the method becomes even more elusive. Still, as with other techniques, it is the *how* that counts more than the *what*. The question of the right attitude on the part of the meditator is the hardest for meditation teachers to transmit, and though it is the object of most supervision, may be apprehended only through practice.

It might be said that the attitude, or "inner posture," of the meditator is both his path and his goal. For the subtle, invisible *how* is not merely a *how to meditate* but a *how to be*, which in meditation is exercised in a simplified situation. And precisely because of its elusive quality beyond the domain of an instrumentality that may be described, the attitude that is the heart of meditation is generally sought after in the most simple external or "technical" situations: in stillness, silence, monotony, "just sitting." Just as we do not see the stars in daylight, but only in the absence of the sun, we may never taste the subtle essence of meditation in the daylight of ordinary activity in all its complexity. That essence may be revealed when we have suspended everything else but *us*, our presence, our attitude, beyond any activity or the lack of it. Whatever the outer situation, the inner task is simplified, so that nothing remains to do but gaze at a candle, listen to the hum in our own ears, or "do nothing." We may then discover that there are innumerable ways of gazing, listening, doing nothing; or, conversely, innumerable ways of *not* just gazing, not just listening, not just sitting. Against the background of the simplicity required by the exercise, we may become aware of ourselves and all that we bring to the situation, and we may begin to grasp experientially the question of attitude.

While practice in most activities implies the development of habits and the establishment of conditioning, the practice of meditation can be better understood as quite the opposite: a persistent effort to detect and become free from all conditioning, compulsive functioning of mind and body, habitual emotional responses that may contaminate the utterly simple situation required by the participant. This is why it may be said that the attitude of the meditator is both his path and his goal: the unconditioned state is the freedom of attainment and also the target of every single effort. What the meditator realizes in his practice is to a large extent how he is failing to meditate properly, and by becoming aware of his failings he gains understanding and the ability to let go of his wrong way. The right way, the desired attitude, is what remains when we have, so to say, stepped out of the way.

If meditation is above all the pursuit of a certain state of mind, the practice of a certain attitude toward experience that transcends the qualities of this or that particular experience, a mental process rather than a mental content, let us then attempt to say what cannot be said, and speak of what this common core of meditation is.

A trait that all types of meditation have in common, even at the procedural level, gives us a clue to the attitude we are trying to describe: all meditation is a *dwelling upon* something.

While in most of one's daily life the mind flits from one subject or thought to another, and the body moves from one posture to another, meditation practices generally involve an effort to stop this merry-go-round of mental or other activity and to set our attention upon a single object, sensation, utterance, issue, mental state, or activity.

"Yoga," says Patanjali in his second aphorism, "is the inhibition of the modifications of the mind." As you may gather from this statement, the importance of dwelling upon something is not so much in the *something* but in the *dwelling upon*. It is this concentrated attitude that is being cultivated, and, with it, attention itself. Though all meditation leads to a stilling of the mind as described by Patanjali, it does not always consist in a voluntary attempt to stop all thinking or other mental activity. As an alternative, the very interruptions to meditation may be taken as a temporary meditation object, by dwelling upon them. There is, for example, a Theravadan practice that consists in watching the rising and falling of the abdomen during the breathing cycle. While acknowledging these movements, the meditator also acknowledges anything else that may enter his field of consciousness, whether sensations, emotions, or thoughts. He does it by mentally naming three times that of which he has become aware ("noise, noise, noise," "itching, itching, itching") and returning to the rising and falling. As one meditation instructor put it: "There is no disturbance because any disturbance can be taken as a meditation object. Anger, worry, anxiety, fear, etc., when appearing should not be suppressed but should be accepted and acknowledged with awareness and comprehension. This meditation is for dwelling in clarity of consciousness and full awareness."

The practice described above is a compromise of freedom and constraint in the direction of attention, in that the meditator periodically returns to the "fixation point" of visual awareness of his respiratory movements. If we should take one further step toward freedom from a pre-established structure, we would have a form of meditation in which the task would be merely to be aware of the contents of consciousness at the moment. Though this openness to the present might appear to be the opposite of the concentrated type of attention required by gazing at a candle flame, it is not so. Even the flame as an object of concentration is an ever-changing object that requires, because of its very changeability, that the meditator be in touch with it moment after moment, in sustained openness to the present. But closer still is a comparison between the observation of the stream of consciousness and concentration on music. In the latter instance, we can clearly recognize that a focusing of attention is not only compatible with, but indispensable to, a full grasp of the inflections of sound.

Our normal state of mind is one that might be compared to an inattentive exposure to music. The mind is active, but only intermittently are we aware of the present. A real awakening to the unfolding of our psychic activity requires an effort of attention greater and not lesser than that demanded by attending to a fixed "object" like an image, verbal repetition, or a region of the body. In fact, it is because attention to the spontaneous flow of psychological events is so difficult that concentrative meditation *sensu stricto* is necessary either as an alternative or a preliminary.

Attending to one's breath, for instance, by counting and remaining undistracted by the sensations caused by the air in one's nose, is a much more "tangible" object of consciousness than feeling-states and thoughts, and by persisting we may discover the difference between true awareness and the fragmentary awareness that we ordinarily take to be complete. After acquiring a taste of "concentrated state" in this situation and some insight into the difficulties that it entails, we may be more prepared for the observation of "inner states."

Such a "taste" can be regarded as a foretaste, or, rather, a diluted form of the taste the knowledge of which might be the end result of meditation. In the terminology of Yoga, that ultimate state is called *samadhi*, and it is regarded as the natural development of *dhyana*, the meditative state, itself the result of an enhancement or development of *dharana*, concentration. Dharana, in turn, is regarded as a step following *pranayama*, the technique of breathing control particular to Yoga, which entails just such a concentrative effort as the spontaneous breathing of Buddhist meditation.

The process leading from simple concentration to the goal of meditation (*samadhi, kensho*, or whatever we may want to call it) is thus one of progressive refinement. By practicing attention we understand better and better what attention is; by concentrating or condensing the taste of meditation known to us we come closer and closer to its essence. Through this process of enhancing that *attitude* which is the gist of the practice, we enter states of mind that we may regard as unusual and, at the same time, as the very ground or core of what we consider our ordinary experience. We would have no such "ordinary" experience without awareness, for instance, but the intensification of awareness leads us to a perspective as unfamiliar as that of the world which intensified scientific knowledge reveals to us—a world without any of the properties evident to our senses, materiality itself included.

Awareness, though, is only a facet of that meditative state into whose nature we are inquiring. Or, at least, it is only a facet if we understand the term as we usually do. The meditator who sets out to sharpen his awareness of awareness soon realizes that awareness is inseparable from other aspects of experience for which we have altogether different words, and so intertwined with them that it could be regarded as only conceptually independent from them.

Let us take the classical triad *sat-chit-ananda* according to the formulations of *Vedanta*, for instance. On the basis of the experiential realizations in which we are interested here, these three are our true nature and that of everything else, and the three are inseparable aspects of a unity: *sat* means being; *chit*, consciousness of mind; *ananda*, bliss.

From our ordinary point of view, these three seem quite distinct: we can conceive of being without bliss or awareness, of awareness without bliss. From the point of view of what to us is an unusual or "altered" state of consciousness, on the other hand, the individual sees his very identity in another light, so that he *is* consciousness. His very being is his act of awareness, and this act of awareness is not bliss-ful but consists *in* bliss. While we ordinarily speak of pleasure as a reaction in us to *things*, the meditator in samadhi experiences no distinction between himself, the world, and the quality of his experience because he *is* his experience, and experience is of the nature of bliss. From his point of view, the ordinary state of consciousness is one of not truly experiencing, of not being in contact with the world or self, and, to that extent, not only deprived of bliss but comparable to a non-being.

Special states of consciousness are not more expressible than states of consciousness in general, and are bound to the same limitation that we can only understand what we have already experienced. Since the goal of meditation is precisely something beyond the bounds of our customary experience, anything that we might understand would probably be something that it is not, and an attachment to the understanding could only prevent our progress. This is why many traditions have discouraged descriptions, avoided images or positive formulations of man's perfected state or of the deity, and stressed either practice or *negative* formulations:

> It is named Invisible, Infinite, and Unbounded, in such terms as may indicate not what It is, but what It is not: for this, in my judgment, is more in accord with its nature, since, as the capital mysteries and the priestly traditions suggested, we are right in saying that It is not in the likeness of any created thing, and we cannot comprehend Its super-essential, invisible, and ineffable infinity. If, therefore, the negations in the descriptions of the divine are true, and the affirmations are inconsistent with It. . . .
>
> —Dionysius the Areopagite

> The teacher (Gautama) has taught that a "becoming" and a "non-becoming" are destroyed; therefore it obtains that: *nirvana is neither an existent thing nor an unexistent thing.*"
>
> —Nagarjuna

> Never, never teach virtue . . . you will walk in danger, beware! beware!
> Every man knows how useful it is to be useful.
> No one seems to know how useful it is to be useless.
>
> —Chuang-Tzu

Yet positive formulations of what existence looks or feels like in peak states of consciousness abound. When these are conceptual (as in terms of sat-chit-ananda or other trinities), they constitute the experiential core of theologies, theistic or non-theistic. When symbolic, they constitute true religious art, and some great art that we do not conventionally consider "religious." Both types of expression are important to consider in any attempt like ours, which is not properly one of "expressing" but of determining the psychological characteristics of the meditational state. Moreover, the symbols of the meditative state are part of the practice of meditation itself in some of its forms, and we could not bypass their significance in any account of such disciplines.

Though, theoretically, any meditation object could suffice and be equivalent to any other, particular objects of meditation serve (especially for one not far advanced in the practice) the double function of a target of attention and a reminder of that right attitude which is both the path and the goal of meditation.

Just as our experience shows that certain poems, musical works, or paintings can hold our interest without being exhausted while others soon enter the category of the obvious, typical meditation objects partake of the quality of becoming more rather than less after repeated contemplations. A Buddhist sutra or a Christian litany, the symbol of the cross or the Star of David, the rose or the lotus, have not persisted as objects of meditation on the basis of tradition alone but on the grounds of a special virtue, a built-in appropriateness and richness, which meditators have discovered again and again throughout the centuries. Being symbols created by a higher state of consciousness, they evoke their source and always lead the meditator beyond his ordinary state of mind, a beyondness that is the meditator's deepest self, and the presence of which is the very heart of meditation.

We must not forget, however, that symbols, meditation objects, or "seeds" *(bija)* for meditation are only a technique. In contrast to the *directive* approach to meditation, in which the individual places himself under the influence of a symbol, we find a *non-directive* approach in which the person lets himself be guided by the promptings of his own deeper nature. Instead of letting a symbol shape his experience, he attends to his experience as given to his awareness, and by persisting in the attempt he finds that his perceptions undergo a progressive refinement. Instead of holding on to a rigid form handed down by tradition, he dwells upon the form that springs from his own spontaneity, until he may eventually find that in his own soul lies hidden the source of all traditions.

Still another alternative to the guiding influence of the symbol may be found in a purely negative approach, which is directive too, but only in a restrictive sense: instead of taking an object to dwell upon and identify with, the meditator here puts his effort in *moving away* from all objects, in *not* identifying with anything that he perceives. By departing from the known he thus allows for the unknown, by excluding the irrelevant he opens himself up to the relevant, and by dis-identifying from his current self concept, he may go into the aconceptual awakening of his true nature.

The three types of meditation may be represented as the three points of a triangle (as in Figure 1). At one end of the base (line)

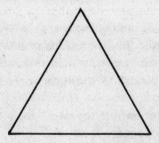

The Negative Way: elimination, detachment, emptiness, centered, the "middle way"

The Way of Forms: concentration, absorption, union, outer-directed, Apollonian

The Expressive Way: freedom, transparence, surrender, inner-directed, Dionysian

Figure 1

is represented meditation upon externally given symbolic objects, and at the other end is the contrasting alternative of meditation upon spontaneously arising contents of the mind. In the former, the person confronts an *other* (idea of God, etc.) upon which he concentrates, in which he sees his own center, with which he identifies, and to which he seems receptive. In the latter, the meditator seeks to become receptive to, and to identify, with *himself*, without the mirror device of the symbol.

In the former approach the individual attempts to interiorize an externally given form, or projects his experience onto it, until his subjectivity is absorbed by the object. In the latter, the individual seeks attunement to an inner form or a formless depth out of which a personal form emerges—in imagery, thoughts, gestures, feelings, or, above all, as an attitude toward the situation at the moment. The former is an assimilative, introjective, or projective process. The latter, a process of expression. One is a formal approach that involves relinquishing of spontaneity, insofar as it keeps the meditator on the path worked by the symbol. The other approach not only does not involve extrinsically given forms, but could be seen as a pursuit of formlessness: the meditator seeks to relinquish expectations, preconceptions, predetermined courses of action, so as to make himself receptive to the promptings of his unprogramed spontaneity. Just as the former is of a hieratic style, the latter is orgiastic; the former entails obedience to a pattern, the latter, freedom from the known; the former is Apollonian, the latter Dionysian.

Different as these two may seem, they converge upon a common end state, for, after all, the forms and symbols that the traditions of mankind offer as starting points for meditation have originated in spontaneity. And, conversely, a surrender to spontaneity leads not to chaos but to the expression of a definite structure that all men share. As Jung showed in the domain of visual fantasy, the images become more "collective"—and therefore similar to the universal patterns of myth—the more the subject explores his presumably individual depth.

In contrast with these two orientations in the task of meditation—one outer-directed and the other inner-directed—the third point in our triangle stands for a purely *negative* approach: not a reaching out or a reaching in but a self-emptying. In this approach the effort is to attain a stillness of the mind's conceptualizing activity, a withdrawal from external perceptions and internal experience alike, to cultivate a detachment toward psychological acting in general. This method is based upon the experiential finding that the state we call wakefulness is in large measure of an inhibiting nature, so that our ordinary mental operations actively preclude or limit the occurrence of states such as those pursued in meditation. If we are able to accomplish nothing more than a stilling of the mind, bringing the goal-directed activity of our ordinary state of consciousness to a standstill, separating temporarily from our ego functions (and still retain consciousness), we may enter an altogether unfamiliar domain of experience without ever having sought it *positively* (*i.e.*, approached it as a goal known through symbolical or conceptual formulations).

2 / Concentrative or Absorptive Meditation

Each of the traditional symbols employed in the different schools of meditation could well be, by itself, the object of an essay larger than the present one. I shall attempt, however, to cast a panoramic glance at some traits shared by the most widespread meditation objects as a means of elucidating the experience elicited by and reflected upon them.

One of the characteristics of the most universal objects of meditation, whether visual, verbal (such as the names of God), acoustical (bell, drum), or other, is what we may call *centrality*. The lotus, the cross, the heart, the sun, a source of light, and many other images more or less explicitly evoke the notion of a center around which actions flow—namely, a center as a point of balance, a source, or an end. Related to the center as a source is the idea of radiation or emanation, also prominent in many of the more widespread meditation objects. Some of these, like white light and fire, are forms of energy and necessarily imply radiation. Others, like the heart, evoke the thought of emanation because of their function as a central mover. Plant symbols, like the lotus, rose, and the seed, express emanation in the aspect of growth; others, like the cross or mandala, express it more directly and geometrically in the pure idea of a center of origin and in vertical and horizontal extension. As to the names of God in different religions, these are also aspects of the ultimate reality, frequently conceived as emanations or extensions of the hidden beyondness of the divine into the field of manifestation. Emanation, be it of goodness, energy, life, consciousness, or existence itself, may also be conceived, in more anthropopsychic terms, as a giving of love. At the same time, though, some symbols convey an understanding of this giving as a self-emptying—such as love or death; the energy and light of the flame being the other side of a sacrifice of that which is burning. Thus the seed must die to become a plant, and the cross, which is the symbol of universal life, is also one of individual surrender and death. In a similar way, only that which makes itself transparent may become full of light, and only that which is empty may be filled. The condition equated with the greatest fullness is also that of nothingness, not in the sense of a nothingness preceding completion, but in that of a void being the ever-present condition, foundation, and ground of fullness. An image that expresses this particularly well is that of the lake of the mind becoming, in its stillness, like a perfect mirror, and in iconography, the invisible or empty center of the mandala and the nothingness at the center of the lotus.

Another aspect of the images that we are considering, not unrelated to those of centrality, radiation, and death-emptiness, is that of order, regularity, and lawfulness. Many symbols convey such lawfulness in their very style, formal and mathematical; others in their inner coherence or allusion to natural processes like growth, radiation, or transformation of energy. The lawfulness of such symbols, simple as an empty circle or complex as a Tibetan mandala, evokes one more aspect of the same single experience that may be viewed as one of giving, of self-emptying, of centering. It is the experience that in theistic formulations is expressed as conformity with God's will and in alternative cognitive maps is expressed as a surrender to a Tao (Way) or Dharma (Law of the Universe).

One particular aspect in which lawfulness is manifested in symbols is in the conciliation of opposites, or, more generally, in the presentation of the unity in multiplicity. Polarity is more explicit in the symbol of the cross, constituted by the intersection of two polarities. It is also explicit in symbols like the Chinese yin-yang and the sacred syllable AUM (the open-mouthed beginning and the close-mouthed ending representing all polarities and dualities). But polarity can also be implicit, as in the symbolism of light, which entails the illumination of a darkness; in that of fire, which must consume something other than itself; or in the mandala-like symbols, which contrast center and periphery, and thus the one and the many.

If we agree that meditation objects are external representations of the "meditation state," and the latter is the meditator's consciousness of himself, we can also say that all object-centered meditation is a dwelling of the individual upon his deepest identity, upon the reflection of himself in the mirror of symbolism. In contrast to this form of meditation, we see in other forms a dwelling upon the self not mediated by symbolism: this is most explicit in Ramana Maharshi's formula of meditating upon the question "Who am I?"[1] and in the "speculation" of medieval platonism. The latter, meaning literally "gazing into a mirror," consisted in concentrating on the pupil of one's own eye, and on one's reflection in it. A reference to this practice is found in the apocryphal Platonic "First Alcibiades," where Socrates relates the Delphic inscription "Know Thyself" to this form of self-contemplation:

> Socrates: but if now the soul wants to know itself, must it not also gaze into the soul, and indeed into its noblest part, that is, where reason and wisdom dwell? This part of the soul resembles the divine. So may it not be that he who turns his gaze thither and learns to recognize everything that is of a divine nature—God and insight by reason—may also, at the same time, learn to know himself with profound recognition?[2]

The centrality of meditation objects is a direct expression of their being a means to our remembrances of the individual's center, the core of his being. In both an inner and an outer sense, they are objects of con-centration. The very word medi-tation refers to a midst or center that we find within us.

Thus, to our former statement that meditation constitutes an exercise of attention, we may add that it is also a practice in centeredness, a practice in being oneself and knowing onself.

But what is this self?

According to the Buddhistic formulation, there is no such thing as "self," and the only image that can convey the experience of attainment is that of sunyata, emptiness. *Sunyata* literally means "no bottom." Just as the center of a mandala is frequently empty, and the center of the cross vanishes into the nothingness of a mathematical point, as the Holy of Holies cannot be entered and the Name of Names cannot be uttered, the core of being is experienced by the meditator's achieving kensho (goal) as bottomless, empty, and endless. It is the night from which proceeds light, the non-being that sustains being, the absence of self at the heart of selfhood.

The "empty" aspect of the meditative state may be seen, at the level of practice, as a direct extension of the concentrative aspect. For concentration intends as exclusion of all activities other than that which medieval mysticism (Jan van Ruysbroeck) calls a mere "staring" and Buddhism calls "bare attention." The actions of "just staring" and "just sitting," and the freedom from thoughts that they intend, represent at the same time a maximization of awareness and the condition of self-abandonment. However, we should not see these two as different phenomena but as inseparable aspects of the whole: awareness *is* receptivity, and "inner silence" must be created before real concentration takes place, a stilling of the mind's lake before it becomes a mirror and can *reflect*. As the Swabian mystic Suso puts it: "If any man cannot grasp this matter, let him be idle and the matter will grasp him."

The culmination of this ego dissolution is achieved in the state called *nirvana* (extinction) in Buddhism and *fana-f'illah* (extinction into God) in Islam. But "extinction" is not another condition but only an *aspect* of the condition to which we have referred as one of awakening (culmination in consciousness) and centering, or identification with the source of one's being. Nirvana is not only the extinction of separateness and illusion but an awakening to reality and the finding of one's identity in the emptiness that contains all things—in themselves impermanent and devoid of self.

The foregoing description of the meditation state as one of awareness-centeredness-emptiness may convey the idea of a condition of feelinglessness, which again would be no more than a half-truth. It is peace (*hesychias*) that the Fathers of the Desert regarded as the landmark of success in their discipline, and equanimity (*upekkha*, sometimes wrongly translated as "indifference") that is the goal of Buddhistic meditation. But, we may ask, do such peace and equanimity signify a lack of feeling or an absence of any reactions toward other beings?

The radiating quality of meditation symbols answers this question in the same way as do the reports from those who have experienced the peak states that we are trying to understand. The enlightened ones are loving and compassionate, and the mystical experience is frequently described as one of deep solidarity with all mankind. Not only the Buddha bears the epithet of "The Compassionate"; in Christianity and Islam, too, love is the most prominent aspect of the godhead, man's highest intuition and experiential realization of the *summum bonum*. "In the name of Allah, the Compassionate, the Merciful . . ." is the formula introducing each chapter of the Koran.

Are equanimity and love, emptiness and compassion, really contradictory? Any close consideration of the matter will show us that, on the contrary, just as in the symbols that depict a growth from an empty center, or in the Tibetan vajra—which is at the same time emptiness, the hardest stone, and a glittering jewel—there is a condition in which equanimity may be seen as the foundation of love, peace as the source of caring, selflessness as the basis for empathy.

In other words, what occurs when the individual relinquishes what he is doing is not inaction but a transpersonal process, which we may see as a much greater action. When he achieves detachment from pleasure and pain, he is not indifferent but free to live and die, and to enjoy the gift of life without caring about gain and loss. If this may sound too abstract, the following anecdote from one of the great Zen masters may show the expression of this state in real life.

The Zen master Hakuin was praised by his neighbors as one living a pure life.

A beautiful Japanese girl whose parents owned a food store lived near him. Suddenly, without any warning, her parents discovered she was with child.

This made her parents angry. She would not confess who the man was, but after much harassment at last she named Hakuin.

In great anger the parents went to the master. "Is that so?" was all he would say.

After the child was born it was brought to Hakuin. By this time he had lost his reputation, which did not trouble him, but he took very good care of the child. He obtained milk from his neighbors and everything else the little one needed.

A year later the girl-mother could stand it no longer. She told her parents the truth—that the real father of the child was a young man who worked in the fish market.

The mother and father of the girl at once went to Hakuin to ask his forgiveness, to apologize at length, and to get the child back again.

Hakuin was willing. In yielding the child, all he said was: "Is that so?"[3]

True indifference is not indifferent. When the individual is able to remove his little ego (moral ideas included) from the course of his deeper nature, the melody played by the gods through his hollow reed is one of goodness and beauty:

> Yu replied: I understand. *The music of earth sings through a thousand holes. The music of man is made on flutes and instruments. What makes the music of heaven?*
>
> Master Ki said: *Something is blowing on a thousand different holes. Some power stands behind all this and makes the sound die down. What is that power?*
>
> —Chuang[4]

> The man in whom Tao acts without impediment
> Harms no other being by his actions.
> Yet he does not know himself
> To be "kind," to be "gentle."
>
> —Chuang[5]

What the Chinese describe as a gentle standing out of the way of the "great blower," or an emptying of the mind, is probably what the more egocentric personality of Western man sees as the violent death of the ego, a self-sacrifice that is the portal to a higher consciousness.

The subject of a conjunction between the experience of love and the acceptance of death is a rich one both at the mythological level and at that of psychological processes. We might say that all love, in that it is a giving of one's self, rests upon a measure of non-attachment, and all life is a consuming of itself.

Perhaps the most significant idea belonging to this domain of love-death is that of sacrifice. We could say that the visible sacrifices that constitute acts of worship in different religions are, like meditation objects, the sacrificer's projections of that state of mind whose aspects are love and self-emptying. "Sacrifice" derives from *sacer facere*, "to make holy," and as usage makes clear, the holy action is one of giving up in pain that is joy. Beyond masochistic distortions of the sacrificial attitude or the understanding thereof, we may see in sacrifice a convergence of the issues of equanimity (transcendence of attachment to pleasure and pain), giving, and death: the giving up of that which is given. The joy of the sacrificer is not a perverse pleasure in pain. If his mind is truly involved in his action, the bliss of the meditation state is a joy *beyond* pleasure and pain, a sense of attunement with the holy that follows upon surrender of personal preference:

> Feelings of heat and cold, pleasure and pain, are caused by the contacts of the senses with their objects. They come and they go, never lasting long. You must accept them.
>
> A serene spirit accepts pleasure and pain with an even mind, and is unmoved by either.
>
> —From the *Bhagavad-Gita*[6]

The detachment from desires encouraged by the Scriptures goes beyond detachment from pleasure and pain and applies to mental formulations of virtue and vice as well. The conventionally virtuous man is no more liberated or open to his true self than the one that is prey to the automatisms of desire. A Hindu saying goes: "A nightingale in a golden cage is no freer than one in a cage of iron." And the Bhagavad-Gita: "The world is imprisoned in its own activity, except when actions are performed as worship of God. Therefore you must perform every action sacramentally, and be free from all attachments to results."[7]

Much of what has been said in the foregoing pages already anticipates that aspect of meditation which is parallel to the lawfulness, regularity, or order of meditation symbols. Non-action that is supreme action, surrender that becomes an attunement to God's will, emptiness that is radiant, death that is eternal life—all these expressions involve the notion of a very *precise* unfolding of experience to which the individual opens himself as he lays aside his habitual patterns of thinking and feeling and his superficial identity. Whereas, from one point of view, his attitudes and experiences may be seen as those of love, from another point of view it is not *his* love, there not being any "self" to do the loving, but only a channel, a field of space where the unfolding can occur. In this sense, the individual can be said to be attuned to a law greater than himself.

> Yet, as a wheel moves smoothly, free from jars,
> *My will and my desire were turned by love,*[*]
> the love that moves the sun and the other stars.
> —Dante[8]

We have briefly looked at meditation as a practice in awareness, intensiveness, self-abasement, love, and in attunement to a regularity, which we may choose to regard as God's law or as the law of our own being. We can also see in meditation the development of that characteristic which we mentioned last among those shared by meditation objects: the coincidence of opposites, and, more generally, unity in multiplicity.

Unity and the solution of conflict as a characteristic of mystical experience is something accepted enough so that we need not discuss it here. What is relevant, though, is to show how the expression of unity relates to the others discussed so far, and constitutes only another way of expressing the single experience that is in itself a unity and a silent center in the midst of our many descriptions.

Let us start by considering an aspect of meditation that we have not emphasized and in which the transcendence of duality is most relevant: the disappearance of the habitual distinction between subject and object.

Just as meditation on an object entails concentration on it, it also entails identification with it. The Zen student *becomes* the *koan*, the worshiper is united with his God, the one meditating on the tradition of enlightenment becomes (to the extent that he succeeds in his meditation) the "enlightened one."

From the conceptual point of view, we look at "attending to"

* The italics are the author's.

and "identifying with" as two fully different processes. But are they so in actual experience? Complete concentration, complete giving of our attention to something, reaches a point where we are, so to say, pure receptivity filled by the object: not a screen or a mind where the object is reflected, not an "I" that perceives, but a nothingness filled by the contemplation; only the object exists, empathetically perceived, as it were, from within. This need not be an experience arrived at through meditation. More appropriately, we might say that meditation aims at the restoration of the *natural* mode of perception that our conceptual distinctions (like that of subject versus object) have blurred. The following excerpt from the work of a contemporary British author illustrates a spontaneous recovery of that lost naïveté which phenomenology sometimes seeks in vain to recover:

This book is an unconventional attempt to discover, for myself and in my own way, what I am and what I amount to in the universe.

What am I? That is *the* question. Let me try to answer it as honestly and simply as I can, forgetting the ready-made answers.

Common sense tells me that I am a man very similar to other men (adding that I am five-feet-ten, fortyish, gray-headed, around eleven stone, and so on), and that I know just what it is like here and now to be me, writing on this sheet of paper.

So far, surely, nothing can have gone wrong. But has my common sense really described what it is like to be me? Others cannot help me here: only I am in a position to say what I am. At once I make a startling discovery: common sense could not be more wrong to suppose that I resemble other men. I have no head! Here are my hands, arms, parts of my trunk and shoulders—and, mounted (so to say) on the shoulders, not a head but these words and this paper and this desk, the wall of the room, the window, the gray sky beyond. . . . My head has gone, and in its place is a world. And all my life long I had imagined myself to be built according to the ordinary human and animal plan!

Where other creatures carry small rounded body-terminals, fairly constant in shape and furnished with such things as eyes and hair and mouth, there is for me a boundless and infinitely varied universe. It looks as if I alone have a body which fades out so that almost the only hints which remain of it above my shoulders are two transparent shadows thrown across everything. (I may call them nose-shadows if I please, but they are not in the least like noses.)

And certainly I do not find myself living inside an eight-inch ball and peering out through its portholes. I am not shut up in the gloomy interior of any object, and least of all in a small, tightly-packed sphere, somehow managing to live my life there in its interstices. I am at large in the world. I can discover no watcher here, and over there something watched, no peep-hole out into the world, no window-pane, no frontier. I do not detect a universe: it lies wide open to me. These ink-marks are now forming on this sheet of paper. They are present. At this moment there is nothing else but this blue and white pattern, and not even a screen here (where I imagined I had a head) upon which the pattern is projected. My head, eyes, brain—all the instruments that I thought were here at the center—all are a fiction. It is incredible that I ever believed in them.[9]

The experience of selfless identification with an object or being is known to all of us in some measure, for it underlies all genuine aesthetic experience, human empathy, and the religious attitude. When we say to somebody "I understand you," we do not mean to convey that we reason and classify his state of mind from without, but that we know it from within. The very word intuition expresses this: *intus-ire*, "to enter," "to place oneself inside."

Aesthetic experience, like that of human empathy, is disinterested, as philosophers of beauty have remarked. The realm of art is divorced from that of practicality. We can only see the play as a play to the extent that we are not personally involved in its slot, and in general we can be open to the sense of beauty when we are free from concern with the useful. The disinterested or gratuitous quality of aesthetic appreciation may help us to understand that of the experience where unity of subject and object reaches a maximum—the state of absorption aimed at by meditation.

Absorption is all that we have enumerated: a concentrated attention, a self-forgetfulness or self-emptying, a giving oneself completely to the matter or situation at hand, a merging with It. If the "It" of the meditator be himself, the resulting experience will be that of merging with himself, and the dissolution of inner duality; if the "It" be God, the experience will be that expressed by St. Paul as "I do not live but Christ lives in me." The attitude of the meditator toward the world was expressively rendered by a Japanese Zen master when he said that we must live with an empty heart, to let the world fill it. The meditator's attitude in face of God is best expressed in Rumi's well-known passage:

> A certain man once came and knocked on the door of a friend.
> "Who are you, faithful one?" his friend asked.
> "I," he answered.
> "Go away," the friend said. "It is not the proper time. There is no place for such a raw fellow at a table like mine."
> . . . then he returned and once more circled about the house of his companion. Fearful a hundredfold, he gently knocked at the door, anxious lest any unmannerly word should escape his lips.
> His friend called, "Who is that at the door?"
> He answered, "You also are at the door, heart-ravisher!"
> "Now," the friend cried, "since you are I, come in, O I! There is not room in the house for two I's."[10]

The perception of unity that characterizes the depth of the meditation state and has been formulated by mystics of all lands entails more than the merging of I and Thou. It is a recognition of oneness in all things and all beings. In monotheistic formulations, all is the expression of one God; in pantheistic renderings of the experience, all *is* God. In non-theistic mysticism, all is a "substance," a thatness, a beingness transcending its own phenomenal manifestations. The oneness of Reality beyond its forms is beautifully expressed in a Sufi tale about an elephant that is brought to a city of blind men:

> The populace became anxious to see the elephant, and some sightless from among this blind community ran like fools to find it.
>
> As they did not even know the form or shape of the elephant they groped sightlessly, gathering information by touching some part of it.
>
> Each thought that he knew something, because he could feel a part.
>
> When they returned to their fellow-citizens eager groups clustered around them. Each of these was anxious, misguidedly, to learn the truth from those who were themselves astray.
>
> They asked about the form, the shape of the elephant: and listened to all that they were told.
>
> The man whose hand had reached an ear was asked about the elephant's nature. He said: "It is a large, rough thing, wide and broad, like a rug."
>
> And the one who had felt the trunk said: "I have the real facts about it. It is like a straight and hollow pipe, awful and destructive."
>
> The one who had felt its feet and legs said: "It is mighty and firm, like a pillar."
>
> Each had felt one part out of many. Each had perceived it wrongly. No mind knew all: knowledge is not the companion of the blind. All imagined something, something incorrect.[11]

In the language of this parable, it would be through an overcoming of blindness that the men could understand that they were confusing the whole with its parts and the being with its attributes, and thus come to see unity where they now experienced diversity. The contemplative act, too, like the overcoming of blindness, may lead to the discovery of a universal whole of which all things are aspects. The absorption of the meditative state is not only one in which the individual becomes the other, but reaches to the essence of the other, which is the essence of everything.

This takes us directly to another characteristic of the meditation object and of the meditative state, which we have not stressed thus far: the religious quality of both. As stated earlier, that essence of all things which is no-thing, that center from which "all" manifests and derives both meaning and value, that essence which the meditator finds in himself by losing himself, is most frequently formulated as "God" or as a cosmic entity of numinous quality. So long has meditation been associated with religion that we take this connection for granted and have ceased to ask whether it is necessary and intrinsic. If meditation is a practice in awareness, in centeredness and equanimity, in attunement to our nature, in the capacity of giving up ourselves and being available to our perceptions, in receptivity and in freedom from preconceptions necessary to reception—does this mean that it is also an act of worship, a religious act?

I think that this question is particularly appropriate at this time when the United States is starting to turn its attention to meditation with a technique-oriented mind developed throughout previous decades, and when we wonder whether feedback training and the control of alpha waves or other brain functions might not perhaps become a substitute for meditation, thus cutting through all theories and theologies and intentions in the person undergoing the discipline.

In examining this aspect of meditation, let us start once more by considering the symbols and their function in practice.

The most widespread meditation objects are the outward expression of a condition of mind after which the individual strives: the self-realized state, the peak of the human condition, the God-man. Emblematic of this are the image of the sitting Buddha, the Bodhisattvas of countless tankas, and the Christ on the cross. These symbols are "religious" to the extent that the inner conditions that they depict are "religious." That some other meditation objects that we have been considering (the lotus, fire, light, heart, etc.) are also emblematic of this mental state that the meditator seeks to cultivate* may be acceptable enough to one who has read the foregoing pages.

In contrast to the symbols that stand for a condition acknowledged as available to man, or even intrinsic to man, another class of symbols stands in the mind of the meditator for the divine being, or spiritual entities outside himself. These objects of meditation, like the names or attributes of God, or the spirits evoked by the magician or shaman, would ordinarily be regarded as religious in the sense that the attitude toward or belief in them and desire for contact or union with them have come to be the very definition of religion.

A contemporary psychologist, with his knowledge of projection, would naturally lean toward the monistic point of view, in which the many images of God conceived by man are regarded as an externalization of his own experience, or aspects of himself.

On the other hand, because of the gap between man's ordinary condition and the God-state, no model could be more true to man's experience than the dualistic one, in terms of which he sees the divine being outside of and beyond himself. Perhaps it is because of this that even in the non-theistic religions the dualistic point of view has a prominent place in the emotional attitude of the seeker of enlightenment. Even though the Mahayana Buddhist may intellectually assert that the "other shore" is this one, his experience is one of aspiration, the intuition of a reality beyond the limitations of his ego, and the feeling of devotion typical of the religious spirit throughout the world.

Moreover, as Lama Govinda has remarked, "Even the Buddha of the Pali texts did not refrain from calling the practice of the highest spiritual qualities (like love, compassion, sympathy, equanimity) in meditation a "dwelling in God" (*brahmavihara*) or in a "divine state.""[12] In this context, the divine is not merely a projection into a beyond of man's object and longing, but a term

---

* To the extent that we may speak of cultivation, because the meditator *is* what he seeks and he seeks what he is.

needed to speak of an actual experience of attainment, and the question naturally arises as to why the most *human* qualities should be ascribed to an entity beyond man. The reason does not lie, I believe, in the mere contrast between man's best and his ordinary condition, a contrast that leads to considering the former as something extraordinary and as the fulfillment of the natural as unnatural. Aside from this and aside from the aptness of the "divine" to symbolize the highest values, the essence of "otherness" may be found in the very essence of man's obedience to his true nature. Our "virtues" have their source in our very being, and their absence in the betrayal of man's true reality. But this "true self" of ours—unlike our self-assertive ego—is but a channel for the expression of natural laws. To the extent that we are "ourselves," we are also a part of the cosmos, a tide in the ocean of life, a chain in the network of processes that do not either begin or end within the enclosure of our skins. This thought, which anyone can grasp conceptually, appears to have been the experiential realization of men of all lands who, in surrendering to their true being, felt, too, that they were becoming part of an organism greater than themselves. Just as if a cell were to understand itself as a small component of a larger organism, so man's experience of true naturalness is inseparable in his mind from that of being supported by greater laws, and of being a mere branch in the tree of life, an individual embodiment of the Way (Tao, the Law; Dharma, God's will). The images of this "greater whole" vary according to their individual interpreters as much as the different parts of the elephant in the Sufi tale. But all, from the nature mystic to the worshiper of a God-outside-the-world, imply the experience of self-as-part, self-as-vehicle or instrument, self-as-field-of-expression-for-the-whole, self-as-channel—which is to say that the experience of self-reality goes hand in hand with the individual's experience of selflessness or emptiness as discussed earlier.

In the Buddhistic outlook, the "self" has been an illusion all along, a conceptual separation of the individual from the matrix of being. According to others, like the Islamic, the ego is pictured as a reality that must die. Yet these are but semantic differences, alternative ways of symbolization. All mysticism acknowledges the underlying experience of self-emptying and a merging with the unity of being. Compare, for instance, the following documents:

1. In Attar's *Parliament of Birds*, when the thirty survivors among the questing birds, after crossing the seven valleys, find the Simurgh, the king whom they were seeking, "the sun of majesty sent forth his rays, and in the reflection of each other's faces these thirty birds (Si-Murgh) of the outer world contemplated the face of the symbol of the inner world. This so astonished them that they did not know if they were still themselves or if they had become the Simurgh. At last, in the state of contemplation, they realized that they were the Simurgh and that the Simurgh was the thirty birds. When they gazed at the Simurgh, they saw that it was truly the Simurgh that was there, and when they turned their eyes toward themselves they saw that they themselves were the Simurgh. In perceiving both at once, themselves and Him, they realized that they and the Simurgh were the same being. No one in the world has ever heard of anything to equal it." And some lines later the Simurgh says, "Annihilate yourselves, then, joyfully and gloriously in Me, and in Me you shall find yourselves."[13]

2. "In archery," said Mumeji, Japanese Master of Archery, "a man must die to his purer nature, the one which is free from all artificiality and deliberation, if he is to reach perfect enjoyment of Tao. Learn how to control the emittance of truth, flowing like an eternal spring . . . this way is a very easy and direct one. The most difficult one is to let oneself die completely in the very act of shooting. To facilitate the death of the lower self, a man must exercise unceasingly to gradually acquire the right attitude."[14]

3. And Richard of St. Victor: "The soul which is plunged in the fire of divine love is like an iron, which at first loses its blackness and then growing to white heat, it becomes like the fire itself. And lastly, it grows liquid, and losing its nature is transmuted into an utterly different quality of being."[15]

The interdependence between the experience of self-emptying and the surrender to God, Tao, Dharma, or Reality can be the basis for understanding the connection between meditation proper and the practices men regard as ritual, cult, or prayer. Meditation emphasizes the cultivation of receptivity, of emptiness; worship (including prayer) emphasizes the establishment of a connection between an ego-imprisoned consciousness and a reality beyond its boundaries. He who prays stands before an "other," and in fact prayer has been defined as "standing in the presence of God." Such a connection, which is the goal of devotionalism, requires, to become effective, a measure of ego loss, which is also the goal of meditation. Conversely, the achievement of receptivity in the meditator implies that the individual becomes transparent toward reality. In the forms of meditation involving an object, visual or imaginary, it is to the reality symbolized therein that the individual makes himself open, thus coming close to the attitude of the worshiper. In forms that do not involve a dwelling upon a divine being, or upon symbols of the ultimate reality or of the self, the individual dwells upon his experience, surrenders to his own existence, becomes receptive to *what is* without the focusing lens of a symbolic construction. Meditation and worship can only artificially be divorced; effectiveness in either leads to the discovery of the other, and most forms of practice contain elements of both. If this is not always obvious, it is because of the unfortunate fate of rituals, which usually become "mere rituals" and of the tendency of objects of worship to become divorced from their true function as instruments of a spiritual exercise, to the point of ending up as mere objects of superstition. By regarding meditation objects as symbols for the meditator's goal—

symbols that are to him the reminders of what he is, symbols that he *becomes* in a process that is at the same time self-emptying and self-expression—we have become aware of several aspects of that subtle action which is meditation beyond its apparent form of external procedure. We have looked at meditation as an exercise in centering, both in the sense of concentration of our energies and in that of finding the center of our being. We have looked at it as an exercise in surrender to our true nature, in receptivity, in naturalness, and in allowing a flow of energies normally buried under our roles, our self-programming, our conscious intentions and preconceptions. We have looked at meditation as an act of unification, both in the sense of transcending the duality of subject and object and in that of standing in equanimity beyond the polarities of our personality. We have seen an element of worship in meditation and noticed that "worship" is only another way of speaking of that single experience of devoted attention to receptive apperception of a being or thing which becomes to us an expression of our own highest values.

In discussing meditation objects up to this point, we have spoken mostly of visual images and ideas, which does not do justice to the whole domain of concentrative meditation. The process of giving one's entire attention to a mental image and identifying with it, for instance, is not qualitatively different from the physical enactment of such an image, and in this way we can understand the use of mudra, postures and gestures evocative of certain inner conditions. And just as an image itself need not be static but may include movement, the physical enactment of images (in the process of which the meditator suppresses his identification with his "object") may take the form of physical movement. Some types of meditation-in-movement have remained such, like dervish and some kinds of Tibetan dancing. Other types, like Tai Chi Chuan, are frequently approached by persons seeking goals (health, self-defense) other than the original ones. Still others, like Indonesian dancing, have evolved into art forms, in

which the aim of entertainment has been developed to the point
where the original purpose of the discipline has been forgotten.

The connection between meditation and the arts is by no
means limited to the field of classical dance and drama, where the
interpreter lends his physical being to an archetypal form, but
extends to all domains of artistic creation. In the case of classical
Indian sculpture, for example, the artist was supposed to engage
in a complex series of inner actions requiring long practice before working with his materials in the outer world:

> The artist (*sadhaka, mantrin,* or *yogin,* as he is variously and
> significantly called), after ceremonial purification, is to proceed to
> a solitary place. There he is to perform the "Sevenfold Office," be-
> ginning with the invocation of the hosts of Buddhas and Bodhisatt-
> vas, and the offering to them of real or imaginary flowers. Then
> he must realize in thought the four (infinite) modes of friendliness,
> compassion, sympathy, and impartiality. Then he must meditate
> upon the emptiness (*sunyata*) or non-existence of all things, for,
> "by the fire of the idea of the abyss, it is said, there are destroyed
> beyond recovery five factors" or ego-consciousness. Then only
> should he invoke the desired divinity by the utterance of the ap-
> propriate seed-word (*bija*) and should identify himself completely
> with the divinity to be represented. Then finally, on pronouncing
> the *dhyana mantra,* in which the attributes are defined, the divinity
> appears visibly, "like a reflection" or "as in a dream," and this
> brilliant image is the artist's model.[16]

Not only is the process of deliberate identification with an
archetype the bridge between meditation and worship and between meditation and art, but it is also at the basis of magical
evocation. Compare, for instance, the following quotation with
the previous one from Buddhist sources:

> Let us describe the magical method of identification. The sym-
> bolic form of the god is first studied with as much love as an artist
> would bestow upon a model, so that a perfectly clear and unshake-
> able mental picture of the god is present to the mind. Similarly,

the attributes of the god are enshrined in speech, and such speeches are committed perfectly to memory. The invocation will then begin with a prayer to the god, commemorating his physical attributes, always with profound understanding of their real meaning. In the second part of the invocation, the voice of the god is heard, and His characteristic utterance is recited.

In the third portion of the invocation, the magician asserts the identity of himself with the god. In the fourth portion, the god is again invoked, but as if by Himself, as if it were the utterance of the will of the god that He should manifest in the magician.[17]

Just as art forms that originated as spiritual disciplines have become divorced from their original intention, much of "magic" can be seen as an empty shell or superstitious mystification of a discipline not different from the one we are concerned with.

To the extent that psychiatry today is assimilating part of what was the function of traditional spiritual disciplines, psychotherapy, too, is incorporating techniques of meditation—deliberately or not. Some psychotherapists have become interested in traditional forms of meditation (Fromm[18] and Heider[19]); others have investigated the psychotherapeutic effectiveness of meditation techniques (Deikman)[20] or have introduced these in their practice. Others have originated psychotherapeutic methods based upon principles similar to meditation, sometimes without intending to imitate or modify traditional forms.

Two types of psychotherapeutic practice are of particular relevance to the discussion of concentrative or absorptive meditation: the psychotherapeutic use of *acting*, as in role-playing, psychodrama, and Gestalt therapy; and the use of suggestion.

The growing incorporation of dramatic resources into psychotherapy probably stems from a recognition that acting, in virtue of its demanding *empathy* from the actor, may be a royal road to intuitive understanding. In acting we understand something by *becoming* it rather than by thinking *about* it. And to identify is —from a different perspective—to establish contact with and express *pre-existing* feelings or experiences in us that match the enacted object.

There is a notable difference between the newer techniques and the attempt of traditional meditators to identify with their object and thus obtain absorption. This difference lies in the choice of the object, which in the traditional forms is typically archetypal and, more, a symbol of integration. In contemporary psychological practice, on the other hand, the typical object is a personification of an aspect of the individual's personality involved in conflict. These contrasting approaches can be characterized as being "the way of ascent" and the "way of descent": the effort to explore, contact, and assimilate the many fragments of the psyche, which may have to be integrated into the Divine Whole versus the direct attempt to identify with the qualities of wholeness.*

The question of similarities and differences between states of concentrative meditation and hypnotic states is an involved one, and I will not discuss it here in detail. But, as in meditation, concentrated attention upon an object and repetition are the main avenues to hypnosis, and in both states the individual may enter a "trance." Whereas in deep hypnosis the individual is usually amnestic of the episode and, in general, hypnotic trance is best described as a state of *restricted* awareness, meditation does not involve amnesia and awareness is expanded, if anything.

Another similarity between suggestion and meditation with an object is that in both cases the individual *places himself under the influence of symbols*—verbal, visual, or other—and experiences the consequent effects of the symbols on his emotions, his body, or states of mind.[21]

Suggestion, as usually practiced in supportive psychotherapy or hypnotherapy, may be regarded as a form of manipulation in which the psychotherapist evokes the desired states in the mind

* This is discussed more fully later. See pp. 65ff.

of a willing subject. In many of the techniques of psychosynthesis (as in self-hypnosis), we may speak of a self-manipulation
in which the individual employs the knowledge of how symbols
may create feeling states. In general, a meditator is one who has
acquired the ability to control inner states—not in the sense of
filtering-suppressing control, but in that of being able to *create* his
mental states.

This ability of self-manipulation may appear to be an alternative
to genuineness; thus, when we speak of "acting" we tend to interpret the word as mere simulation rather than as a creating of
true feelings. Valid as the distinction between deliberateness and
spontaneity may be in terms of subjective experiences, I believe,
however, that at depth we are *always* acting and that there is a
condition of consciousness where the contradiction between deliberateness and spontaneity disappears. At some level, *all* our
mental states are our choice—but "we" do not identify much
with the doer of our actions. The meditator may reach the point
at which he is one with his deeper self, one with the responsible
agent for whom every experience is a choice, all life a conscious
game. Just as the words "speculation" and "reflection" have
shifted in meaning from the original one of non-conceptual receptivity to that of discursive thinking, so has the term "meditation"
itself. In common parlance, "meditate" has come to mean "think
about." In the course of history we have forgotten that it meant
the art of "dwelling upon" topics and ideas. Yet this *dwelling
upon* an idea, which really constitutes meditation, is the very
opposite of *thinking about*. In the highly anti-intellectual tradition of Zen Buddhism, meditation on thought forms has a prominent place (at least in the Rinzai school) in the form of koan
practice.

A koan is a meditation object that, in spite of being presented
to the medium of thought, still defies any attempt to think about
it. It is a statement that at the same time expresses a state of consciousness and is cryptic to the reasoning mind, so that it can be

apprehended only through intuition. Or, more precisely, it is apprehended by him who shares the understanding from which it sprang. Isshu Miura, in commenting on a verse of Fu-Daishi, quotes: "If, on coming upon expressions such as these, you feel as if you were meeting a close relative face to face at a busy crossroad and recognizing him beyond a question of a doubt, then you can be said to understand the Dharmakaya.* But if you use common sense to conjecture about it, or run hither and thither trying to follow the words of others, you would never know the Dharmakaya."[22]

Zen students are encouraged not to discuss their koan practice among themselves, and, anyhow, such a discussion is regarded as something as intimate and subtle as that of one's way of making love. Without going into the intimacy of the meditative process, it may be of interest to read what D. T. Suzuki has written of his autobiographical experience with the first two koans that he received in his instruction. The following quotation emphasizes the total involvement of the meditator with his task, to the point where it becomes a matter of life or death. This is a point that I have not stressed enough and that might be overlooked in a treatment of meditation as a mere "exercise." Dr. Suzuki tells us how for about a year he worked unsuccessfully on his first koan until his teacher died. The roshi that succeeded changed the earlier koan to *Mu* and then

> There followed for me four years of struggle, a struggle mental, physical, moral, and intellectual. I felt it must be ultimately quite simple to understand *Mu*, but how was I to take hold of this simple thing? It might be in a book, so I read all the books on Zen that I could lay my hands on. The temple where I was living at the time, Butsunichi, had a shrine attached to it, dedicated to Hojo Tokimune, and in a room of that shrine all the books and documents belonging

---

* "The realm which is revealed to us when we see into our true nature," according to one of many definitions. The understanding of the Dharmakaya is the content and objective of many koans.

to the temple were kept. During the summer I spent nearly all my time in that room, reading all the books I could find. My knowledge of Chinese was still limited, so many of the texts I could not understand, but I did my best to find out everything I could about *Mu* intellectually. . . . Then in the way of moral effort I used to spend many nights in a cave at the back of the Shariden building where the Buddha's tooth is enshrined. But there was always a weakness of will power in me, so that often I failed to sit up all night in the cave, finding some excuse to leave, such as the mosquitoes.

I was busy during those four years with various writings, including translating Dr. Carus's *Gospel of Buddha* into Japanese, but all the time the koan was worrying at the back of my mind. It was, without any doubt, my chief preoccupation, and I remember sitting in a field, leaning against a rice stack and thinking that if I could not understand *Mu* life had no meaning for me. . . .

It often happens that some kind of crisis is necessary in one's life to make one put forth all one's strength in solving the koan. This is well illustrated in a story in the book *Keikyoku Soden, Stories of Brambles and Thistles*, compiled by one of Hakuin Zenshi's disciples, telling of various prickly experiences in practising Zen.

"A monk came from Okinawa to study Zen under Suio, one of Hakuin's great disciples and a rough and strong-minded fellow. It was he who taught Hakuin how to paint. The monk stayed with Suio for three years working on the koan of the sound of one hand. Eventually the time for him to go back to Okinawa was fast approaching, and he had still not solved his koan; he got very distressed and came to Suio in tears. The Master consoled him, saying, 'Don't worry. Postpone your departure for another week and go on sitting with all your might.' Seven days passed, but still the koan remained unsolved. Again the monk came to Suio, who counselled him to postpone his departure for yet another week. When that week was up and he still had not solved the koan, the Master said, 'There are many ancient examples of people who have attained satori after three weeks, so try a third week." But the third week passed and still the koan was not solved, so the Master said, 'Now try five more days.' But the five days passed and the monk was no nearer solving the koan, so finally the Master said, 'This time try three more days, and if after three days you still have not solved the koan, then you must die.' Then, for the first time, the monk decided to devote the whole of whatever life was left to him to solving the koan. And after three days he solved it."

The moral of this story is that one must decide to throw absolutely everything one has into the effort. "Man's extremity is God's opportunity." It often happens that just as one reaches the depths of despair and decides to take one's life, then and there satori comes. I imagine that with many people satori may have come when it was just too late. They were already on their way to death. . . .

This crisis or extremity came for me when it was finally settled that I should go to America to help Dr. Carus. . . . That winter might be my last chance to go to sesshin, and if I did not solve my koan then, I might never be able to do so. I put all my spiritual strength into that sesshin.

Until then I had always been conscious that *Mu* was in my mind. But so long as *I* was conscious of *Mu* it meant that I was somehow separated from *Mu*, and that is not a true samadhi. But towards the end of that sesshin, about the fifth day, I ceased to be conscious of *Mu*. I was one with *Mu*, I identified with *Mu*, so that there was no longer the separateness implied by being conscious of *Mu*. This is the real state of samadhi.

But this samadhi alone is not enough. You must come out of that state, be awakened from it, and that awakening is Prajna. That moment of coming out of the samadhi and seeing it for what it is —that is satori.

. . . I would like to stress the importance of becoming conscious of what it is that one has experienced. After kensho I was still not fully conscious of my experience. I was still in a kind of a dream. This greater depth of realization came later while I was in America, when suddenly the Zen phrase . . . "the elbow does not bend outwards" became clear to me. "The elbow does not bend outwards" might seem to express a kind of necessity, but suddenly I saw that this restriction was really freedom, the true freedom, and I felt that the whole question of free will had been solved for me."[23]

The "irrational quality" of the koan has a parallel in the Sufi use of jokes as meditation objects. The humorous effect of jokes is precisely linked to that paradoxical quality in them of a break in logical consistency that is still not a break in coherence at a non-logical level of understanding. There is a whole corpus of literature consisting of stories attributed to the seemingly foolish wise man Nasrudin, many of which have spread throughout the world as jokes to which nobody gives a second thought. Here is a Middle Eastern version of a familiar story, told in the words of Idries Shah:

> On one occasion a neighbor found [Nasrudin] down on his knees looking for something.
>
> "What have you lost, Mulla?"
>
> "My key," said Nasrudin.
>
> After a few minutes of searching, the other man said, "Where did you drop it?"
>
> "At home."
>
> "Then why, for heaven's sake, are you looking here?"
>
> "There is more light here."[24]

Though the story makes enough sense at a first reading to elicit a humorous response, the reader might be interested in exploring its meaning further by devoting a few minutes of exclusive attention to the situation depicted. Furthermore, he might ponder on the possible meaning of losing the *key*, of the statement that it lies at *home*, of *searching* for it where there is more *light*. He may find it useful for this end to enact the story in his mind, and *be* Nasrudin, the key, the home, the light, the friend. Last, he might recapitulate by inquiring to what extent Nasrudin's predicament is his own, "trying it on for size." "*I* am searching for the key in the wrong place," etc. These Nasrudin stories are given much importance in some Sufi orders. "The use to which the tales of Nasrudin are put in Sufi circles," writes an informant, "shows that the intention of the teacher is to develop in the student the form of thinking which is different from customary patterns. . . . Certain levels of human understanding cannot be attained, it is claimed, until the brain can work in more than one way. This is the equivalent of what in some systems is a 'mystical illumination process' but the Naqshbandis seem to hold that the brain is prepared by degrees without this illumination being as violent an experience as in other methods."[25]

When the seed idea constituting the meditation object is one that can be put in a few words, repetition of such words may serve as a means for the meditator to avoid distraction. Just as concentration in breathing is important, among other things, for its being a more concrete act of awareness than that of inner states, so, too, concentration on a verbal repetition lends a tangible support to the object of meditation, and this helps to ensure continuity in awareness.

Repetition of words or phrases may be vocal, subvocal, written, or in the medium of visual imagery. Still, the nature of the practice in each case is beyond the mechanical appearance of its outward form. As in all meditation, the goal of the exercise is the absorption of the individual in the idea upon which he dwells, and no amount of repetition would substitute for the right attitude and perhaps the proper guidance. The following autobiographical passage from Mohammed Alawi is revealing as to the "inner dimensions" of such a practice. Speaking of his teacher, he says:

His way of guiding his disciples, stage by stage, is varied. He would talk to some about the form in which Adam was created and to others about the cardinal virtues, and to others about Divine Actions, each instruction being especially suited for the disciple in question. But the course which he most often followed, and which I also followed, was to enjoin upon the disciple the invocation of the single name with the distinct visualization of its letters until they were written in his imagination. Then he would tell him to spread them out and enlarge them until they filled all the horizon. The dhikr would continue in this form until the letters became like

light. Then the Sheikh would show the way out of this standpoint
—it is impossible to explain in words how he did so—and by means
of this indication the spirit of the disciple would quickly reach
beyond the created universe provided that he had sufficient preparation and aptitude—otherwise there would be need for purification
and other spiritual training. At the above-mentioned indication, the
disciple would find himself able to distinguish between the Absolute
and the relative, and he would see the universe as a bowl or lamp
suspended in a beginningless endless void. Then it would grow
dimmer in his sight as he persevered in the invocation to the ac-
companiment of meditation, until it seemed no longer a definite
object but a mere trace appeared. Then it would become not even
a trace, until at length the disciple was submerged in the World of
the Absolute and his certainty was strengthened by Its Pure Light.
In all this the Sheikh would watch over him, and ask him about his
faith and strengthen him in the dihkr degree by degree until he
finally reached the point of being conscious of what he perceived
through his own power. The Sheikh would not be satisfied until this
point was reached, and he used to quote the words of God which
referred to 'one whom his Lord hath made certain and whose
certainty he hath then followed up on direct evidence.'

When the disciple had reached this degree of independent perception, which was strong or weak according to his capability, the
Sheikh would bring him back again to the world of outer forms
after he had left it, and it would seem to him the inverse of what it
had been before, simply before the light of his inward eye had
dawned. He would see it as *Light Upon Light,* and so it had been
before in reality.[26]

The practice of oral repetition is widespread in the form of
mantras and litanies, in recitation of sutras, in kirtan (chanting
of divine names, in Hinduism), the Nembutsu, in the practice
of Pure Land Buddhism, and in certain forms of prayer. Its highest development is probably to be found in Sufi circles, where
the exercise holds a prominent role and is known as *dhikr,* which
means repetition and also remembrance. This is an apt double

meaning, for the notion of "remembrance" is as appropriate to the psychological aspect of the exercise as "repetition" is to the physical or literal. In the Moslem tradition the utterance of the name of God is related to God's injunctions through the hand of the prophet: "Remember your Lord in yourself with compunction and awe. . . . Remember Me and I will remember you." In these we can see what we have pointed out as an aspect of meditation throughout these pages: meditation is a summoning up within oneself of a state of being that is not something to be created but our deepest reality. For this reality of ours to awaken, on the other hand, "we" must stand aside. This, translated into the complete words of the dhikr, means that the zakir (remembrancer) gives his attention more and more to the meaning of what is said, until he "is not so much busy with the dhikr (remembrance) as with the mazkur (the one invoked or remembered)."[27] This double movement of affirming the transcendent unity of existence and denying the attachments of the ego to partial reflections of the One Truth is the content of one of the most widespread forms of dhikr: the repetition of the words of the Prophet Mahomet: "LA ILAHA ILLA'LLAH" (There is no god but God).

The following passage from *Najmeddin Daya*, a thirteenth-century Sufi classic, is most explicit on both the outer and inner aspects of the repetition:

Having prepared a room which is empty, dark, and clean, in which he will, for preference, burn some sweet-scented incense, let him sit there, cross-legged, facing the qibla (direction of Mekka). Laying his hands on his thighs, let him stir up his heart to wakefulness, keeping a guard on his eyes. Then with profound veneration he should say aloud: LA ILAHA ILLA'LLAH. The LA ILAHA should be fetched from the root of the navel, and the ILLA'LLAH drawn into the heart, so that the powerful effects of the Zikr (dhikr) may make themselves felt in all the limbs and organs. But let him not raise his voice too loud. He should strive, as far as possible, to damp and lower it according to the words 'Invoke thy Lord in thyself humbly and with compunction, without publicity of speech.' . . .

After this fashion, then, he will utter the Zikr frequently and intently, thinking in his heart on the meaning of it and banishing every distraction. When he thinks of LA ILAHA, he should tell himself: I want nothing, seek nothing, love nothing ILLA'LLAH—but God. Thus, with LA ILAHA he denies and excludes all competing objects, and with ILLA'LLAH he affirms and posits the divine Majesty as his sole object loved, sought and aimed at.

In each Zikr his heart should be aware and present (hazir) from start to finish, with denial and affirmation. If he finds in his heart something to which he is attached, let him not regard it but give his attention to the divine Majesty, seeking the grace of help from the holy patronage of his spiritual Father. With the negation LA ILAHA let him wipe out that attachment, uprooting the love of that thing from his heart, and with ILLA'LLAH let him set up in its place the love of Truth (God).[28]

In reading the account above, in which the *content* is emphasized, one might overlook the importance ascribed to the *form* or phonetical aspect of most verbal repetition.

The names of the deity and divine attributes and emanations (just as those of the angels, demons, or djinn invoked by the magican) are highly important in all traditions as a key to the success of the theurgic operation. The particular name of the spiritual force is like a key that may unlock its power, and in this light we may understand the importance attached by Egyptian priests to words uttered under certain conditions (remarked by the distinguished Egyptologist Sir E. A. Wallis Budge) or of the secret pronunciation of the tetragrammaton.*

The thought that words and sounds may have a "power" may be understandable and acceptable to a modern mind if formu-

* Israel Regardie mentions a legend according to which "he who knows the correct pronunciation of YHVH, called the Shemha-Mephoresh, the Unpronounceable Name, possesses the means of destroying the universe, his particular universe, and hurling that individual consciousness into samadhi."[29]

lated in terms such as the following: the "powers" invoked by the words are states of consciousness and aspects of our psyche.* In a natural symbolism, there is a relationship between these and specific sounds, as there is between these and specific gestures, postures, colors, parts of the body, and elements of nature. To some extent, this is something that every good poet recognizes and uses implicitly when he chooses the appropriate phonetic expression for his ideas.† A word is a conventional symbol in that a given meaning is arbitrarily ascribed to a given string of sounds. But words are also *natural* symbols in that they their sound structure evokes in us a certain feeling state or an atmosphere of associations. In the first sense, a word is an intellectual symbol; in the second, a feeling symbol—*i.e.*, the bearer of a direct experience.

The use of the purely phonetical and non-intellectual aspect of word symbolism has apparently reached its maximum development in the Hindu tradition of Mantra Yoga and is also an important component of Vajrayana (Tibetan Buddhism). According to the mantra shastra, each element or category of the universe has its own natural sound, which is called its seed (*bija*). Each one of the elements has its mantra, and new mantras arise from the combination of these. Each deity has a mantra, and every mantra a deity. AUM has been called the queen of all mantras, and their source as well. There exists a whole literature on the significance of AUM and the technique of meditation thereon.

The phonetic aspect of a poem may be highly expressive to one who understands its words, so that form then becomes to the

* Francis Barrett, the British forerunner of Eliphas Levi, states in *The Magus:* "All the spirits, and as it were the essences of all things, lie hid in us, and are born and brought forth only by the working, power (will) and fantasy (imagination) of the microcosm."[30]

† Even in the natural structure of languages there seems to be a component of phonetic symbolism not to be explained as mere onomatopoeia. In a study that has become a classic, Roger Brown demonstrated that when English-speaking subjects were presented with pairs of antonyms in English, Chinese, Hindu, and Czech, they were able to match the English to appropriate terms of the other languages unknown to them with a degree of success beyond chance.[31]

content what blood is to the body. On the other hand, the same sounds will be without expressive value to one who does not have an understanding of the language. In a similar fashion, the claim that certain sounds are better than other sounds, expressions, and remembrances of certain experiences does not imply that the effectiveness of mantra is independent of the meditator's knowledge of its significance. In other words, mantras are not expected to be "magical" in the sense of being mechanically effective. Sir John Woodroffe, who devoted much attention to the subject, states quite explicitly: "The utterance of a mantra without knowledge of its meaning, or of the mantra method, is a mere movement of the lips and nothing more. The mantra sleeps. There are various processes preliminary to and involved in its right utterance. . . ."

Mantra, like visual symbols, postures, or ideas, are mere screens for the meditator to project aspects of his goal. The quality of the screen counts, but no meditation object is a real meditation object while it remains a mere object.

If we now return to a consideration of the dhikr described earlier, we will notice that the exercise is more than the repetition of certain words. It is obvious from the description that, like many other forms of meditation (in the broad sense used in this work), the exercise represents a coherent composite of several elements: among others, an attitude of repentance and purity, a feeling of veneration, a quality of awareness or "wakefulness," a selfless humility, love of God, and detachment from all other affections.

Even in an outer sense, this form of dhikr is more than the repetition of a formula, for "the LA ILAHA should be fetched from the root of the navel, and ILLA'LLAH drawn into the heart, so that the powerful effects of the dhikr may make themselves felt in all the limbs and organs." This aspect constitutes a bridge between the mantric aspect of the dhikr (verbal repetition) and still another type of concentrative meditation, which we will discuss here only briefly in spite of (and because of) its particular importance—that in which the meditation objects are certain areas of the body and their related functions or aspects of existence.

Meditation on the body "centers," the chakras of the Hindu and Tibetan systems, and the lataif[33] of the Arabic system, constitutes a complex spiritual science (just as that of the mandala or mantra), but elements of this knowledge are widespread as components of other types of meditation. Just as the dhikr is frequently a composite exercise bringing together into a coherent whole a number of different techniques, so are most forms of meditation. Even the utterly simple practice of counting the breath in the Zen tradition brings together quite a number of technical components: sustained awareness of breathing; spontaneity of the breath function not affected by watchfulness (a form of nondoing); stillness; an enactment of the posture of the sitting Buddha at the moment of enlightenment as a means to evoke the meditator's basic identity or Buddha nature; a posture of the hands (*maha mudra*) signifying the union of opposites, or specifically the identity of samsara and nirvana; the direction of attention to the belly region, so that the body is perceived as *centered* in an area that constitutes its natural center, and so on.

In many of these composite practices the body is given a special importance. Even when it is with images, ideas, or sounds that the meditator is concerned, these are considered to be located within the body, or as related to it, so that it could be said that his body becomes the temple for his ritual.

An example of the above may be found in the "Prayer of the Heart" of the Christian tradition. This prayer, which constituted the basic discipline of the early Fathers of the Church (and was later cultivated particularly by the Hesychast monks of Mount Athos), may well called the Christian dhikr. The following passages from St. Simeon the New Theologian (contained in the *Philokalia**) should make this apparent:

---

* An ascetic-mystical anthology, compiled in the eighteenth century, probably by Macarius of Corinth and Nicodemus of the Holy Mountain, and first published in Venice in 1782. It contains writings of the Fathers of the Christian Church of the first millennium.

There are three methods of attention in prayer, by which the soul is uplifted and moved forward, or is cast down and destroyed. Whoever employs these methods at the right time and in the right way, moves forward. . . .

Attention should be linked to prayer as inseparably as body is linked to soul. . . . Attention should go on ahead, spying out the enemy, like a scout. . . .

The distinctive features of the first method are as follows: if a man stands in prayer and, raising his hands, his eyes and his mind to heaven, keeps in mind Divine thoughts, imagines celestial blessings, hierarchies of angels and dwellings of the saints, assembles briefly in his mind all that he has learned from the Holy Scriptures and ponders over all of this while at prayer, gazing up at heaven, and thus inciting his soul to longing and love of God, at times even shedding tears and weeping, this will be the first method of attention and prayer.

But if a man chooses only this method of prayer it happens that, little by little, he begins to pride himself in his heart, without realizing it; it seems to him that what he is doing comes from God's grace. . . .

This method contains another danger of going astray; namely, when a man sees light with his bodily eyes, smells sweet scents, hears voices and many other like phenomena. Some have become totally possessed, and in their madness wander from place to place. . . .

The second method is this: a man tears his mind away from all sensed objects and leads it within himself, guarding his senses and collecting his thoughts, so that they cease to wander amid the vanities of this world; now he examines his thoughts, now ponders over the words of the prayer his lips utter, now pulls back his thoughts if, ravished by the devil, they fly toward something bad and vain, now with great labour and self-exertion, strives to come back into himself, after being caught and vanquished by some passion. The distinctive feature of this method is that it takes place in the head, thought fighting against thought. In this struggle against himself, a man can never be at peace in himself, nor find time to practise virtues in order to gain the crown of truth. Such a man is like one fighting his enemies at night in the dark; . . . because he himself remains in the head, whereas evil thoughts are generated in the heart. He does not even see them, for his attention is not in his heart. . . .

Truly the third method is marvelous and difficult to explain. . . . If someone observes perfect obedience towards his spiritual father, he becomes free from all cares, because once and for all he has laid all his cares on the shoulders of his spiritual father. Therefore, being far from all worldly attachments, he becomes capable of zealous and diligent practice of the third method of prayer, provided he has found a true spiritual father, who is not subject to prelest. . . .

The beginning of this third method is not gazing upward to heaven, raising one's hands, or keeping one's mind on heavenly things; these, as we have said, are the attributes of the first method, and are not far removed from prelest. Neither does it consist in guarding the senses with the mind and directing all one's attention upon this, not watching for the onslaughts of the demons on the soul from within. . . .

Proceeding in this way you will smoothe for yourself a true and straight path to the third method of attention and prayer which is the following: the mind should be in the heart—a distinctive feature of the third method of prayer. It should guard the heart while it prays, revolve, remaining always within, and thence, from the depths of the heart, offer up prayers to God. (Everything is in this; work in this way until you are given to taste the Lord.)

. . . As to other results which usually come from this work, with God's help, you will learn them from your own experience, by keeping your mind attentive and in your heart holding Jesus, that is, His prayer—Lord Jesus Christ, have mercy upon me! One of the holy fathers says: 'Sit in your cell and this prayer will teach you everything.'[34]

The same source offers other descriptions and indications as to breathing, aside from those of the repetitive prayer and the attention directed to the heart area. The following is a passage from the Patriarch Callisotis and his fellow-worker Ignatius of Xanthopoulos:

"You know, brother, how do we breathe: we breathe the air in and out. On this is based the life of the body, and on this depends its warmth. So, sitting down in your cell, collect your mind, lead it into the path of the breath, along which the air enters in, constrain it to enter the heart together with the inhaled air, and keep it there. Keep it there, but do not leave it silent and idle; instead give it the following prayer: 'Lord, Jesus Christ, Son of God, have mercy upon me.' Let this be its constant occupation, never to be abandoned. For this work, by keeping the mind free from dreaming, renders it unassailable to suggestions of the enemy and leads it to Divine desire and love."[35]

One particular element of Nadi Yoga, which frequently occurs in association with apparently dissimilar practices, is its first stage: that of centering, or focusing attention, in the lower abdomen.* This region is called in Japanese *hara*, a word that signifies not only the center of the body but also the center of the soul, and is a prominent concept in the culture of that country. According to Durkheim:

There are master schools that make *hara* the sole object of their exercise, while every master art in Japan considers that it is necessary to possess it in order to achieve "success" in whatever one is doing. To a Japanese, what a man experiences in the "center of being" is none other than the unity of life, bearing all, permeating all, nourishing and enfolding all.[36]

When we deal with spiritual disciplines that involve the manipulation of images or sounds, we can conceive these as "symbolic" and say that the symbol evokes a psychological reality, or that the individual in his meditative absorption "becomes" what the symbol represents. When we deal with the domain of anatomical objects of meditation, can we consider these as merely symbolic? Is, for instance, a condition of physical cen-

---

* Some methods emphasize the solar plexus (as in the position of hands in Za-Zen), while others choose a point under the navel, and others the "root chakra."

teredness in the abdominal area a mere symbolic expression of a psychological or spiritual centeredness, or is the psychophysical parallelism the expression of the fact that each single condition of being is mirrored in the domain of both psyche and soma?

If we think that we *are* our body, we will have no trouble understanding the powers of the body-centered techniques of meditation in affecting the individual's state. If, on the other hand, we prefer to regard physical localizations as symbolic of inner states, we cannot fail to see that this is a symbolism more natural and "closer to home" than any other. In this symbolism, our whole body stands for our "self" (as we ordinarily imply when we say, for instance, "Don't touch me!") and different regions of the body relate to different domains of experience.*

In the Tantric tradition of India and Tibet, the body is seen as a field of a double polarity: one, the right-left (*ida* and *pingala*, "sun" and "moon"; *ha-tha*, involution-evolution); and the other, above-below, (consciousness and power, spirit and matter). The spiritual work consists in the unification of these opposites and the attainment of the center of a symbolic cross. The integration of this double polarity "is experienced in successive stages, namely in successive chakras, of which each represents a different dimension of consciousness, and in which the higher dimension includes the lower one without annihilating its qualities."[38]

More precisely, the body is regarded as comprising in the vertical plane three regions: head, chest, and abdomen, and in each of these are located the chakras that express particular specializations of the character of each region. The systems of Hindu and Buddhistic Tantras here diverge. The former speaks of three chakras in each of the extreme regions, which, added to the heart chakra, give a total of seven. The Buddhistic tradition,

* The work of Sheldon might be taken as an indication that this is more than symbolism.[37]

on the other hand, takes into account only two chakras each in the head and in the abdominal region, and thus deals with a system of five.*

The chakras are regarded as positive and negative (and, in the Hindu Tantras, neutral) particularizations of the functions expressed by the three regions of the body. This type of body symbolism is quite natural, and one that is implicit in our current speech when we say that a person "has guts" or "is kind-hearted," or that somebody "lives in his head." Here is a brief characterization of the lower, upper, and middle regions in the words of the Lama Angarika Govinda:

> Lower: A terrestrial plane, namely that of earth-bound elementary forces of nature, of materiality, corporality, an emphasis on the "materialized past";
>
> Upper: The cosmic or universal plane of eternal laws, of timeless knowledge (which from the human point of view is felt as a "future" state of attainment, a goal yet to be attained), a place of continuous spiritual awareness of the Infinite, as symbolized in the boundlessness of space and in the experience of the Great Void (*sunyata*) in which form and non-form are equally comprised;
>
> Middle: The human plane or individual realization, in which the qualities of terrestrial existence and cosmic relationships, the forces of the earth and of the universe, become conscious in the human soul as an ever-present and *deeply felt* reality. Therefore, the Heart Center becomes the seat of the seed-syllable HUM in contradistinction to the OM of the Crown Center.[39]

The formulations of the Taoist system of meditation are quite similar. There are in man three currents or rivers (called "seed," "breath," and "spirit"), which are in correspondence, but not identical, with their physical manifestations and in turn are influenced by them. These three "humors," which might be rendered as a force of generation, a vital force, and a spiritual

---

* Vajrayana Buddhism eliminates the *swadhist chakra* (the gential center) and its upper correspondent, *ajna chakra* (between the eyebrows).

force, must be united to generate the immortal man, the "diamond body." In accordance with this conception, "There are three points of departure for meditation . . . , namely the 'three fields of cinnabar' . . . or fields of the alchemical elixir: the 'upper' field is in the middle of the forehead, seat of the 'radiance of our essential nature' . . . ; the 'middle' field is in the heart, the true source of the cinnabar-red elixir and of the conscious soul . . . ; and the 'true' field is in the middle of the body (approximately from the navel to the kidneys) seat of the vital force . . . and of the lower soul. . . ."[40]

For the sake of clarity, we have been dealing separately with different areas of symbolization in which the meditator may dwell, different sense-modalities in which he may find the reflection of his "object." But here it may be appropriate to note that the most elaborate meditation systems take advantage of the correspondence between different domains. This might seem to contradict one of the characteristics of meditation indicated earlier: that of one-pointedness of attention or concentration. We can understand how this is not really so if we make a distinction between the perceptual basis of the meditation object, which may be called the *apparent object*, and the experiential meaning conveyed by it, which constitutes the *object itself*. Only at the latter level of meaning can the meditator achieve identification with his "object." In fact the "object" has been himself all along, so that what he does in the process of such unification is to *re-absorb* the meaning projected into the image, sound, or other symbol, and experience it fully as himself.

When we consider the case of meditation techniques involving a single sensory object—visual, motoric, musical, mantric, somatic—concentration on the evoked meaning coincides with concentration on the percept, and we may speak of "concentration" in the usual technical sense. When we consider multi-media meditation, though, concentration on the meaning upon which the different symbolic media converge is paralleled by the division of attention among the images, sounds, actions, etc., that may be involved in that particular sadhana. Yet that apparent division of attention is only superficial: the simultaneous meditation objects that a person contemplates (*i.e.*, bija, mantra, and chakra) are *in essence* the same (if not complementary aspects to be united in a more encompassing whole).

Though some of the practices described in the foregoing pages are, as we have remarked, composites that bring together a number of technical devices, a further example may give a fuller picture of the systematic use of a multisymbolic approach to meditation. This is a Tibetan practice, whose object is the generation of the "inner fire" and in which one may see the superimposition of devotionalism, meditation on the breath, contemplation of images, Chakra Yoga, and mantra:

> After the Sadhaka [artist] has purified his mind through devotional exercises and has put himself into a state of inner preparedness and receptivity; after he has regulated the rhythm of his breath, filled it with consciousness and spiritualized it through mantric work, he directs his attention to the Navel Centre (*Manipura*), in whose lotus he visualizes the seed-syllable RAM and above it the seed-syllable MA, from which latter emerges *Dorje Naljorma* (Sanskrit: *Vajra-Yogini*), a *Khadoma* of a brilliant red colour surrounded by a halo of flames.
>
> As soon as the meditator has become one with the divine form of the *Khadoma* and knows himself as *Dorje Naljorma*, he places the seed-syllable A into the lowest, the seed-syllable HAM into the highest, Centre (the "thousand-petalled Lotus" of the Crown Centre).
>
> Thereupon he arouses, by deep conscious respiration and intense mental concentration, the seed-syllable A to a state of incandescence; and this, being fanned and intensified with every inhalation, grows steadily from the size of a fiery pearl to that of a fierce flame, which through the middle *nadi* finally reaches the Crown Centre from where now the white nectar, the Elixir of Life, issues from the seed-syllable HAM (which the meditator has placed and visualized in this Centre) and while flowering down, penetrates the whole body.
>
> This exercise can be described in ten stages: in the first the

susumna, with its rising flame, is visualized as fine as a hair, in the second stage as thick as a little finger, in the third of the thickness of an arm, in the fourth as light as the whole body, *i.e.*, as if the body itself had turned into a *susumna* and had become a single vessel of fire. In the fifth stage, the unfolding vision attains its climax; the body ceases to exist for the meditator. The whole world becomes a fiery *susumna*, an infinite, raging ocean of fire.

With the sixth stage begins the reverse process of integration and perfection; the storm abates and the fiery ocean is re-absorbed by the body. In the seventh stage the *susumna* shrinks to the thickness of an arm; in the eighth to the thickness of a small finger; in the ninth to that of a hair; and in the tenth it disappears altogether and dissolves into the Great Void (Sanskrit: *sunyata*) in which the duality of the knower and the known is transcended and the great synthesis of spiritual completeness is realized.[41]

At this point we may draw a distinction between two types of meditation objects according to the domain of perception to which they belong. On the one hand, there are those that we examined first and found to express centrality, radiation, emptiness, etc., and that may be taken to express the totality of man's being or essential nature (the cross, OM, fire, etc.). On the other hand, there are meditation objects that are more restricted in meaning, standing for more particular aspects of man's psyche (the crescent, the syllable AH, water).

Most mantra, chakras, and images correspond to *specific* facets of man's appearance, which will eventually become the object of unification with complementary aspects through a meditative process like the one quoted above, or through a ritual operation. In terms of these strategies we may distinguish contrasting systems of meditation. In one, the individual evokes the ultimate goal, the center of his being, the object of his highest aspiration, and most exalted state. In the other, his goal appears to be less ambitious, for he is evoking only a part of his being, and for that very reason his operation is more likely to succeed. The ultimate goal, though, even in this approach, is the bringing together into an encompassing totality of all the faculties or experiences first meditated upon one after another.

In the Tibetan exercise of gtum-mo, for instance, the end result is expressed in the symbol of integration: "The fire of spiritual integration which fuses all polarities, all mutually exclusive elements arising from the separateness of individualization, this is what the Tibetan word *gtum-mo* means in the deepest sense, and what makes it one of the most important symbols of meditation."[42] The approach here is different from that of Vedic ritual, where absorption in the sacrificial fire is both the end and the beginning. In the Tibetan practice described by Govinda, the fire is the result of the polarity and union of two opposite principles, symbolized in A and HAM. A is the seed-syllable of the female or mother principle, and HA that of the male or father principle. A is wisdom (*prajna*) and HA love; the final M, written in Tibetan as a dot (*bindu*), symbolizes the union. Moreover, the symbolic action of unification is expressed in one more aspect of the sadhana under discussion:

> ". . . the seed-syllable A which represents the principle of cognition in the above-mentioned meditative practice, and which the Hinduistic chakra system characteristically associates with the Centre of inner vision (ajna chakra), is to be visualized in the lower centre, namely at the entrance of *susumna* (the Root Centre is here not to be contemplated), while the seed-syllable HAM, here representing the creative principle or Elixir of Life, is visualized in the Crown Centre. This visualization is a symbolic anticipation of the aim, as may be seen from the fact that only when the heat of the flaming A reaches the HAM, the latter is activated and liquefied . . . into the degenerative force of an enlightened consciousness which fills the thousand-petalled lotus and, overflowing from it, descends into all the other centres.[43]

Systems like the one above, and Tantras on the whole, might appear as unwarrantedly complicated when contrasted with the simplicity of the Christian mystic's way to *ekstasis* or the practice of *shikan-taza* in Zen Buddhism. But such complexity is merely another expression of the understanding that simplicity is not as simple to achieve as it might seem. To invoke the highest goal requires a knowledge of the goal. To dwell upon the deity requires an experience of the sacred. To "see into one's nature" requires a previous breakthrough into reality.

There is in classical Buddhism a meditation exercise called the "recollection of nirvana" or the "recollection of peace," in which the meditator should in solitude and seclusion "recall the qualities of nirvana," which is defined as the appeasing of all ill, with the words: "As far as there are dharmas, conditioned or unconditioned, dispassion has been thought as the highest of these dharmas, *i.e.*, the sobering of thought-intoxication, the removal of thirst, the uprooting of clinging, the halting of the round (of samsara), the extinction of craving, dispassion, stopping, Nirvana (Anguttara Nikaya, 1134). Like the other five 'recollections,' though, the text informs us that this one *"can be properly and successfully accomplished only on the level of sainthood."*[44] This parallels the statement of alchemists that in order to make gold, one must have gold.

In addition to this type of meditation, which has the potential of leading into full trance, Buddhistic scriptures of the same school describe many others that are conceived as preliminaries, their aim being less distant. It is illustrative to consider the list presented by the fifth-century Buddhaghosa in his "Path of Purity" ("Visuddhimagga"):

Ten Devices: 1. earth; 2. water; 3. fire; 4. air; 5. blue; 6. yellow; 7. red; 8. white; 9. light; 10. enclosed space.

Ten Repulsive Things: 11. swollen corpse; 12. blueish corpse; 13. festering corpse; 14. fissured corpse; 15. gnawed corpse; 16. scattered corpse; 17. hacked and scattered corpse; 18. bloody corpse; 19. worm-eaten corpse; 20. skeleton.

Ten Recollections: 21. the Buddha; 22. the Dharma; 23. the Samgha; 24. Morality; 25. Liberality; 26. Devas; 27. Death; 28. What belongs to the body; 29. Respiration; 30. Peace.

Four Stations of Brahma: 31. Friendliness; 32. Compassion; 33. Sympathetic joy; 34. Even-mindedness.

Four Formless States: 35. Station of endless space; 36. Station of unlimited consciousness; 37. Station of nothing whatsoever; 38. Station of neither perception nor non-perception.

One Perception: 39. of the disgusting aspects of food.

One Analysis: 40. into the four elements.[45]

According to Edward Conze:

Two only among the forty are always and under all circumstances beneficial—the development of friendliness and the recollection of death. The remainder are suitable only for some people, and under quite definite circumstances. The recollection of Buddha, for instance, demands strong faith, and even-mindedness presupposes great proficiency in the "Stations of Brahma" which precede it. In this way, some of the meditations may be outside a person's range, others may meet with insuperable resistance, others again may fulfill no useful purpose. Because, as such, the exercises have no value in themselves. They are only cultivated as antidotes to specific unwholesome and undesirable states.[46]

We find a similar situation if we turn to classical yoga. In his twenty-first sutra, Patanjali says: "It [samadhi] is closest to those who desire it intensely." And in the twenty-third, he adds that samadhi can also be attained by self-surrender to God (*isvara-pranidhana*). This is a statement that has puzzled commentators, for Shamkya philosophy, in terms of which Patanjali's Yoga is formulated, is atheistic. On the other hand, it is not upon surrender to isvara that Patanjali lays emphasis as a means of enlightenment, but on the techniques of Astanga Yoga, which is based upon the development of concentration and will. Still, he cannot bypass the existence of that universal experience, which is the heart of the devotional path. Mircea Eliade answers his own question as to Patanjali's need to introduce isvara by saying that isvara corresponds to an experimental fact; in fact, isvara may provoke samadhi if only the yogi practices the exercise called isvara-pranidhana, that is to say, if he takes isvara as the goal of his actions. In attempting to bring together and classify all the valid techniques of yoga in the "classical tradition," Patanjali could not dismiss unusual experiences only obtained through concentration on isvara. That is: aside from the traditions of an exclusively "magical" Yoga which only appeals to will and the personal resources of the ascetic, there was another tradition, a "mystical" one, in which the last stages of Yoga practice were facilitated, at least, by means of a devotion . . . toward a God.[47]

Just as the "mystical" tradition (in the restricted sense) reaches upward in affirmation, the "magical," which we might better call "technical" or perhaps "theurgic," stresses a deepening in the contemplation of our present level of experience, or even a furrowing into an underworld upon which our experience is based. This reaching downward is no doubt the source of the "devilish" associations to the Tantric and magical traditions, as well as the source of some real dangers. This way of descent, immortalized by Dante in his journey through hell, is that of establishing contact with the repressed and suppressed, with those "dormant powers" without which no unity of being would be possible.

A medieval medallion with the text of the famed Emerald Tablet of Hermes Trismegistus bears an inscription that expresses in condensed form the leading idea of the journey of descent. It is an acrostic on the word "vitriol," the Latin for the corrosive sulphuric acid: *Visita Interiora Terrae Rectificando Invenies Occultum Lapidem.* (Visit the inside of the earth. In rectifying you will arrive at the secret stone.) The philosopher's stone, which is the goal of the alchemistic pursuit and which has the virtue of turning "baser metals" into "gold," is to be found through a "corrosive" action upon the earthy side of existence rather than by aspiring toward the lofty heights.

The expressions of this movement of descent in the spiritual disciplines of mankind have been various. One aspect of it is what Dante's hell obviously represents: a journey of self-exploration. Here contemplation is not directed to symbolic embodiments of the spiritual goal nor to particular aspects of the psyche, but toward experience unmediated by symbols. A serene, impartial observation of what we are, not limited to or biased by what we judge as "good," cannot help leading to a re-evaluation of what we are, and eventually to a "seeing into our true nature." The second embodiment of the strategy of descent is in the use of symbolic forms to awaken the inhabitants of our dark underworld from their slumber. Professor Tucci writes:

> The ancient phantoms, the memory of a primitive and far-off world, the monsters and strange figures of primeval gods, the fruits of barbarous and cruel intuitions live on in the depths of our souls and it would be vain to attempt their suppression. They would re-appear unexpectedly on the edge of our subconscious. Gnosis does not deny them, does not drive them back, but *guides* them, as guests of the senses, toward more noble paths, or *transforms* them.

The point of view on which this operation is based is an optimistic one that sees all the undesirable drives in the human personality as a mere imbalance or misapplication of natural forces that are not evil in themselves. The archetypal images used to personify and summon up the forces, therefore, are images that serve as models that direct them to their proper channels. In general, the symbolism of dark deities that mankind has created may be seen in this light. When the Greek genius conceived Dionysus as a mad god, it was seeing godliness even in human madness, and bowing in trust to the forces of chaos within the individual soul. Only today are we beginning to think that this may be after all the most satisfactory way of dealing with and "curing" psychosis.* When the Hindus conceived of Shiva, the destroyer, they were acknowledging the destructive aspect of

* See pp. 106ff.

any creative action, and the positive—even indispensable—role of aggression in life. It can be expected that meditation on Shiva would lead the individual to the assimilation of his insight and to his finding a constructive course for his own aggressive potential. The "dark" figures of Dionysus, Persephone, and others, the idea of descent to a netherworld and the process of psychological "death" prior to renewal, were dominant in the Mysteries of antiquity, and it is small wonder that these pagan rites (or what remained of them through the European Middle Ages) came to be seen by Christian eyes as satanic masses and cults of the devil. European Christianity, with its asceticism, was an attempt to reach God by transcending nature; the Mystery religions, quite the opposite, found the universal soul-spirit *in* nature and attempted a synthesis in which natural man would be included and exalted.

A third aspect of the way of descent in meditation is the importance given to the body. The upward-reaching West, with its pointed cathedral spikes and its Faustian striving, has apparently wanted a short-cut to heaven, and in spite of Jesus' statement that the kingdom of heaven is within, this has mostly been envisaged as above the body. Accordingly, whenever physical techniques were employed in Christian mysticism, they met some criticism and did not become part of the main historical tradition.* By contrast, the East has always given great importance to psychophysiological techniques as a means of enlightenment.

The East in general has asserted what only the esoteric tradition has maintained in the West: that man, and specifically the body, is a microcosm reflecting the macrocosm. In the body dwell all the gods, but they must be awakened. Or, in the language of the Alexandrian Gnostics, the body is the cross to which our Christ-nature is nailed, the tomb in which our spirit lays imprisoned.

* We find, for instance, comments by Church authorities to the effect that the breathing exercises of the Hesychasts were something of the devil.

There is a passage in the Surangama Sutra where Buddha ties one knot after another in a handkerchief, and after each he asks his disciple Ananda, "What is this?" After having tied the seventh knot and heard an identical answer from Ananda, Buddha explains that not all knots are the same because of the order in which they have been tied. "If we wish to untie a knot, we must first find out how the knot was tied. He who knows the origin of all things, knows also their dissolution. But let me ask you another question: Can all the knots be untied at the same time?

"No, Blessed Lord! Since the knots were tied one after another in a certain order, we cannot untie them, unless we follow the reverse order."

To start with the last knot, in the Buddhist darshan, means to start with the body, and within the body (in the chakra system) with its most bodylike region, the foundation, or lower area. The contrast between East and West in this last aspect is also suggestive of the predominant spirit of the respective cultures: Western man, in his ambition to fly out of his body, has identified with the head or, at lowest, with the heart. Orientals, with no less spiritual ambition, have stressed the importance of attaining rootedness in the body first and have cultivated the feeling of the center of gravity in the belly. This experience, which might appear to be a matter of trivial psychological gymnastics, has proved to be an exercise of far-reaching consequences. As may be seen from the following description by Professor Rousselle, the pursuit of centeredness on the abdominal region is the dominant element in the method of Taoistic meditation:

1. Choose a quiet room, neither dark nor bright. In a bright room, one is disturbed by outward images, in a dark room, by inner images.
2. Choose a comfortable position, which the body will not be compelled to change soon, a sitting position. Crossing of the legs in the traditional tailor's posture is quite unnecessary for anyone not

accustomed to it. On the contrary, it is a good idea to set the feet firmly on the ground.

3. Hold the back straight (supported by a back rest if desired) and the head high but bent backward a little, so that the tip of the nose is vertically over the navel and the "light of the eyes" can easily be directed toward the body's center (solar plexus), *i.e.*, so that consciousness can easily be directed toward the unconscious.

4. Keep the eyes half closed. The same would be true of entirely open or entirely closed eyes as of bright or dark rooms. The eyes —their gaze converging over the tip of the nose—are directed toward the solar plexus.

5. Hold the hands together, as in the Chinese greeting—the right hand forms a fist which is held clasped by the left. This represents a *communio naturarum* of the yin and yang.

6. Before beginning to meditate, breathe from three to five times, deeply, slowly and evenly, so that the "sea of breath" (*ch'i hai*) is stimulated in the abdomen. In this way you will avoid being disturbed in the course of meditation by the need to take a deep breath. During meditation, pay no attention to breathing. The mouth must be closed, you must breathe entirely through your nose.

7. Look reverently at the picture of the Master (in the student's certificate). Thus you will be in his presence as it were, and will keep yourself open to meditation with confidence.

8. Banish all thought. A total emptiness of mind is created. Meditation consists in "letting go." It is not the surface consciousness but the creative genius of the deep psyche that should speak to us.

9. This emptiness of thought is facilitated by its positive counterpart, which consists in directing consciousness toward the body's center, *i.e.*, the unconscious.

10. You now enter upon the first of the three preparatory stages of meditation. All thoughts are bound fast in imagination to the body's center (*eros!*) like monkeys at the foot of a tree. The bond between *logos* and *eros* paralyzes the "monkey" thoughts. Consciousness by an act of the imagination is shifted to the solar plexus, i.e., the unconscious. This fixation is called *ting* (c.f., in Indian Yoga, dharana).

11. This produces a certain degree of relaxation, though there is still a faint striving to hold fast. This second preparatory stage of release or silence is called *ching*.

12. One now attains the third stage, in which there is no further effort or tension, the state of peaceful beatitude (*an*).

Now at last the stage has been reached in which something can "happen" to you. What you now experience is the content of your meditation—but images and ideas must be expelled at once! It is impossible to guess beforehand what this content will be. Certain temporary disturbances of the meditation will occur, but these are actually an indication that you have meditated correctly.[48]

It would be artificial to separate completely the two approaches that we are outlining, one of ascent and the other of descent; one of contemplating unity and the other of exploring multiplicity; one, a knocking at the door of the heart of things, and the other a starting at the periphery. There are systems like the meditation on the sephira in European Cabala, or the meditation on mandalas, in which these two movements are like in-breath and out-breath. The mandala, for instance, is a "cosmogram" or "psychogram" to which the meditator journeys with the mind from the multiplicity of the fourfold periphery to the center, and from the center again into the periphery, thus bringing about his own unification and relating from his center to the multiplicity of light.

Still, the predominance of one or another approach in some methods justifies raising the question of their comparative merit. May any one be said to be more appropriate than the other, in general, or are the "mystical" and "technical" ways appropriate to different kinds of men? Opinions as to the unparalleled merit of this or that particular system of meditation are easy to find in any school, and the great number of discordant statements may be a reason to doubt their impartiality. Devotional mystics, for instance, tend to regard the whole idea of technique as foreign to the spiritual domain, and frequently conceive the higher states of consciousness as gifts of grace that may not be earned. "The grace of contemplation," says Bernard of Clairvaux, "was granted only in response to longing, and importunate desire." And even this desire is a gift of divine grace; it is not man who seeks God but God who seeks man. The prayer of Christian mystics is *oratio infusa*, imparted, inspired from above.

But even if the illumination of grace be God's gift, can we make ourselves receptive to it? Empirical research is still to be carried out to ascertain whether the gifts received by a Christian devotionalist or by a Sufi, a Pure Land Buddhist, or a yogi are comparable.

Aside from the possibility of one or another type of meditation being more effective in general, or more appropriate to a certain type of individual, there is the possibility that the ways of descent and ascent may be suited to different stages of spiritual unfolding. One of the most memorable expressions of this is to be found in the *Divine Comedy*. Dante describes how, soon after waking up halfway along the course of his life and finding himself in a dark forest, lost, he saw the rays of the sun illuminating the summit of a mountain.

> Then I looked up, and saw the morning's rays
> Mantle its shoulder from that planet bright
> Which guides men's feet aright on all their ways.[49]

When he proceeded, full of hope, to walk toward the higher goal, however, he found that the enterprise was impossible. His way was obstructed by three successive animals, so terrifying that he realized that he had to give up the attempt of climbing. At this point, in his despair, Virgil appeared to him to guide him, but Dante's journey would now be *un altro viaggio: another* journey. The short way to the "Mount Delectable from which grows the beginning of all joy" being barred, he would have to take that long detour through the Kingdom of the Dead: he would have to *descend* before being able to *ascend* (the Mountain of Purgatory). In his version of the spiritual quest, the descent into hell is the very means of overcoming the obstacles to his ascent: for each of the animals blocking the way, there will be a corresponding region or level in the underworld. The journey through hell is thus analytical and introspective: it is one of confrontation with the passions, the moving forces of one's life in their chaotic actuality. It is an enterprise of pure awareness. The ascent of Mount Purgatory, by contrast, is an act of striving and of devotion in which the soul is lifted by remembrance of its goal.

Is this the path of only one individual, Dante Alighieri, or is there a truth in it that applies to the human condition in general? Should we think of the journeys into multiplicity and into unity, into the given and into the possible, into the soul and into God, as successive states rather than as parallel ways? If so, the way for a given individual would depend upon his station along the path.

Another contrast to be seen among the forms of object meditation described thus far (not unrelated to what has just been discussed) is that between techniques that involve varying degrees of support in the physical world. Thus, at one end of the gamut, we find exercises like concentration on a single mental image. Close to the other end, there are practices like the Tibetan meditation, mentioned above, that involve simultaneous use of breathing, visualization, mantra, and chakra Yoga. Yet, here the images are still internalized, the sound silent, the chakras used merely as aids to the location of visual images. Much richer in sensory experience is the practice of the European occultist who, wanting to invoke Hermes, stands within an octagon surrounded by inscriptions peculiarly relevant to Hermes' nature, in an environment where color predominates and where burns the incense storax.

In commenting precisely on this ceremony, Israel Regardie draws attention to the contrast that we are examining, which he equates with that between mysticism and magic:

Mysticism ordinarily conceives of the senses as barriers to the light of the soul, and that the presence of the latter is debarred from manifestation by reason of the disruptive influence and turbulence of the senses and mind. In magic, however, the senses are considered to be, when under control, the golden gateways through which the King of Glory may come in. In the work of invocation, every sense and each faculty must be made to participate.[50]

On the other hand, as we have commented in regard to mantra, a ritual can be psychologically effective only if the actions and perceptions that it involves are saturated with meaning. Then we may ask: if the meaning is what counts, why complicate meditation with unnecessary images, actions, sounds, or paraphernalia? There is an Oriental tale that brings the point home.

A conventionally minded dervish, walking along the shore of a lake, heard another dervish give the dervish call incorrectly uttered. Considering it a duty to correct the unfortunate person who was mispronouncing the syllables, for this was probably someone who had had no guidance and was probably "doing his best to attune himself to the idea behind the sound," he hired a boat and traveled to the island from where the loud shout came. He corrected the other dervish, who thanked him, and felt satisfied with his own good deed. After all, it is said that a man who could repeat sacred formulas correctly could even walk on the waves.

While he was thinking like this, he suddenly saw a strange sight. From the island the other dervish was coming toward him, walking on the surface of the water. "Brother," he said to him when he was close enough, "I am sorry to trouble you but I have come out again to ask you the standard method of making the repetition you were telling me, because I find it difficult to remember it."[51]

If the essence of meditation is in an attitude, why so many rituals and techniques? The answer can be the same as to why employ symbolic forms in general. Why books, if what counts is meaning and not the words? Why music, if what counts is feeling and not the sound?

The ideal of meditation should be such a firm grasp on the "meaning" that forms become unnecessary,* such a direct contact of the person with reality that he needs no technique. What is the use of the scaffold once the house has been built?

Symbols serve to indicate something beyond themselves, but symbols can also become veils, usurping the place of that which they symbolize. Religious and artistic forms, philosophical *Weltanschauungen*, all stem from certain experiences or from the elicitation of experiences. Yet most religious and artistic images and philosophical forms have become petrified symbols, mere icons that do not speak any more.

Aware of the propensity of individuals to become attached to dead husks and substitute the word expressing the image for the spirit behind it, some mystical traditions have emphasized forms of meditations that bypass symbols, rituals, and ideas. In these, the attitude is all important, and the object may be anything or nothing.

True, in doing away with objects and procedures we do away with the danger of mistaking the issue and taking the outer trappings for the real aim. But how can this all-important attitude be communicated? It is easy to write at length about this or that *technique* of meditation, but how are we to describe a meditation without technique? This becomes as difficult as painting the smile of the Cheshire cat without the cat.

The simpler the meditation object becomes, the less prone the meditator is to fall in love with any counterfeit substitute of his heart's desire, and the more he is on his own in the search, unsupported by a language of forms. Christian mystics speak

* In his essay on contemplation in Christian mysticism, Heiler states: "Contemplation is directed toward the ultimate, the highest, the absolute, toward God in His totality and infinity, in 'His unutterable plenitude.' In contemplation, the spirit gazes into an abyss, an ocean, a dazzling sun. All concrete conceptions and imaginings, all *corporales similitudines*, are left far behind; banished are all the religious and cultic symbols; even the humanity of the Son of God, the child in the manger, the sufferer on the Cross, are left behind."[52]

of prayer as "the practice of the presence of God," yogis speak of "detachment," Moslems of "surrender." All these expressions and others point to *one* elephant, but an abyss lies between these words and the experience that constitutes their confluence. What does the meditator have if he has no symbols to guide him toward the ineffable goal?

The answer, I think, is twofold: (1) the knowledge of what is *not* his goal, so that he may progress by elimination and outgrowing; and (2) the prompting from his own essence, which sleeps within him and has in its very nature the answers that "he," identifying in himself with his learned roles and cultural heritage, does not know.

The first idea is the backbone of what we shall deal with in the following chapter as "The Negative Way." The second is behind the methods that I describe in Chapter IV as the "Way of Surrender," the "Expressive Way," or the "Way of the Prophets."

3 / The Negative Way

The negative way may seem opposite to the previously described approaches to meditation (upon externally given objects or upon internally arising mental contents), but this is only superficially so. Moreover, *the "negative" dimension of the meditation may be considered to be the invisible backbone sustaining both the concentrative and the expressive way of attunement.* It may be readily seen, in fact, that the concentrative effort involved in meditation upon a *single* object is of an eliminative nature. It is also clear that those forms of meditation involving the development of receptivity toward the unfolding of inner experience imply a passivity possible only through an active effort to eliminate the intrusion of thought on imagination. The practice in "letting go" that this meditation entails, in the sense of "surrendering to" or "allowing," cannot be completely divorced from a letting go in another sense, which is the essence of the negative way: letting go of habits, preconceptions, and expectations; letting go of control and of the filtering mechanisms of ego.

Because the negative or eliminative dimension of meditation is present in both forms implying concentration upon either external or spontaneously emerging "inner" objects (as withdrawal from sensory activity and as passive attention) many of its technical forms coincide with those described in the previous chapter or with those that will be described in the last chapter of this essay. Consequently, I shall concentrate in the following pages on those practices which may be regarded as most characteristic of the negative or eliminative way of approach, and which come, therefore, closest to a pure expression of this direction in spiritual technology.

Yoga is defined by Patanjali at the opening of his sutras as "the *inhibition* of the modifications of the mind." The full accomplishment of this inhibition is attained only in the final stage of samadhi;* however, the eliminative effort is a basic aspect of each one of the "limbs" of yoga, including those that precede meditation proper. I particularly want to stress this aspect in the case of the first two—*yama* and *niyama*—because of the light that this may shed on the spiritual significance of a pervasive aspect of ethics throughout the world.

Yama, the first limb or step of Yoga, comprises vows of abstention or self-restraints: non-violence, non-lying, non-misappropriation, non-craving for sensual enjoyment, non-possessiveness. If we consider the connection between these vows (equivalent to some of the Mosaic commandments) and later phases of yoga, we may understand the broader implications of an extension of meditation into the domain of interpersonal behavior, comparable to the extensions of meditation into ritual philosophy and some art forms considered earlier.

The real point of *yama* is not at all in "morality," as usually understood, in a vision of the good life for society or in the achievement of happiness; but, like Yoga as a whole, in the conquest of the Great Illusion. To this end, the follower of

---

* The term *samadhi* is not employed for a specific state of mind but for a range of "super-conscious" states, which Patanjali classifies in different manners.

this path is required to give up his attachment to the world. *Ahimsa* (non-violence), for instance, is, in its highest expression, utter *transcendence* of the need to harm, and no mere rule of conduct; in the same way *asteya* means not only abstention from stealing, but from misappropriation of privileges, from esteem, from personality traits—a practice in giving up numerous forms of attachment. One function of the external observance of *yama* is to make apparent the subtler aspects of each vow by observing its obvious aspects. It is with inner levels of abstention that the yogi is essentially concerned. Thus, through abstinence from lying he will become more aware of his subtler lies, and in dealing with these he will be able to know his truth and develop intuition. Similarly, by means of a rule of sexual continence he will place himself in a position where he can understand the extent and nature of his cravings for sensuous enjoyment,* and not deceive himself by taking a substitute to be the goal that he really seeks.

In contrast with yama, or self-restraint, *niyama*, the second limb of Yoga, is usually formulated in positive terms. Yet the essence of the observances, like that of the restraints, is detachment, and the eliminative aspect is prominent in both.

Purity, the first observance, is eliminative by definition. As a commentator on Patanjali put it: "Purification means *elimination* from the vehicles belonging to an individual of all those elements and conditions which prevent them from exercising their proper functions and attaining the goal in view. . . ."

Contentment, the second observance, is "the capacity to remain satisfied whatever may happen"; it is based upon "perfect *indifference* to all those personal enjoyments and other considerations which sway mankind." Again, this can only be the outcome

---

* It is important to stress that it is the *craving* for enjoyment and not the enjoyment of the senses itself that yoga seeks to overcome. Pleasure stems from the experience of the present, whereas desire is linked to a projection into the future and suggests a lack of acceptance of the present.

of an eliminative process whereby attachments are relinquished or identification with them transcended.

The third observance, austerity, comprises a variety of practices—fasting, feats of self-discipline, specific vows, etc.—which distinctly involve *privations* of various sorts—food, comfort, sleep, etc. As in the previous observances, the ultimate aim is a condition of equanimity independent from physical, emotional, or even mental satisfactions, a state in which "consciousness abides in itself" and is experienced as independent from all psychophysiological mechanisms. As set forth by Patanjali, Kriya Yoga (the practice of austerity and the remaining two observances, self-study and surrender to God) is practiced for attenuating the *klesas* and bringing about samadhi.

The *klesas*—a term that may be translated as "afflictions" or "roots of pain"—constitute a fundamental aspect of Yoga philosophy and are most relevant to our discussion of the eliminative attitude in meditation. According to Yoga, in fact, the *klesas* are precisely that which *must be eliminated:* ignorance (*avidya*) or lack of awareness of reality; the sense of I-am-ness (*asmita*); attractions and repulsions toward objects; and the desire for life (or fear of death).

Avidya, as explained by Pantanjali, is the root-klesa that causes the self (*atman*), which is unconditioned and eternal, to mistake its true identity. Deprived by maya of the knowledge of its self-sufficient nature, the atman becomes enmeshed in matter and, more particularly, in the flux of his psychological phenomena: perceptions, feelings, thoughts. From this condition derives the second *klesa*, asmita, which Patanjali defines as a blending together of consciousness (*purusa*) and cognition (*buddhi*).

I. K. Taimni remarks in his commentary to the sutras that the word *asmita* derives from *asmi*, which in Sanskrit means "I am":

"I am" represents the pure awareness of self-existence and is therefore the expression . . . of pure consciousness or the purusa. When the pure consciousness gets involved in matter and, owing to the power of maya, knowledge of its real nature is lost, the pure "I am" changes into "I am this," where "this" may be the subtlest vehicle through which it is working, or the grossest vehicle, namely, the physical body. The two processes—namely, the loss of awareness of its real nature and the identification with the vehicles—are simultaneous."[1]

Detachment in the context of the yogic world view, when properly understood, is not a matter of less participation in the world, but one that bears on the experience of identity. This becomes clear if one considers that even the overcoming of desires and aversions (which constitute the following *klesas*) is seen as conducive not to inaction but to a different *stance* toward action. The *Bhagavad-Gita*, which is perhaps the most articulate work in the Indian tradition with regard to this subject, describes the attitude of the karma yogin* in terms of *duty*, in contrast with ordinary actions that are dependent upon the pleasure or pain that they bring about. In the latter case, the action is motivated by the attachment or aversion of the doer toward the fruits of his action; in the former, the condition of the doer is such that he experiences each action as its own reward.

Far from being a specific trait of Yoga, the pursuit of detachment is an aspect of every spiritual tradition. Furthermore, in a less technical sense (which has all too frequently led to wrong understanding), detachment is a trait in every major religious system.† It is the marrow of the Christian repudiation of "the world,"‡ for instance, and is inseparable from the Far Eastern formulations of Emptiness. And, just as in Yoga, the practice of detachment in daily life (in the form of vows and observances) constitutes a foundation for the detachment of *ekagrata*, the one-pointedness of the mind required in meditation. In other tradi-

* The yogan who follows the discipline of liberation through action.
† Practical asceticism, which may be seen as an unformulated practice in detachment, is also a generalized trait of shamanism.
‡ The *Encyclopedia of Biblical Quotations* lists under "world" nothing but negative pronouncements.

tions, too, the seemingly ethical manifestations of the practice constitute a necessary foundation for a more radical experience of transcendence.

The identity between detachment as an attitude in daily life* and detachment as an attitude in meditation is poignantly conveyed by an episode in the life of Zen Master Bokusan:

> During the civil disturbances of the nineteenth century a fugitive samurai took refuge in the temple of Soto Zen Master Bokusan. Three pursuers arrived and demanded to know where he was. "No one here," said the Zen master. "If you won't tell us, then let's cut off your head," and they drew their swords to do so. "Then if I am to die," said the Zen master, "I think I'll have a little wine." And he took down a small bottle, poured it, and sipped with evident relish.
>
> The samurai looked at one another. Finally they went away. Bokusan was repeatedly asked about this incident, but did not want to discuss it. Once however he said: "Well, there is something to be learnt from it. When those fellows came, I did not do what they wanted, but neither did I quarrel with them or plead with them. I just gave up their whole world and had nothing to do with them. And after a time I found they had gone away.
>
> "Similarly when people complain that they are overwhelmed with passions and wrong thoughts, they should know that the right way is not to quarrel nor to plead or argue. Simply give up all claim on their world and have nothing to do with them, and after a time you will find that they have gone away."[2]

Seen from without, the negative way can be easily taken to express a hateful denial of joy, of nature, and of the human body. This misinterpretation is more than understandable, since the outward actions that constitute such a discipline in different lands have served for centuries as a channel for a collective aber-

---

* A cross-cultural examination of spiritual exercises involving detachment in action would probably be an endeavor of no less scope than the present one on meditation techniques—ranging from painful puberty ordeals to sophisticated exercises in dis-identification.

ration. Fear, inhibition, self-hate, shame, guilt—they all find expression and apparent justification in the "virtuous" front provided by a life of "renunciation." It was to this psycho-pathological trait in the Western world that Nietzsche addressed himself through his Zarathustra when he said that those who talk of celestial hopes are poisoners, whether they know it or not:

> Offending God was once the greatest offense, but God died and with him died his offenders. To offend the earth is now the dreadest thing: to esteem the entrails of the unknowable higher than the aim of the earth! Once the soul looked down contemptuously at the body; the greatest thing of all was this contempt. The soul wanted the body lean, hideous, starved. By such means it sought to escape the body and the earth. Oh, but that soul was itself lean, hideous, and starved: cruelty was the debauchery of that soul.[3]

In spite of historically prevalent forms of pseudo-detachment, pseudo-humility, pseudo-serenity, etc. (where these and other classical "virtues" have become *tokens* of virtue in a purely extrinsic sense altogether incompatible with their true nature), it is not difficult to see that these false interpretations derive their very existence from a true model. Detachment, serenity, and purity (to choose the more denying of them all) are aspects of that ideal condition of the psyche that we have seen as being the aim of meditation and that we have been examining from different angles.

A measure of non-attachment is the source of a healthy individual's ability to stand on his own, not mistaking his identity with that of an owner of given things or a performer of a certain role. It is also the source of a basic independence from others, which is, in turn, the prerequisite for true relationships. A measure of non-attachment to one's own moods and whims is involved in that attitude of psychological health which we define as "ego strength"—the ability to stand above oneself—which goes hand in hand with the capacity to accept pain, discomfort, and frustration rather than repress or avoid them. More radically than any standard of mental health, though, the negative way arises from an implicit acknowledgement that man's optimal state of consciousness is one of *total* detachment: such total surrender of man to his cosmic duty that not even attachment to life or fear of death can deviate him from his path. In terms of such an aspiration we cannot be surprised at the small and great degree of unpleasantness imposed by styles of meditation in which this component predominates.*

The practice that tackles most directly the question of not doing (and the underlying ego annihilation) is one that cannot properly be called a technique:

> This Ch'an† is the supreme Ch'an of seeing one's Buddha-nature instantly. But if this is so, why should one bother to practice the so-called Seven Days' Meditation? [You must understand that] people's capacity to practice the dharma is deteriorating all the time. Nowadays people have too many distracting thoughts in their minds. Therefore the Patriarchs have designed special methods and techniques. . . ."   —Discourse of Master Hsu Yun.[4]

Among the techniques, though, none comes closer to being a pure expression of wu-wei (non-action) than that which Japanese Zen calls shikan-taza, a term approximately translated as "just sitting."

Not long ago, Shrinyu Suzuki Roshi, the abbot of Tassajara Zen Monastery in Big Sur, California, was invited to Stanford University to demonstrate Zen meditation. He laid his pillow on the floor, bowed in salutation to it, sat, and then explained that in Za-Zen the back is held straight, the ears in a line with the shoulders, the hands are placed over the belly, forming a mudra—as he was indicating—the eyes, half closed, are focused on a spot about three feet in front of the meditator. Thereupon he started to meditate and did not address his audience again

---

* Some of the martial arts of the Far East, the theme of which is—from one point of view—the cultivation of serenity, may literally involve the confrontation of death.

† "Ch'an" is the Chinese equivalent for "Zen," from which the latter, Japanese expression derives.

until the end of an hour, when he bowed to the people remaining and departed.

If Suzuki Roshi's non-lecture is not explicit enough, perhaps its message may be brought into the light by statements that he has voiced on other occasions. Some of his statements may be intriguing or not understandable at all to one unacquainted with Zen or the experiences with which Zen deals. Nevertheless they come closer to explaining the inner dimension of "just sitting" than any scholarly and logically careful exposition could. The following excerpts are from a lecture he delivered during a sesshin in the summer of 1966:

"Most of you are beginners, so it may be rather difficult for you to understand why we practice Za-Zen or meditation in this way. We always say, 'just sit,' and if you do, you will find out that Zen practice—just to sit—is not so easy. Just to sit may be the most difficult thing. To work on something is not difficult; but not to work on anything is rather difficult. When we have the idea of 'self,' we want some reason why we work on something. But if you do not have any idea of self, we want some reason why we work on something. But if you do not have any idea of self, you can remain silent and calm whether or not you work on something. You will not lose your composure. So to remain silent and calm is a kind of test you will receive. If you can do it, it means you have no idea of self. If your life is based on the usual idea of self, what you do will not be successful in its true sense. It will be success in one way, but in another you are digging your own grave. So to work without the idea of self is a very important one. It is much more important than making a good decision. Even a good decision based on a one-sided idea of self will create difficulties for yourself and others. . . .

"All the difficulties you have in Za-Zen should not take place outside your mind. Your efforts should be kept within your mind. In other words, you have to accept the difficulty of not being other than what you are. You should not try to make some tentative particular efforts based on your small mind—like, 'My practice should be better.' *My* practice, you say, but Za-Zen is not your practice. It is Buddha's practice. Your effort is based on big mind, which you cannot get out of. If your small self begins to act without the care of big mind, that is not Zen. What you should do should be well taken care of by big mind."[5]

And at a lecture at Zen Mountain Center, in 1968, Suzuki said:

"I want to explain shikan-taza, what it means *just to sit*. Some monks said to a Zen master, 'It is very hard. How is it possible to sit somewhere where there is no hot and no cold weather?" The master answered, 'When it is hot, you should be hot Buddha. When it is cold, you should be cold Buddha.' This is Dogen Zenji's understanding of the story. Actually, the master said, 'When it is hot, you should kill hot. When it is cold, you should kill cold.' But if you say, *kill*, the *kill* is extra. If you say to obtain enlightenment, the *obtain* is extra. Dogen was very direct when he said, 'When it is hot, you should be hot Buddha. When it is cold, you should be cold Buddha.' That is what shikan-taza, just to sit, means.

"When your practice is not good, you are poor Buddha. When your practice is good, you are good Buddha. And *poor* and *good* are Buddhas themselves. *Poor* is Buddha and *good* is Buddha and *you* are Buddha also. Whatever you think, say, every word becomes Buddha. I am Buddha. *I* is Buddha, and *am* is Buddha, and *Buddha* is Buddha. Buddha. Buddha. Buddha. Buddha. Whatever you say. Then there are no problems. There is no need to translate it into English, no need to be bothered with fancy explanations of Buddhism. Everything is Buddha: lying down is Buddha, each word is Buddha. If you say Buddhabuddhabuddhabuddhabuddha, that is our way, that is shikan-taza. When you practice Za-Zen with this understanding, that is true Za-Zen. Even though we say just to sit, to understand it is difficult, and that may be why Dogen Zenji left us so many teachings. But this does not mean that the teachings are difficult. When you sit, you know what he means without thinking and without expecting anything from it. When you accept yourself as a Buddha, or accept everything as an unfolding of the absolute teaching, the truth, the first principle, or as a part of the great being, when you reach this understanding, whatever you think or see is the actual teaching of Buddha and whatever you do is the actual practice of Buddha. Problems arise because you are trying to do something, or because you think that nothing will arise because of doing something, or because you feel that you can rely on something. . . .

"Masters who understand the Soto way may give you the koan *Mu* instead of telling you just to sit. *Just to sit!* There is no difference and *just to sit* will be various kinds of koans. There may be thousands of koans, and just to sit includes them all. This is the direct way to enlightenment, liberation, nirvana, or whatever you say."[6]

Another form of meditation involving the negative approach to a high degree is that known in Buddhism as "insight meditation" or the *vipassana method* (in contrast to absorptive meditation, which leads to the jhanas—trance states characterized by a suspension of thought and tranquility rather than insight).

The practice of the vipassana method, although amply described in Buddhist texts, was apparently forgotten until this century, when the Burmese monk Mahasi Sayadaw "rediscovered" it, and taught it. Presently it is the dominant form of meditation in Burma, and from that country it is spreading to other Buddhist centers of the world.[7]

The term "insight" (vipassana) used to designate this method may be misleading, for it tends to suggest an active intellectual pursuit, which is not part of this technique. The practice is designed to lead the meditator to insight into the "three characteristics of existence": impermanence (*anicca*), suffering and insufficiency (*dukkha*), and impersonality (*anatta*). Yet this insight, which will crown his practice, is not the fruit of discursive thought but of *direct observation* of experience.

The basis of the vipassana method is in the practice of what Buddhist scriptures call "right-mindfulness" or "foundations of mindfulness." Right-mindfulness is the seventh factor of the "eightfold path leading to the extinction of suffering," which itself constitutes the fourth of the Four Noble Truths of Buddhism.

Right-mindfulness rests upon two faculties called in Buddhist texts "bare attention" and "clear comprehension." Sometimes, however, "mindfulness, (*sati*) is used in association with the expression "clear comprehension" (*sampajanna*), and in such instances, as Nyaponika Thera has pointed out, "mindfulness applies pre-eminently to the attitude and practice of bare attention and a purely receptive state of mind."

"Bare attention" provides the key to the distinctive methods of satipatthana, and "accompanies the systematic practice from its very beginning to the achievement of its highest goals." It is in bare attention that we find the characteristic orientation of the *negative way*.

The very expression "*bare* attention" indicates the eliminative aspect of the practice, which consists in the mere registering of sense impressions, feelings, or mental states "without reacting to them by deed, speech, or mental comment. . . . By cultivating a receptive state of mind, which is the first stage in the process of perception, bare attention *cleans* the mind, and prepares the mind for subsequent mental processes." The cleansing aspect of the practice is repeatedly stressed in the Pali texts. The foundations of mindfulness are "for the purification of beings."

Bare attention, which might be thought of as a mental operation leading to an impoverishment of experience, may, on the contrary, reveal the complexity of the world when not masked by our simplifying labels. Nyaponika Thera comments that the individual

will first find out that, where he believes himself to be dealing with a unity, *i.e.*, with a single object presented by a single act of perception, there is multiplicity, *i.e.*, the whole series of physical and mental processes presented by corresponding acts of perception, following each other in quick succession. He will further notice with consternation how rarely he is aware of a bare or pure object without any alien admixture. For instance, the normal visual perception, if it is of evidence of any interest to the observer, will rarely present the visual object pure and simple, but the object will appear in the light of added subjective judgments: beautiful or ugly, pleasant or unpleasant, useful, useless, or harmful. If it concerns a living being, there will also enter into the preconceived notion: this is a personality, an égo, just as "I" am, too! . . . It is the task of bare attention to *eliminate** all those alien additions from the object proper that is then in the field of perception.[8]

How bare attention may be the foundation of insight is suggested by the statement (in the commentary to the Sutta Nipata) that "only things well examined by Mindfulness can be understood by Wisdom, but not confused ones." Also, "bare attention first allows things to speak for themselves, without interrupting." This injunction implies very specially the suppression of fantasy or daydreaming, "which by its tough and sticky substance of endlessly repetitive character crowds the narrow space of present consciousness giving no chance for its shaping, and making it, in fact, still more shapeless and slack."

The outline of the vipassana method is summed up in the opening of Buddha's discourse on the foundations of mindfulness—the Maha Satipatthana Sutta.

The four areas of contemplation indicated in the quoted text quoted above—the body, the feelings, the mind, and mind-objects—are treated in detail in the rest of the sutra. Mindfulness of the body, for instance, comprises mindfulness of breathing, mindfulness of postures and movements, and several exercises in which the meditator contemplates the body from specific points of view. The practice of breathing meditation (*anapana sati*) is a cornerstone of the whole method and is dealt with in detail in the Vinaya and the Sutta Pitakas (the instructions are also included in Buddhaghosa's "Path of Purification").

I have already described in Chapter 1 a modified form of the

* Italics the author's.

practice of mindful breathing, introduced in modern times by the Burmese meditation master Mahasi Sayadaw. In this exercise the meditator attends to the sensations of the rising and falling of the abdomen rather than to the tactile sensations of air passing through the nose, as described in the sutras. Just as it was appropriate to discuss this method in connection with the role of concentrated attention in meditation, it will be a relevant illustration of the principle of spontaneity and relinquishment of intentional control, which is the subject matter of Chapter 4. This points up the statement made at the beginning of this chapter that the negative approach is not only compatible with the other two dimensions of meditation, but constitutes their backbone.

Just as the absorptive aspect of meditation has its parallel in contemporary psychotherapy, so the negative aspect has a parallel, which is striking because of its resemblance to the satipatthana method: the exercise of the "awareness continuum" in Gestalt therapy.

As in the Buddhist practice of mindfulness, the object of this exercise that is central to Gestalt therapy is simple awareness. The creator of the method, Frederick S. Perls, even insisted: awareness of the *obvious*. As in the satipatthana method, awareness of the obvious involves suppression of fantasy, minimization of conceptual activity, and the elimination of anticipation or reminiscences. "I have one aim only," says Perls, "to impart a fraction of the meaning of the word *now*. To me, nothing exists except the now. Now = experience = awareness = reality. The past is no more and the future not yet." Compare this with Nyaponika Thera's statement: "Right-mindfulness recovers for man the lost pearl of his freedom, snatching it from the jaws of the dragon Time. Right-mindfulness cuts men loose from the fetters of the past, which he foolishly tries even to re-enforce by looking back frequently, with eyes of longing, resentment, or regret. Right-mindfulness stops man from chaining himself even now to the imaginations of his fears and hopes, to anticipated events of the future. Thus, right-mindfulness restores to man a freedom that is to be found only in the present."[9]

The difference between Gestalt therapy and the satipatthana method is that in the former the exercise in awareness is verbalized, and this makes supervision possible. It is precisely such corrective supervision that makes it, more than an awareness training (as it is sometimes called), a *therapy*.

Other than pointing out the connection the Gestalt therapeutic exercise with meditation in general (for it is an exercise in awareness) and, specifically, with the negative way (for it involves the elimination of thought, fantasy, memory, and anticipation), I will not say more of the psychotherapeutic procedure.[10]

4 / The Way of Surrender and Self-Expression

The way of Za-Zen may be regarded as the way of surrender of personal preferences: an emptying oneself of preconceptions (in the intellectual aspects), greed (in the emotional), and self-will, in order to discover that enlightenment bypasses or is not dependent on the satisfactions of those habits that we call our personality. As well as the movement of surrender or letting go *of* something, we can also see that there is place in meditation for an attitude of surrender *to*.

This might seem an attempt doomed to failure, if we consider that any surrender to our preferences is likely to leave us subject to those impulses in our personality that constitute the very prison or vicious circle that we want to transcend. If saying "No" to our little ego proves to be effective, could saying "Yes" to it be effective as well? In this, as in other things, paradoxes seem to be more compatible with empirical reality than with logical reasoning, and experience indicates that surrender *to* impulse may not be the blind alley that it seems to be.

An anecdote may be appropriate here to suggest how a respectful attitude toward the spontaneous urge of the moment may become a key to the meditation process. This is a story about an ancient Hindu king who was very attached to his riches, and yet, having developed a feeling of the nothingness of his vast wealth, was eager to meditate in order to apprehend the timeless reality. A yogi gave the king instructions:

The king sat down to meditate in earnest, but whenever he tried to fix his mind upon the eternal, it went blank. Pretty soon, without his knowing it, his imagination began to hover around his beautiful bracelet, of which he was particularly fond. Before his admiring gaze, the real bracelet began to sparkle in all the colors of the rainbow. As soon as he found himself in that fantasy, he fought his way back to God. But the harder he tried to fix his mind upon God, the bigger was the disappointment he experienced. God invariably changed in his mind into the bracelet. With much humility, the king now went to the yogi for further instructions. The yogi knew how to turn the weakness itself into a source of strength. He said to the king, "Since your mind is so much attached to the bracelet, start right there. Meditate upon the bracelet. Contemplate its beauty and gorgeous colors. Then inquire into the source of that beauty and those colors. The bracelet is, in its objective essence, a configuration of energy vibrations. It is the perceptive mind which lends it its beauty and color. Therefore, try to understand the nature of the mind which created the world as you see it."[1]

The decision to meditate upon the bracelet, in this story, aligns with what we have called the way of descent, the contemplation of individual aspects of reality rather than of its unity—in symbol or direct experience. Although the king's greater attraction toward his precious object removes him from the One and draws him to one of the Hundred Thousand Things, is not each of these worldly objects also an echo of the One?

In contrast to the way of detachment, which would have us see the whole world as maya, we may instead develop an attitude of reverence toward all of existence, and trust in the compass that life has placed in our hearts. If we thus follow our feelings, rather than constrain them, we are most likely to find that our preferences of today become obsolete in the face of tomorrow's; the music that we now enjoy, the books that nourish us, the women or men that we feel in resonance with, may become trite, exhausted of meaning, too obvious or shallow to our future perceptions, likings, and needs. Yet that shift of attitude, which would make our present feelings seem indiscriminate or lacking in orientation, would have taken place precisely through satiation, not through denial. Just as in life we grow by outgrowing, and we outgrow by living something out completely, our perceptions may be refined by giving in to our inner voices to the fullest degree.

Athough the attitudes called for by the concentrative and by the receptive ways appear as perfectly logical opposites, this need not be so in actual experience. It would be better to view them as divergent ways that converge upon the same goal. They may be experienced as divergent at the beginning of the journey but as aspects of the same attitude when the meditator is approaching higher states of consciousness. In these, empathy with an attractive object leads to a state of desirelessness—the very gratuitousness of beauty and detachment makes the world more alive and not dead. As Ch'an Master Hsu Yun has put it: "Oh, friends and disciples, if you do not attach yourselves to the Ten Thousand Things with your minds, you will find that the life-spark will emanate from *everything*."[2]

The borderline between the negative attitude of "just sitting" and that of surrendering to experience is a very delicate one indeed, and one that may be discerned most clearly in the case of visions, revelations, physical sensations that commonly take place in meditation. In the Japanese Zen tradition, these are all called *makyo* (meaning "diabolical phenomena"), and while not considered inherently bad, they are regarded as a potential obstacle to Za-Zen. According to the Za-Zen Yojinki, "The disciple may develop the faculty of seeing through solid objects as though they were transparent, or he may experience his own body as a translucent substance. He may see Buddhas and Bodhisattvas. Penetrating insights may suddenly come to him, or passages of sutras which were particularly difficult to understand may suddenly become luminously clear to him. Yet," the book goes on to say, "these abnormal visions and sensations are merely the symptoms of an impairment arising from a maladjustment of the mind with the breath."[3]

The indifference of Zen masters to these phenomena may be surprising to the disciple, and hard to understand for anyone not familiar with the Way of Emptiness. *Makyo* may be experienced as highly rewarding and desirable, and are valued in other religions. Yet this attitude of Zen toward unusual contents of consciousness does not differ from its attitude with regard to contents of consciousness in general—the aim being awareness of awareness in itself: the direct grasping of mind by mind.* This was made explicit by Yasutani Roshi, the Japanese Zen master who has lectured extensively in the United States. He has pointed out that makyo has a general as well as a specific sense:

> Broadly speaking, the entire life of the ordinary man is nothing but makyo. Even such Bodhisattvas as Monju and Kannon, highly developed though they are, still have about them traces of makyo; otherwise they would be supreme Buddhas, completely free of makyo. One who becomes attached to what he realizes through satori is also still lingering in the world of makyo. So, you see, there are makyo even after enlightenment. . . ."[4]

The attitude that is recommended in face of makyo is therefore no different from that which characterizes Zen in general: detached awareness. The issue deserves special mention only because the exceptional nature of the phenomena might seem to

---

* The word *hsin*, frequently translated as "mind," may be rendered also by "heart" or "consciousness."

call for an exception. For instance, cases are reported of persons who have written down things that turned out to be prophetically true, or who felt in communication with divine beings. The Zen view of these states, though, is that they constitute a mixture of reality and unreality, falling short of true enlightenment. They indicate progress in the practice of meditation, and yet they would not be part of a more concentrated state.

> Just as dreams do not appear to a person in deep sleep but only when he is half-asleep and half-awake, so makyo do not come to those in deep concentration or samadhi. Never be tempted into thinking that these phenomena are real or that the visions themselves have any meaning. To see a beautiful vision of a Bodhisattva does not mean that you are any nearer becoming one yourself, any more than a dream of being a millionaire means that you are any richer when you awake. Hence there is no reason to feel elated about such makyo. And similarly, whatever horrible monsters may appear to you, there is no cause whatever for alarm. Above all, do not allow yourself to be enticed by visions of the Buddha or of gods blessing you or communicating a divine message, or by makyo involving prophecies which turn out to be true. This is to squander your energies in the foolish pursuit of superstition.[5]

These very phenomena against which Zen warns its followers as deceptive surrogates of enlightenment are the substance of the trance states cultivated by the alternative approach to meditation. The domain of surrender or letting go is typically that of visionary experience, automatic movements, the release of dormant physical energies, inspired utterance, automatic writing, spirit possession.

Yet if we consider these superficially contrasting attitudes closely enough, we may see where they meet. On one hand, the way of detachment, in its ripeness, cannot help being permissive; a suppressive effort would entail attachment to a preference or perception and would fall short of non-action. (It is no coincidence that makyo appear in Za-Zen. This is because this system cultivates a state of undistracted receptivity, and though the meditator is warned not to become attached to his visions, he is not told to suppress them but to persist in the stance of both not doing and allowing, which characterizes Shikan-taza.) On the other hand, a complete surrender cannot fail to involve detachment, for a greedy interest in the attainment of certain mental states would cease to be surrender altogether. We might say that there is a condition of *openness to experience*, expressed by both detachment and surrender.

In the actual experience of meditation, though, this meeting point of detachment and surrender may take a long time to attain. And so we see, in its less perfected stages, a sharp contrast between a dry asceticism of the mind* and a tumultuous Dionysian spirit; between the serene spirit of the monk and the seeming madness of the prophet; between the pursuit of emptiness and the phenomena of possession by gods or cosmic forces.

Possession by gods, spirits, or energies is, indeed, the most characteristic experience in the domain of spirituality that we are discussing at this point, just as an equanimity transcending all feeling and thought is most characteristic of the Apollonian way (see Figure 1, p. 16). Possession also differs from the absorptive way of meditation insofar as in possession there is no *union* of subject and object† (which the word *samadhi* reflects—*sam*, meaning "together" or "with" in Sanskrit), but a state in which the subject entirely disappears and becomes a mere channel. As in the case of the individual in absorption he may say, "I am God," but it is not he but the entity speaking through him that says "I." Also, in spite of the abysmal difference between a possession state and the ordinary state of hypnotic trance, it seems legitimate to inquire as to whether both depend on a similar propensity within the person to be in a dissociated state—*i.e.*, a state in which the habitual role, style, and center of consciousness are relinquished, and a different personality role, style, and state of consciousness

---

* As in countless instances among the Fathers of the Desert in Christianity and in the history of Hinayana Buddhism.

† See quotations pp. 28–29 and pp. 30–31.

are adopted, frequently without knowledge or memory of this having happened.

When contrasting the orgiastic-prophetic dimension of the revelatory state with the dimension of detachment and equanimity that we discussed before, we may say that the main difference between them is the importance ascribed to *content*. Everything the Zen monk would consider makyo—imagery, feelings, voices, etc.—here is likely to become the very goal of the meditation. The inner vision, idea, or inspired utterance of the shaman, sybil, or prophet, is frequently regarded not as a by-product of an individual quest but as a self-sufficient end of one's function in the community: a channel for revelation.

From this angle we may also contrast the revelatory and concentrative ways of meditation. While both forms are content-centered, they differ (especially in the degraded forms of each) in the relative accent placed on the social or individual role (product versus person, message versus state), and, more radically, in the contrast between the structural content of the former and the unstructured, inwardly determined content of the latter. While a Christian may attempt to apply the idea of death and resurrection to his own life and inwardly enact an "imitation of Christ," the Dionysian Bacchae would abandon themselves unconditionally to the workings of their deeper nature, there to find, without seeking it, the eternal rhythm of death and resurrection.

Perhaps the best illustration for much of what I have been saying is to be found in shamanism, which, as a whole, embodies the orgiastic-revelatory aspect of experience as much as Buddhism embodies the dimension of emptiness. Not only is shamanism in general a mysticism of possession, but the shaman's trance is usually content-oriented. A shaman* that may properly be called

---

* The shaman performs the roles of priest, medicine-man, prophet, artist, and is not to be confused with the formal priest or medicine-man who exists in some cultures in addition to the shaman. What distinguishes the shaman is his ability to "transport himself to other worlds", *i.e.*, to experience altered states of consciousness.

so is not a seeker of enlightenment or an individual who indulges in altered states of consciousness as part of a discipline for personal development. He is one who has attained communication with the supernatural (a spirit world, in most shamanistic conceptions) and may act as a mediator between spirits or gods and man, making the desires of each known to the other. In this, he may be called a primitive prophet. Apparently his ecstasy is not for himself but for others: his patients, his disciples, or the community at large. Yet we must not forget that in his becoming a mouthpiece of the gods he fulfills *his* calling—and some reports indicate that a shaman that has no occasion to shamanize tends to become ill.

In no instance better than in that of shamanism can we discern the archetypal—inwardly prompted—nature of the symbols that later religions have crystallized into standard forms.

Ideas such as the journey to the underworld, ascent to heaven, death and resurrection, are not mere *ideas* in shamanism but actual experiences that are renewed generation after generation. In countries as far apart as Australia, South America, and the Arctic Circle, these are echoed with the same freshness of spirit. Constancies such as these are generally interpreted as an indication of a shamanistic "tradition," spread by migrations. But do we not overstate, perhaps, the necessity of tradition in our experiential ignorance of the archetypal domain? It is quite possible that the essence of the tradition may lie in a tradition of no-tradition: the fostering of an openness (which perhaps is more easy in preindustrial cultures than in ours) whereby the individual can discover in himself all that his ancestors did not enforce upon his world view. Consider, for instance, the following account of his initiatory experience by a Siberian shaman who, far from seeking it, plunged into it with no apparent expectations:

A. A. Popov gives the following account concerning a shaman of the Avam Samoyed. Sick with smallpox, the future shaman remained unconscious for three days and so nearly dead that on the third day he was almost buried. His initiation took place during the time. He remembered having been carried into the middle of a sea. There he heard his Sickness (that is, smallpox) speak, saying to him: "From the Lords of the Water you will receive the gift of shamanizing. Your name as a shaman will be Huottarie (Diver)." Then the Sickness troubled the water of the sea. The candidate came out and climbed a mountain. There he met a naked woman and began to suckle at her breast. The woman, who was probably the Lady of the Water, said to him: "You are my child; that is why I let you suckle at my breast. You will meet many hardships and be greatly wearied." The husband of the Lady of the Water, the Lord of the Underworld, then gave him two guides, an ermine and a mouse, to lead him to the underworld. When they came to a high place, the guides showed him seven tents with torn roofs. He entered the first and there found the inhabitants of the underworld and the men of the Great Sickness (syphilis). These men tore out his heart and threw it into a pot. In other tents he met the Lord of Madness and the Lords of all the nervous disorders, as well as the evil shamans. Thus he learned the various diseases that torment mankind.

Still preceded by his guides, the candidate then came to the Land of the Shamanesses, who strengthened his throat and his voice. He was then carried to the shores of the Nine Seas. In the middle of one of them was an island, and in the middle of the island a young birch tree rose to the sky. It was the Tree of the Lord of the Earth. Beside it grew nine herbs, the ancestors of all the plants on earth. The tree was surrounded by seas, and in each of these swam a species of bird with its young. There were several kinds of ducks, a swan, and a sparrow-hawk. The candidate visited all these seas; some of them were salt, others so hot he could not go near the shore. After visiting the seas, the candidate raised his head and, in the top of the tree, saw men of various nations: Tavgi Samoyed, Russians, Dolgan, Yakut, and Tungus. He heard voices: "It has been decided that you shall have a drum (that is, the body of a drum) from the branches of this tree." He began to fly with the birds of the seas. As he left the shore, the Lord of the Tree called to him: "My branch has just fallen; take it and make a drum of it that will serve you all your life." The branch had three forks, and the Lord of the Tree bade him make three drums from it, to be kept by three women, each drum being for a special ceremony—the first for shamanizing woman in child-birth, the second for curing the sick, the third for finding men lost in the snow.

The Lord of the Tree also gave branches to all the men who were in the top of the tree. But, appearing from the tree up to the chest in human form, he added: "One branch only I give not to the shamans, for I keep it for the rest of mankind. They can make dwellings from it and so use it for their needs. I am the Tree that gives life to all men." Clasping the branch, the candidate was ready to resume his flight when again he heard a human voice, this time revealing to him the medicinal virtues of the seven plants and giving him certain instructions concerning the art of shamanizing. But, the voice added, he must marry three women (which, in fact, he later did by marrying three orphan girls whom he had cured of smallpox).

And after that he came to an endless sea and there he found trees and seven stones. The stones spoke to him one after the other. The first had teeth like bears' teeth and a basket-shaped cavity, and it revealed to him that it was the earth's holding stone; it pressed on the fields with its weight, so that they should not be carried away by the wind. The second served to melt iron. He remained with these stones for seven days and so learned how they could be of use to men.

Then his two guides, the ermine and the mouse, led him to a high, rounded mountain. He saw an opening before him and entered a bright cave, covered with mirrors, in the middle of which there was something like a fire. He saw two women, naked but covered with hair, like reindeer. Then he saw that there was no fire burning but that the light came from above, through an opening. One of the women told him that she was pregnant and would give birth to two reindeer; one would be the sacrificial animal of the Dolgan and Evenki, the other that of the Tavgi. She also gave him a hair, which was to be useful to him when he shamanized for reindeer. The other woman also gave birth to two reindeer, symbols of the animals that would aid man in all his works and also supply his food. The cave had two openings, toward the north and toward the south; through each of them the young women sent a reindeer to serve the forest people (Dolgan and Evenki). The second woman, too, gave him a hair. When he shamanizes, he mentally turns toward the cave.

Then the candidate came to a desert and saw a distant mountain. After three days' travel he reached it, entered an opening, and came upon a naked man working a bellows. On the fire was a cauldron "as big as half the earth." The naked man saw him and caught him with a huge pair of tongs. The novice had time to think, "I am dead!" The man cut off his head, chopped his body into bits, and put everything in the cauldron. There he boiled his body for three years. There were also three anvils, and the naked man forged the candidate's head on the third, which was the one on which the best shamans were forged. Then he threw the head into one of three pots that stood there, the one in which the water was the coldest. He now revealed to the candidate that, when he was called to cure someone, if the water in the ritual pot was very hot, it would be useless to shamanize, for the man was already lost; if the water was warm, he was sick but would recover; cold water denoted a healthy man.

The blacksmith then fished the candidate's bones out of a river, in which they were floating, put them together, and covered them with flesh again. He counted them and told him that he had three too many; he was therefore to procure three shaman's costumes. He forged his head and taught him how to read the letters that are inside it. He changed his eyes; and that is why, when he shamanizes, he does not see with his bodily eyes but with these mystical eyes. He pierced his ears, making him able to understand the language of plants. Then the candidate found himself on the summit of a mountain, and finally he woke in the yurt, among the family. Now he can sing and shamanize indefinitely, without ever growing tired.[6]

The resemblance between shamanistic experience and the mystic experiences encountered in the "higher religions" goes beyond mere content, striking as this aspect may be (cf., death-resurrection theme in Osiris, Attis, Adonis, in the Tibetan Tchöd ritual, and the journeys to the other world of Aeneas, Enoch, Mohammed, St. Paul, and others). Also, the psychological character of the shamanistic experience is fairly constant and is the prototype of that which we recognize in prophets and other inspired men of more recent cultures. The aspect of the shamanistic experience is one that the individual expresses either as a separation of the soul from the body (so that it may visit other places and levels of existence), or as a penetration of his soul-free body by other spirits (animal, demonic, or angelic); possibly, by both at the same time. The Greeks gave names to these two concepts: the flight from the body they called ἔκστασις (ecstasy), and the penetration by the spirits, ἔνθεος (enthusiasm—literally, "in God," or "God within"). The quality that inspires such interpretations seems to link together experiences that are remote in time, place, or cultural setting. The resemblances may be even more apparent from the frequent physical or visible concomitants of this type of experience: the seer's frenzy, his seeming madness taking the form of agitation, his convulsive movements, glossalalia,* lack of regard for his social image or physical safety, followed by a period of calm and, later, of forgetfulness for the whole event. Compare, for instance, the following descriptions:

Even as she spoke, neither her features nor her complexion remained the same, nor was her hair confined within her braid; her bosom heaved, and her wild heart was stolen with frenzy; her stature was longer to the sight, her voice no longer human: so soon she was inspired by the breath of the god as it came ever nearer . . . at length no longer submitting herself to Phoebus, the prophetess rages furiously in her cavern, if so be, she may succeed in flinging off the mighty god from her bosom. All the more he plies her frenzied mouth, subduing her wild heart and fashions her to his will by constraint.—*Aeneid*, Book vi.

* From the Greek, "speaking in tongues."

[When David fled to Samuel for protection] Saul sent messengers to take David: and when they saw the company of the prophets prophesying, and Samuel standing as appointed over them, the Spirit of God was upon the messengers of Saul, and they also prophesied. [Saul sent messengers three times,] then went he also to Ramah . . . and the Spirit of God was upon him also, and he went on, and prophesied, until he came to Naioth in Ramah. And he stripped off his clothes also, and prophesied before Samuel in like manner, and lay down naked all that day and all that night.

—I Samuel 19

And when the day of Pentecost was fully come, they were all with one accord in one place. And suddenly there came a sound from heaven as of a rushing, mighty wind, and it filled all the houses where they were sitting. And there appeared unto them cloven tongues like as of fire, and it sat upon each of them. And they were all filled with the Holy Ghost, and began to speak with other tongues, as the Spirit gave them utterance. And there were dwelling at Jerusalem Jews, devout men, out of every nation under heaven. . . . And they were all amazed, and were in doubt, saying one to another, What meaneth this? Others mocking said, These men are full of new wine.

—Acts of the Apostles 2

In spite of the constancy of the characteristic of the possession trance, however, it seems necessary to draw a distinction between states of greater or lesser *quality*, in terms of the level of experience to which they relate, or the excellence of their content. This distinction is acknowledged in all cultures and attributed to the nature of the entities by whom the individual is possessed. Islamic thought, for instance, draws a distinction between inspiration by jinn or by angels, and Mahomet himself is said to have distrusted his own states at the beginning, regarding them as the workings of jinn rather than divine revelation. Even among jinn, distinctions in quality are drawn. Whereas some are regarded as the inspirers of poets or of soothsayers (*'arraf*, who sometimes gives his oracles in verse), others inspire the less profound utterances of the diviner (*kahin*, who will give inspiration on practical issues such as the finding of lost objects).*

Though frequently the individual will maintain connections with a specific entity (jinni, spirit helper, "familiar spirit," etc., according to the tradition), or with entities at a given level of mystical realization, there are exceptions in the instances of shamans who declare themselves to be in contact with *many* spirit helpers and who will attend to matters as different in scope as divination related to hunting and the leading of the souls of the dead. Even in the case of such a High Prophet as Elisha, we find an instance in which he was asked for an oracle on where to find a water supply:

> . . . And it came to pass, when the minstrel played, that the hand of the Lord came upon him.
>
> And he said, Thus saith the Lord, Make this valley full of ditches.
>
> For thus saith the Lord, Ye shall not see wind, neither shall ye see rain; yet that valley shall be filled with water, that ye may drink, both ye, and your cattle, and your beasts.
>
> —II Kings 3

Not only can we discern differences in "level" among instances of revelation, ranging from the stage clairvoyant to the prophet, but differences in quality at a given level—stylistic differences that might be likened to the different colors of the spectrum.

Plutarch draws this distinction for us when he classifies inspiration or "enthusiasm" into the diviner, prompted by Apollo; the Bacchic frenzy, prompted by Dionysus, Cybele, and Pan; the warlike frenzy of Ares; the poet's frenzy, inspired by the Muses; and the most fiery of all, the frenzy of love.[7]

---

* To the more orthodox Muslims, only the Prophet is regarded as divinely possessed—his words being inspired by the Archangel Gabriel. In this we see the tendency of all orthodoxies to substitute the realization of the individual for that of the savior, rather than seeing their highest exemplar as the embodiment of a universal ideal and possibility. Thus, other instances of God-incarnation in the Moslem world (like the Sufi Hallaj) were considered heretical.

Today we may want to call the Greek gods "archetypes," regarding them, as Jung puts it, as "organs of the psyche"[8] comparable to those in our body. Notwithstanding this shift in point of view (which turns the gods from personalities to forces within us), Plutarch's classification holds for what we know of possession in all cultures, regardless of the names or interpretations given to these states.

One last important distinction is that drawn by many cultures with regard to the good or the evil nature of possessing entities.

At least in the Judeo-Christian and Moslem worlds, the tendency to interpret all possession as caused by devils or the Devil seems to have run parallel to the establishment of a formalized orthodoxy. Whereas jinn appear to have been regarded as amoral in early times, they later came to be seen more and more as shaitans (satans), and while there is no record of possession by demons in early Jewish history, that is the only type of possession reported by the authors of the Gospels.

We may assume that both the positive regard for possession and the frequency of the phenomenon increased again in the Christian world as a consequence of the experience of the Apostles on the day of Pentecost. From the writings of St. Paul we may infer that the effects of the Holy Spirit were well known during his time. (Consider, for instance, the admonition in the Epistle to the Ephesians: "Be not drunken with wine, wherein is riot, but be filled with the Spirit.") Ecstatic prophecy, nevertheless, was viewed with suspicion by the early Church, and when it was revived by Montanus in the second century, he and his followers were exterminated as heretics. The sayings of Montanus ring of the prophetic spirit of all times and places:

> Man is like a lyre, and I [the Holy Spirit] play him like a plectrum. Man sleeps; I [the Holy Spirit] am awake.

The attitudes and interpretations the Church adopted with regard to the revival of possession in medieval witchcraft are too well known to call for more than a brief mention. Only with the Reformation did this phenomenon find a modest place in Christianity: in the early meetings of the Quakers in seventeenth-century England and, in present practice, as the religious core of minor sects such as the Pentecostals.

This historical digression is most relevant to the question of technique in the path of surrender for, if the "devil" is the misinterpretation of the "god" (because of our rigid assumptions and imperfect surrender), doesn't this make possession by the devil the unavoidable first step for one who shares this bias? In other words, in surrendering to his own nature, the individual may at first experience the emergence of unconscious intrusions of "devilish" nature, and only later come to "shake hands" with what, after all, was nothing other than his own energies, his constructive potential.

I am not thinking specifically of "devil-worship," though some historical forms of it may be related to this process, but of a more general principle: the conversion of "negative" into "positive" forces, or the recognition of a constructive power in what at first seems destructive. A typical instance of this is to be found in the shamanistic approach to helping spirits, which are often perceived at first as threatening, but which must be "tamed" in the overcoming of the shaman's nervous crisis.

Among the Angmagssalik Eskimos, what often takes the form of a shaman's spontaneous crisis is probably no different in nature (though perhaps in degree) from the crisis that the shaman is able to bring about in his function as a healer. Just as he has been able to come to terms with seemingly destructive forces (by giving in or riding with them), he is able to guide others on a similar journey. This entails a redirecting of the drives that are manifested in the form of mental or psychosomatic disease, and is essentially a process of giving such drives a channel of *expression:* dancing, imagery, drawing, dramatization, the emotionally expressive medium of gibberish (glossalalia). In being expressed, the "spirit" will have fulfilled its calling: once accepted, it will not need anymore to knock at the door of the individual's consciousness in the form of an ailment.

If we consider this situation in which religion, medicine, and art meet, we might well say that only in allowing himself to be *possessed by the spirit* (in dance, song, etc.) can the person *express himself*, and, consequently, create and become cured. Only in being taken over by a genie, can he become a genius.*

A particularly interesting instance of the transmutation of disease into constructive expression is afforded by the Zar cult of Iran, Ethiopia, Egypt, and Arabia, observable to this day. This is a form of healing practice in which the patient (afflicted by what we would regard as emotional or psychosomatic disturbances) *is regarded as possessed* from the outset, and in his being persuaded that in this possession lies the root of his sickness, he is also prompted to open up to the expression of the possessing entity. In the Zar healing ceremony the patient falls into a trance during which the intruding spirit in him can speak and make its demands clear. If satisfied, it agrees to leave the patient in peace.

The interpretation of disease as possession is far from being a rarity. Not only is it a common belief in the Middle East of today, but it was prevalent in Egyptian and Babylonian antiquity. We may regard the process that takes place in the Zar cult (or similar practices) as one of *surrogate* expression: under the special circumstances of the ceremony and, particularly, under the pretext of an alien spirit in his body, the patient may express *himself*, say what *he* wants, satisfy his postponed needs. But does not the *idea* of possession amount here to a powerful therapeutic technique, without which the cathartic process would have needed perhaps years on the psychoanalytic couch?

---

* The word "genius," which we now use to denote a certain type of excellence, derives from the notion of a possessing genie or jinn. To "have" genius once meant to have a helping spirit, a daimon.

The same interpretation is reported in other cultures (Greenland, Australia) as one of being swallowed by a monster and emerging out of it as a new man (cf. Jonah), or being taken to the underworld, torn apart and put together again, killed and resurrected:

> The first thing the disciple has to do is to go to a certain lonely spot, an abyss or a cave, and there, having taken a small stone, rub it on the top of a large one, the way of the sun. When they have done this for three days on end, they say, a spirit comes out from the rock. It turns its face toward the rising sun and asks what the disciple will. The disciple then dies in the most horrible torments, partly from fear, partly from overstrain; but he comes to life again, later in the day.[9]

There are special instances of the use of such personification in contemporary psychotherapy—notably Gestalt therapy and psychodrama—and in these we can see a type of psychological healing not different in essence from that of the shamanistic conversion of an "enemy" into a "helper." By confronting and even taking sides with the hitherto avoided aspects of his personality, the patient learns that these may be expressed in ways not detrimental to his life but, on the contrary, enriching. When this becomes possible, the devious mechanism at the root of his symptoms is no longer necessary.

The sudden flooding of the mind by unconscious (or, better, ego-alien) contents, which is characteristic of the kinds of spiritual practice under discussion, is not only most dramatic but also entails real dangers. The relationship between possession accompanied by visionary phenomena and psychosis can be seen at all levels. Not only do the prophet and the "God-intoxicated" frequently act like madmen, but a specific pathology seems to derive from the failure of the individual to deal with the avalanche of energies awakened by a practice of this type. Moreover, we may be justified in considering many cases of schizophrenia as an outcome of the spontaneous plunging of an immature person into the realm of that kind of experience, which, when properly assimilated, distinguishes the genius from the average man.

The shamanistic process, the cults of Egyptian and Greek Mysteries, the Sufi science of opening the lataif, the practice indirectly alluded to by Western and Taoistic texts on alchemy, all appear to deal with the domain of experience that has the potential of bringing the individual into harmonious contact with his unsuspected dormant powers or, alternately, of turning him into a puppet of forces that he cannot control. One of the reasons for the esoteric nature of many of the techniques employed in these various traditions lies in the dangers of misuse that are inherent in them. A dervish tale illustrates this point. It tells—such is the version of it in the *Arabian Nights*—of a fisherman who brought up a bottle from the ocean in his net. When he opened it a jinn came out and threatened to destroy him, but he managed to trick the jinn back into the bottle and throw it into the ocean. . . .

Many years passed, until one day another fisherman, grandson of the first, cast his net in the same place, and brought up the self-same bottle.

He placed the bottle upon the sand and was about to open it when a thought struck him. It was the piece of advice which had been passed down to him by his father, from *his* father.

It was: "Man can use only what he has learned to use."

And so it was that when the jinn, aroused from his slumbers by the movement of his metal prison, called through the brass: "Son of Adam, whoever you may be, open the stopper of this bottle and release me: for I am the Chief of the Jinns, who know the secrets of miraculous happenings," the young fisherman, remembering his ancestral adage, placed the bottle carefully in a cave and scaled the heights of a near-by cliff, seeking the cell of a wise man who lived there.

He told the story to the wise man, who said: "Your adage is perfectly true: and you have to do this thing yourself, though you must know how to do it."

"But what do I have to do?" asked the youth.

"There is something, surely, that you feel you want to do?" said the other.

"What I want to do is to release the jinn, so that he can give me miraculous knowledge: or perhaps mountains of gold, and seas made from emeralds, and all the other things which jinns can bestow."

"It has not, of course, occurred to you," said the sage, "that the jinn might not give you these things when released; or that he may give them to you and then take them away because you have no means to guard them; quite apart from what might befall you if and when you did have such things, since 'Man can use only what he has learned to use.'"

"Then what should I do?"

"Seek from the jinn a sample of what he can offer. Seek a means of safeguarding that sample and testing it. Seek knowledge, not possessions, for possessions without knowledge are useless, and that is the cause of all our distractions."

Now, because he was alert and reflective, the young man worked out his plan on the way back to the cave where he had left the jinn.

He tapped on the bottle, and the jinn's voice answered, tinny through the metal, but still terrible: "In the name of Solomon the Mighty, upon whom be peace, release me, son of Adam!"

"I don't believe that you are who you say and that you have the powers which you claim," answered the youth.

"Don't believe me! Do you not know that I am incapable of telling a lie?" the jinn roared back.

"No, I do not," said the fisherman.

"Then how can I convince you?"

"By giving me a demonstration. Can you exercise any powers through the wall of the bottle?"

"Yes," admitted the jinn, "but I cannot release myself through these powers."

"Very well, then: give me the ability to know the truth of the problem which is on my mind."

Instantly, as the jinn exercised his strange craft, the fisherman became aware of the source of the adage handed down by his grandfather. He saw, too, the whole scene of the release of the jinn from the bottle; and he also saw how he could convey to others how to gain such capacities from the jinn. But he also realized that there was no more that he could do. And so the fisherman picked up the bottle and, like his grandfather, cast it into the ocean.

And he spent the rest of his life not as a fisherman but as a man who tried to explain to others the perils of "Man trying to use what he has not learned to use."

But, since few people ever came across jinns in bottles, and there was no wise man to prompt them in any case, the successors of the fisherman garbled what they called his "teachings," and mimed his descriptions. In due course they became a religion, with brazen bottles from which they sometimes drank housed in costly and well-adorned temples. And, because they respected the behaviour of this fisherman, they strove to emulate his actions and his deportment in every way.

The bottle, now many centuries later, remains the holy symbol and mystery for these people. They try to love each other only because they love this fisherman; and in the place where he settled and built a humble shack they deck themselves with finery and move in elaborate rituals.

Unknown to them, the disciples of the wise man still live; the descendants of the fisherman are unknown. The brass bottle lies at the bottom of the sea with the jinn slumbering within.[10]

The danger of psychosis that besets the legendary sorcerer's apprentice is today a matter of great interest, because we are beginning to see that not only is psychosis the outcome of a failure of the ego (to deal with the unconscious) but also a state of potentialities greater than those of the normal states. Julian Silverman has remarked on how a shaman undergoes, as part of his initiation process, something that we would diagnose as a psychotic state.[11] He is not hospitalized for it and "treated," but, quite to the contrary, his state is respected and allowed to follow its natural course. The consequent question is then: are not some of the syndromes that we treat as schizophrenic, tumultuous, and even cataclysmic, stages of development that we are, for lack of trust, interrupting instead of allowing them to take a positive course?

A new approach to psychosis, now gaining adherents, is more respectful than the traditional, and we may therefore hope that definitive answers to the question are not too far away.* At any rate, from the facts known to us now, it may be said that practices in surrender of control (such as mediumship) *may* lead to psychotic states and that temporary states akin to psychosis are part of the inner journey of *some* shamans, mystics, and artists.

Aside from the esoteric character of some practices, there are a number of factors that make it difficult to write on techniques pertaining to the revelatory dimension of meditation. One such factor relates to the nature of the defining attitude. Because of its openness to the promptings from one's deeper nature, and its attunement to one's inner voices, the way may be expected to be a highly *individual* one. Indeed, if we seek analogies for the shamanistic way in the modern world, the closest might be found in the life of some artists, whose endeavor has been to follow their "calling" or vocation. Their attunement to themselves (or, if we prefer, to what wanted expression through them) cannot in general be divorced from their process of expression, so that their art is at the same time a result and a discipline. When the Greeks spoke of the poet as one possessed by the Muses, they were not merely indulging in a metaphor. For many, the visionary or clairaudient experience was as true as that which Socrates reported in speaking of his daimon, and this has continued to be true among a number of artists in our own tradition.

Dante writes: "I am one who when Love inspires me, takes

* An international conference on the value of psychotic experiences was held at Esalen Institute in 1968, and a forthcoming book edited by J. Silverman will present a summary of the more important contributions.

note; and I go on setting it forth after the fashion which Love dictates within me." In Whitman we read:

> Oh, I am sure they come from Thee, the urge, the order, the unconquerable will, the potent, felt, interior command, stronger than words. A message from the heavens, whispering to me ever in my sleep.

They are both speaking of the true experience of *inspiration*, which most people today have come to regard as little more than a figure of speech. Such experiences do not differ in essence from that which Alfred de Musset describes in the following terms: ". . . it is not work. It is merely listening. It is as if some unknown person were speaking in your ear."

Another factor that makes description of techniques of meditation difficult is that the effectivness of any technique seems to depend on an extra-technical factor of "personal contagion."

The infectious nature of possession by devils throughout history is well established, and it is impressive to read documents such as those of the epidemic of Loudun, showing how even apparently sane priests sent to perform exorcisms became affected by the prevalent state.[12]

What is true with regard to unwanted devil possession is apparently as true with regard to states that are welcomed and cultivated. Among many peoples, trance is a collective phenomenon in which the state of the more experienced is believed to facilitate that of the novices. The Kung Bushmen of the Kalahari Desert, for instance, understand the possessing entity not as a spirit but as an energy* (also called a "medicine") originally given to man by God and now maintained by direct *transmission* from man to man. According to Dr. R. Lee, who has studied the trance dances, the practicing curers spend much of their time implanting "medicine" into the bodies of their trainees.[13]

---

* Interestingly, not unlike the Taoist elizir or the Power of Kundalini Yoga, this is a "medicine" that lies in the pit of the stomach and, when heated up, rises in the form of vapors through the spinal column.

That the direct transmission of a spiritual energy, or the possibility for a divinely inspired individual to bring another into contact with his seemingly supernatural source of inspiration, is well recognized in the different mystical traditions can be seen in stereotyped expressions that have lost their original significance, such as the notion of "blessing," or the Christian formula of insufflation during baptism, "Receive ye the Holy Spirit." In other instances, however, it is a matter of a non-verbal process by which a spiritual master may actually initiate a disciple to a new domain of experience. The following passage of the Sufi Master Ibn' Arabi —known as a "disciple of Khidr"—tells of his own initiation to the state of communion with the cosmic entity that the Sufis equate with the Holy Spirit, with the Angel Gabriel, and with the historical Elijah:

This consociation with Khidr was experienced by one of our *shaikhs*, the *shaikh* 'Ali ibn 'Abdillah ibn Jami, who was one of the disciples of 'Ali al-Mutawakkil and of Abu Abdillah Qadib Alban. He lived in a garden he owned in the outskirts of Mosul. There Khidr had invested him with the mantle in the presence of Qadib Alban. And it was in that very spot, in the garden where Khidr had invested him with it that the *shaikh* invested me with it in turn, observing the same ceremonial as Khidr himself had observed in conferring the investiture upon him. I had already received this investiture, but more indirectly, at the hands of my friend Taqiuddin ibn Abdirrahman, who himself had received it at the hands of Sadruddin, *shaikh* of *shaikhs* in Egypt, whose grandfather had received it from Khidr. It was then that I began to speak of the investiture with the mantle and to confer it upon cerain persons, because I discovered how much importance Khidr attached to this rite. Previously I had not spoken of the mantle which is now well known. This mantle is for us indeed a symbol of confraternity, a sign that we share in the same spiritual culture, in the practice of the same *ethos*. It has become customary among the masters of mysticism that when they discern some deficiency in one of their disciples, the *shaikh* identifies himself mentally with the state of perfection he wishes to communicate. When he has effected this identification, he takes off the mantle he is wearing at the moment of achieving this spiritual state, and puts it on the disciple whose spiritual state he wishes to make perfect. In this way the *shaikh* communicates to the disciple the spiritual state he has produced in himself, and the same perfection is achieved in the disciple's state. Such is the rite of investiture, well known among us; it was communicated to us by the most experienced, among our *shaikhs*.[14]

For each type of concentrative meditation, one is likely to find a corresponding type of expressive meditation. Meditation on externally given visual images has its correspondence, among the expressive techniques, in the contemplation of spontaneously arising imagery; meditation on a verbal formula crystallizing a definite state of mind (such as the koan) has in it the formulation of the hitherto unformulated state of the meditator. To traditionally stereotyped dance forms will correspond a form of dancing in which the individual aims at becoming transparent to the music and letting the dance, so to speak, do itself.*

Even in the domain of breathing we can contrast the two approaches. On the one hand, we find formalized exercises like pranayama,† which involve control of the breath and the surrender of spontaneous preference in favor of a pre-established rhythm; on the other hand, we have a practice that involves the relinquishing of control and a surrender of preference in favor of a spontaneity in the breathing process that originates in a level deeper than that of conscious choice. Even in this simple psychophysiological sphere we thus find a correspondence between the two approaches, a confluence that religions have described as the doing of God's will: the way of the Law, given from without, and that of Revelation, from within; the unfolding of the Divine seed planted in man's innermost nature.

---

* There are, however, exceptions: some trance dances (like the Balinese) are stereotyped. In the highly structured movements of Tai Chi Chuan, on the other hand, the aim is spontaneity and the flow of *chi* is an energy conceived in terms similar to those reported by the Bushmen.
† The fourth limb of Astanga Yoga or Raja Yoga.

The breathing exercise may seem, from such a written description, easy to carry out and perhaps trivial. We may tend to believe that "breathing naturally" is the most simple thing to do and that we are already doing it. In fact we *are*, but *only when we are not aware* of breathing. While we go about our ordinary activities, our breathing center—the animal within us—directs our respiratory movements with great wisdom according to the needs of our organism. As soon as "we" notice our breathing, however, "we" cannot hold back from interfering. Our conscious ego is a great manipulator that only through special training can learn to be *merely* aware. The exercise in spontaneous conscious breathing, therefore, is that of becoming a permissive observer, a non-intruding witness of nature—and in that, it is a practice in surrender and in action-in-inaction. This exercise, which is of great importance in the Buddhistic tradition, may be regarded as the simplest conceivable practice in naturalness and the first step toward disciplines in naturalness of movement (such as Zen archery or painting) and in mind-at-large.[15]

The attitude we have described above, which can be characterized as one of letting a process happen and "being breathed by one's breath," becomes, in the domain of visual representation, one of letting imagery unfold without conscious interference. Just as in the case of breathing, we would be wrong in assuming that this is something that we already do in our ordinary daydreaming. Only in *unconscious* daydreaming or in nocturnal dreaming—when "we" are not present—do we let go of control in our imaginary activity, and even then to a moderate degree.

True freedom of the mind is an attitude that many poets and painters have intentionally cultivated. It has led them to feel that their work was creating itself through them. In the domain of pure imagery, however, the situation is simplified by the absence of any technical issue such as that implied by the holding of pencil and brush.

The practice of unstructured contemplation of imagery is so widespread that it encompasses such different examples as the "hunting for visions" of American Indians and the astral scrying of magicians. Under the name of "active imagination," it holds a prominent place in Jungian psychology,[16] and under that of "guided daydream," it is a different version of the practice recently discovered independently by Desoille.[17] Various psychotherapeutic schools today (such as Gestalt therapy and psychosynthesis) make use of the inner-directed display of visual fantasy as occasion suggests and in the context of their characteristic styles. Without forgetting that progress in the ability to let go of voluntary manipulation—in fantasy as well as in breathing—is more a matter of practice and self-observation than of sophisticated techniques, it is useful to keep in mind certain conditions, such as the necessity of sustained, concentrated attention to the unfolding of imagery. Muscular relaxation may also facilitate the practice, and, as with any form of training extending over time, regularity is important to success. With persistent practice, even persons who are not good visualizers are likely to notice a gradual shift in the quality of their imagination. While not unlike habitual daydreams at first, their productions will tend to resemble more and more those of the natural dream in their spontaneity and apparently irrational quality. Finally, as this level is also left behind, fantasies of a mythical quality, reflecting the archetypal level of the mind, become more prominent.

Techniques of letting go of control in the domain of fantasy are by no means the only ones that have found their way into psychotherapy. Indeed, most of psychotherapy today consists of variations upon the underlying motif of liberation of man's organismic tendencies from the prison of his conditioning.

The basic technique of psychoanalysis—"free association"—is the perfect reflection, at the conceptual level, of the practice of non-interfering observation that we encountered in the breathing exercise described earlier. The specific contribution of psychoanalysis to the attainment of this freedom is in the participation of the second person who witnesses the process: the activity known as "analysis of resistances." For, just as it may take devoted attention to discover that our "natural" breathing is not natural and our "spontaneous" fantasies are controlled, it may be necessary for us to develop a deeper insight in order to understand that our "free association" is unfree. According to Sandor Ferenczi, who may be called one of the fathers of the psychoanalytic technique, when a person attains the ability to free-associate, his analysis may be deemed completed. From this point of view, the technique of psychoanalysis is, like techniques of meditation in general, both a path and a goal.

A similar strategy of de-structuring individual behavior in order to facilitate the emergence of inner structure or style represents the foundation of several schools of group psychotherapy, from group psychoanalysis to encounter. The basic rule in all of these is self-expression, and the goal that of letting self-identity emerge from the superimposed socially patterned behavior that we have come to regard as "self."

One more instance of the way of expression and liberation in the province of psychotherapy is to be found in certain ways of employing psychoactive drugs. As with other techniques, the use of drugs to induce trance states appears to be of great antiquity and is generally found in association with shamanistic practice. The association of Dionysian rites with wine is well known, and it appears from various descriptions that the trance of the sybil at the Delphic Oracle was aided by her inhalation of the vapors of the chasm and of the fumes of laurel. There are indications, too, that some drug was employed at the Mysteries of Eleusis. "I have tasted, I have drunk the *cyceon*," says an oft-quoted statement by the Mystai (initiates).

Just as drugs have been traditionally employed as catalysts to achieve self-expressive and prophetic attitudes, so their most promising place in contemporary psychotherapy seems to be in connection with the techniques aiming at unfolding suppressed spontaneity. For instance:

1. The use of intravenous amphetamines or MDA in order to elicit recall of repressed traumatic memories and feelings.

2. The use of harmaline or ibogaine as facilitators of the guided fantasy or similar practices and, in general, as bridges to the archetypal domain.[18]

3. The use of LSD and related drugs to induce a state of temporary unlearning of perceptual or social stereotypes, in which the individual may become receptive to his unconditioned or true needs and reactions.[19]

It is no wonder that several forms of practice in letting go to our deeper propensities are now to be found in the field of psychotherapy, for psychotherapy as a whole (as most frequently conceived today) aims at liberating the individual from what hinders from within his expression or realization.[20]

As to the relationship between art and therapy as ways of expression and liberation, it may be said that art centers in the issue of expression, and therapy in that of removing the blocks to expression, but any sharp boundary between the two processes can only be artificial. The shaman was at the same time an artist and a healer, and today we seem to be entering a stage of decompartmentalization of disciplines through which we can understand their original unity. More specifically, art-education disciplines are becoming therapies, and therapy is seen as both an art (rather than a medical technique independent of the inner states of the "patient") and a means of liberating the artist in the patient.

Another technique that deserves special attention is the one that has attracted many adherents all over the Western world today as a consequence of the influence of the Indonesian Bapak Subuh. The main practice carried out in different branches of Subud is called *latihan* and consists, precisely, in a surrender of control. The words that are generally used at the beginning of a session define the practice as a specific form of isvara-pranidhana*: "Let us surrender to the will of God." The specificity of the context lies in the fact that it is carried out in groups of either men or

* See p. 63.

women, and that a restriction is placed on the possible impulse to touch or address other persons in the group.

The phenomena typical of the latihan are mostly those already described: ecstatic experiences, visionary experiences in the form of hallucinations or eidetic imagery, possession or manifestations related to possession, such as automatic movements, glossolalia, inspired singing, spontaneously unfolding rituals. Otherwise the latihan may take the form of a serene receptive state akin to that in Za-Zen, or a tranquil attunement to what the individual perceives as God's will. Alternatively, it may be an experience of purification through the awareness of lack of attunement, either in that very moment or, more generally, in the individual's ordinary life.

According to Idries Shah, the latihan is a Sufi exercise not to be recommended as a single practice divorced from its original context or expert supervision.[21] Perhaps this is a statement valid for all the exercises mentioned, because they can represent a way both out of or into mental disease. They are ways of liberation through chaos, ways to consciousness via the unconscious, and, as Jung has pointed out about deep psychotherapy, there is the danger of remaining paralyzed in the depths and not returning.

The *latihan* is no exception to the expressive way in general, in that it may be an avenue to psychotic experience. Even psychoanalysis can be such an avenue, and it is not uncommon for psychotic experiences, elicited by the analytic process, to be the prelude to the definitive cure. However, the *latihan* (like the ingestion of drugs) may not only be a particularly ample gateway to the other side of the mind, but call for the complement of highly skilled guidance.

What I am saying of techniques of surrendering control in general is particularly true, I believe, of a technique that has received little attention in professional circles but whose potential danger might well be turned into usefulness. This is automatic writing.

Automatic writing is a phenomenon not known to most persons, and yet it is susceptible of being experienced by many (and perhaps most). It is done by holding a pencil over a sheet of paper without attempting to write, but only waiting for an involuntary movement to develop. If the experiment is engaged in with some persistence, it is very likely that the subject will find that his hand moves by itself, "as if guided by an invisible power." This may lead, at first, to illegible scribbling, but in the course of time it will take the shape of writing that can be understood. The experience is most likely to be successful when a question is posed by the subject, either aloud or mentally, and when this question is one whose answer deeply concerns him. Then the writing will have relevance to the question, and it is likely to impress the subject as an answer not formulated by himself. Moreover, as in the phenomenon of possession or in some deliberately induced hypnotic states, the person who writes sometimes does not know the content of his writing at all until a statement is completed.*

After persistent practice in automatic writing, however, texts dealing with personal matters often tend to be replaced by more impersonal or transpersonal ones, generally associated with the emergence of definite answering personalities (regardless of whether these are interpreted or not as "spirits" by the subject). When this occurs, it can be said that automatic writing has led to a more complete expression of the possession syndrome, with the dangers or the blessings, whichever may be the case.

I want to describe in some detail two instances of an inner saga triggered by automatic writing. Both cases are what may be called *monumenta psychologica* and show the organic interrelationships among a number of features of the expressive way and its states.

* The interested reader may find useful technical information on the procedure in a book by Dr. A. Mühl,[22] who employed it in a psychotherapeutic context. As Dr. William Alanson White puts it in his introduction to the work, she had employed automatic writing "for discovering what was going on in the mind of her patients which was inaccessible to ordinary questioning."

The first case is that of Ludwig Staudenmeier, a professor of experimental chemistry, who in 1910 published a long essay entitled "Die Magie als experimentelle Naturwissenschaft" (Magic as an Experimental Science).[23] He was a methodical person with a critical mind, who started experimenting with automatic writing out of scientific curiosity. Once that Pandora box of his mind was opened, his life became a struggle to master the forces he had unleashed in his own psyche.

Staudenmeier was persuaded by a friend to try automatic writing. After several failures, his friend encouraged him to go on, until finally his pencil described "the strangest loops and curlicues." Later, and in spite of his skepticism, letters began to form and answers to the questions he was formulating. Though different spirits claimed to be involved in the writing, Staudenmeier doubted this, for he realized that his own thoughts were involved in the answers. "Nevertheless," he wrote, "I absolutely had the impression of having to do with a being utterly alien to me. At first I could tell in advance what was going to be written, and from this there developed in time an anticipated 'inner' hearing of the message; . . . as the spiritualists say, I had become an 'auditory medium.' "[24]

Some of the voices that Staudenmeier described are similar to those reported by most mediums as well as schizophrenics with auditory delusions:

If the end the inner voice . . . made itself heard too often and without sufficient reason, and also against my will; a number of times it was bad, subtly mocking, vexatious, and irritable. For whole days at a time this insufferable struggle continued entirely against my will.

Often the statements of these so-called beings proved to be fabrications. Opposite the house where I live a strange tenant was just moving in. By way of test I asked my spirits his name. Without hesitation I received the reply: Hauptmann von Müller. It later proved that the information was completely false. When in such a case I afterward reproached them gently, I often elicited this sincere reply: "It is because we cannot do otherwise, we are obliged to lie, we are evil spirits, you must not take it amiss!" If I then became rude they followed suit.

"Go to blazes, you fool! You are always worrying us! You ought not to have summoned us! Now we are always obliged to stay near you!" When I used stronger language it was exactly as if I had hurled insults at a wall or a forest: the more one utters the more the echo sends back. For a time the slightest unguarded thought that passed through my mind produced an outburst from the inner voices.[25]

In the course of time, some of the voices became highly individualized and endowed with some characteristics more related to possession than to hallucination. The three most persistent of these he called "my highness," "the child," and "Roundhead." Here are some of Staudenmeier's descriptions of the first two:

Later there were manifested in a similar manner personifications of princely or ruling individuals, such as the German Emperor, and furthermore of deceased persons such as Napoleon the First. At the same time a characteristic feeling of loftiness took possession of me; I became the lord and master of a great people, my chest swelled and broadened almost without any action on my part, my attitude became extremely energetic and military, a proof that the said personification was then exercising an important influence. For example, I heard the inner voice say to me majestically: "I am the German Emperor." After some time I grew tired, other conceptions made themselves strongly felt and my attitude once more relaxed. Thanks to the number of personalities of high rank who made their appearance to me, the idea of grandeur and nobility gradually developed. My highness is possessed by a great desire to be a distinguished personality, even a princely or governing personality, or at least—this is how I explain after the event—to see and imitate these personalities. My highness takes great interest in military spectacles, fashionable life, distinguished bearing, good living with abundant choice beverages, order and elegance within the house, fine clothing, an upright military carriage, gymnastics, hunting and other sports, and seeks accordingly to influence my mode of life by advice, exhortations, orders and threats. On the other hand, my highness is averse to children, common things, jesting and gaiety, evidently because he knows princely persons almost exclusively by their ceremonial attitude in public or by illustrations. He particularly detests illustrated journals of satirical caricatures, total abstainers, etc. I am, moreover, somewhat too small for him.

Another important role is played by the "child" personification: "I am a child. You are the father. You must play with me." Then childish verses are hummed. "The little wheel goes thud, thud, thud," "Comes a little flying bird." Wonderfully tender childishness, and artless ways such as no real child would show in so marked and touching a manner. In moments of good humour I am called Putzi, or else he says simply, "My dear Zi." When walking in town I must stop at the toy-shop windows, make a detailed inspection, buy myself toys, watch the children playing, romp on the ground, and dance in a ring as children do, thus consistently behaving with an entire absence of loftiness. If on the request of "the child" or "the children" (at times there occurred a division into several kindred personalities), I happen to pause in a shop and look over the toy counter, this personification bubbles over with joy and in a childish voice cries out ecstatically: "Oh, how lovely! It's really heavenly!"

Since the "child" personification has acquired a greater influence over me, not only has my interest in childish ways, toys, and even shops increased, but also my search for childish satisfactions and the innocent joys of the heart, a fact which acts upon the organism, rejuvenating and refreshing it, and driving away many of the cares of the grown man, accustomed more and more to use his intelligence. In the same way a number of other personifications also have a beneficial effect upon me. For example, my interest in art and understanding of artistic things have increased considerably. Particularly remarkable and characteristic of the profound division which takes place in me is the following fact: that whereas my interest in art was formerly very slight, especially as regards that of antiquity and the Middle Ages, certain of my personifications are passionately interested in these latter and have continually impelled me to devote attention to them."[26]

Staudenmeier's experiments led him to a number of discoveries that I will not detail in this context—in spite of their being more extraordinary than mere possession experiences. As for the self-perfecting quest into which he stumbled unwillingly, he apparently failed to reach his goal. At least we know that two and one-half years before his death, at the age of sixty-six, he wrote in a postcard to a friend: "I am continuing with my work with desperate energy, but it is very slow and difficult. Although all four of the recalcitrant centers have received ample blows in their personifications partly from one another and partly from me, they fall back again and again into their old errors so that it really takes the patience of a lamb to persevere."[27]

The second case of a life profoundly affected by automatic writing is that of another scientist whose pursuit of knowledge became a pursuit of wisdom and a spiritual quest. The difference from Staudenmeier is that in this instance we can speak of a completed development, in the same sense that, in shamanism, the initiate not only plunges into seeming madness but emerges from it "reborn" before undertaking his work.

I am speaking of Emanuel Swedenborg, who may be called a modern shaman, not only because of the nature of his journey, his visionary experiences, and the multiplicity of his interests and gifts, but because his whole spiritual adventure unfolded from his following the bent of his inner nature.

Swedenborg, mineralogist, physicist, biologist, philosopher, and adviser to the Swedish government in the early eighteenth century, has been one of the few men of encompassing genius in the history of Europe. William Blake, Goethe, Heine, Balzac, Emerson, Henry James, the Brownings, and many other writers have praised him or acknowledged a debt to his ideas, while his scientific theories foreshadowed what dozens of specialists were to confirm in the following years. He was the first, for instance, to formulate the idea of cerebral localizations and to describe the functions of the brain cortex. Also, a hundred years before the neuronal structure of the brain cortex had been observed, he attributed the primary functions of nervous control to little oval particles in the gray matter. Arrhenius, in an introduction to the cosmological section of Swedenborg's *Prodromus Principiorum Rerum Naturalium*, concluded:

> If we briefly summarize the ideas which were first given expression by Swedenborg, and afterwards, though usually in a much modified form—consciously or unconsciously—taken up by other authors in cosmology, we find them to be:
>
> The planets of our solar system originate from the solar matter—taken up by Buffon, Kant, Laplace, and others.
>
> The earth and the other planets have gradually removed themselves from the sun and received a gradually lengthened time of revolution, a view again expressed by G. H. Darwin.
>
> The suns are arranged around the Milky Way, taken up by Wright, Kant, and Lambert.
>
> There are still greater systems in which the milky ways are arranged, taken up by Lambert.[28]

Swedenborg's early stage of spiritual development may be seen as that of a gnani-yogin. He was at first a scientist who turned his attention more and more to the basic questions of science (such as the nature of matter, or the mind-body problem) until, at the age of forty-two, he established a great synthesis of the knowledge of his time in the three big volumes of his *Opera Philosophica et Mineralia*. Driven through this work to consider the nexus between the infinite and the finite, eternity and time, he produced next a book entitled *Of The Infinite*. In the second part of this book, far from the a-religious stance that was characteristic of his early career, he proposed that the true divinity in man is an acknowledgment of the existence of God, "and the sense of delight in the love of God." His interest now turned to the "science of the soul," to complete which, he said, "all the sciences are required that the world has ever eliminated or developed." His reflections on this matter constitute the content of two volumes that he completed at the age of fifty-one and that bear the title *The Economy of The Animal Kingdom.* (This is a gross mistranslation from his Latin original; "animal" here stands for his word *anima*—"soul." The title should be "The Organization of the Soul's Kingdom," that is, the body).

It was apparently during this time that Swedenborg had the first clear-cut indications of an order of experience other than that with which he was familiar. He became very interested in his dreams, of which he started to keep a journal, and he discovered an ability to cut off his sense impressions when he wanted to think intensely. Perhaps of greater importance is his statement that when men of science who have the power of synthesizing, "after a long course of reasoning make a discovery of the truth, straightaway there is a certain cheering light, a joyful confirmatory brightness, that plays round the sphere of their mind; a kind of mysterious radiation—I know not whence it proceeds—that darts through some secret temple of the brain." The following quotation from later writing probably refers to the same experience, or to the development of it in subsequent years:

. . . a flame of diverse sizes and with a diversity of color and splendor has often been seen by me. Thus while I was writing a certain little work hardly a day passed by for several months in which a flame was not seen by me as vividly as the flame of a household hearth; at the time this was a sign of approbation, and this happened before spirits began to speak with me viva voce.[29]

Experiences of this type, culminating in a vision of Christ, profoundly changed Swedenborg and resulted in a book entitled *Of The Worship and Love of God.* After this, not even his writing would be his own: his next eight volumes were, as he said, *inspired:* "Nay have I written entire pages, and the spirits did not dictate the words, but absolutely guided my hands, so that it may [be assumed to be]* they who were doing the writing."

Signe Toksvig, author of an appreciative biography of Swedenborg, writes of *The Word Explained:* "There probably never has been anything written so overpoweringly alien to normal interest as these Biblical commentaries by Swedenborg, nor anything more foreign to the results of modern Biblical research. Neither has anything served so much to conceal the true greatness of the man. No one who chances to meet him first in these earnest crossword puzzles can be blamed for turning quickly away."

There are indications that some of the contents of the exegesis were repulsive to his own mind. Yet Swedenborg respected it all as *revelation*, for "these words were written by my hand, and dictated by Isaac, the father of the Jews. . . ." Other parts were written by Jacob, by Abraham, by Moses, or by "the Messiah himself through Abraham."

But, according to Toksvig, Swedenborg early began to lose faith in the declared identities of the spirits, and it is evident that he was worried by their claim that "they were doing the dictation." At the end, he came to believe that the spirits claiming to be Biblical patriarchs were truly impostors. Yet his own writing continued,† now inspired by more trustworthy entities. In a diary entry of this period he stated that he did not accept any "representation, vision or discourse" from spirit or angel without reflection on them "as to what thence was truthful and good." Since "truthful" and "good" were to him from the Lord, he could say that he had been instructed "by no spirit or by any angel but by the Lord alone from whom is all truth and good."

This is an important statement. No longer does Swedenborg

* The original source is unclear at this point.
† The eight volumes of *Arcana Coelestia*, written during this period, were a new attempt to explain the inner meaning of Genesis and Exodus.

equate the fruit of inspiration with truth, nor does he leave this decision to reason alone. The ability to *discriminate* truth, like the confirmatory light experienced during his writing in earlier years, is in itself a gift of intuition. *He* could only say, "*I know.*" During the later decades of his life he produced his most profound works, in which he *brought together* his highly uncommon inspiration with his ordering, critical mind. Through the years his discrimination became more subtle, we may surmise, so that he could be enriched by messages beyond his reasoning faculties and still be a creator and master of his world picture. Thus, when a friend asked him how many he had succeeded in persuading of the truth of his doctrines, he could say, after reflection, that he thought he had "about fifty in this world and about the same number in the other."[30]

I have given what might seem inordinate attention to these two illustrations of automatic writing because of their bearing on much of what I have touched upon in this chapter. Both Staudenmeier and Swedenborg are instances of visionaries and men who experienced possession states; both illustrate the unleashing of unsuspected forces within their own psyches; both raise the question as to the boundaries between mysticism and schizophrenia; and both evidence what we regard as supernatural or "psychic" abilities.*

Beyond all this, these two lives illustrate another more fundamental feature of the dimension of spontaneity that we have been discussing: they were solitaries who learned everything from their own experience and inspiration. In contrast to individuals who have trodden the way of meditation on symbolic forms or the way of emptiness, they are eminently free from tradition, finding guidance only within themselves. And, we may add, only individual instances can properly illustrate the way of

---

* Staudenmeier could cause action at a distance and was able to impress an image on a photographic plate; Swedenborg was well known for feats of clairvoyance that have become historical.

expression. *What* is expressed may be in the final analysis the same for each enlightened prophet, all the disciples of Melchizedek being prompted by a selfsame inner spirit. And yet their ways are unique, and their process of realization directed by their peculiar background and situation. Their way is essentially *the way of vocation,* that of listening to their inner voice, and their path one of gradual approximation. Had Swedenborg not taken down the messages of the spirit-world imposters, would he have been able to know them for what they were, and receive the more refined messages of later years?*

The way of forms is based upon the predication: "Here is a truth: assimilate it; make it yours." The way of expression starts out from the opposite prospect: "The truth lies within you, and you can find it only by forgetting the ready-made answers."

These are two attitudes that bear upon life in general, not merely upon the sphere of meditation. An extension of the assimilative and unitive approach is an attitude of respect for established forms and feelings of reverence for crystallized wisdom. The formalist is typically pious. The corresponding extension of the way of expression to life at large is that self-assurance and disrespect for established forms which is frequently part of the personality of a genius and has given rise to the stereotype of the artist as a rebellious man. By questioning established knowledge those who have followed the way of expression have been able to contact—to a greater or lesser extent—the source of all answers without intermediaries, and thus have given new words, sounds, shapes to the eternal truth.

The same two attitudes may be seen in education, where the formalistic declares: "I have a truth. Listen!"; and the permissive, trusting a natural development within the individual, holds

---

* It is interesting to note that the phenomenon of intrusion is commonplace in spiritualistic circles. A remarkable instance of it may be found in William Yeats's work, "A Vision," completed after years of automatic writing frequently interrupted by "false teachers."

that the child can be nourished but cannot be guided without risk of interference or conditioning.

These attitudes may be found again in ethics, as a trust in absolutes, principles, and laws on the one hand, and a trust in free choice and responsibility on the other. In politics, they take the extreme forms of theocracy and democracy; in cultural styles, those of traditionalism and individualism, past-orientation and present-orientation.

In all these spheres today we seem to be passing from a state of formalism to one of relinquishing forms and seeking inner orientation. Our culture seems to be at a point of transition where the old forms are dying and people do not want new ones but seek to grasp the meaning that the older traditions have failed to express through excessive repetition.

Humanity is increasingly aware of the prison it has built for itself, and individuals want to be freed from what they are made to swallow whole by their environment. Because of this, man's metaphysical drive is leading him in the direction of expression, liberation, revelation from within.

Epilogue

I set out in this essay to show the unity of meditation beyond its forms. I believe that I have clearly shown, if not a unity, a tri-unity: the way of absorption, the way of emptiness, and the way of surrender constitute, each one of them, a major direction of the spirit at the heart of a number of disciplines—in the province of meditation and beyond.

I have also attempted to show that these mutually complementary directions of the spirit—this disciplined concentration, in letting go and in freedom—are only apparently (or conceptually) exclusive of each other. On the contrary, successful meditation requires the simultaneity of purposefulness, spontaneity, and detachment. To clarify still further how a single form of meditation may contain a balanced admixture of the three components, I want to give one more example: the Chinese practice of wu-hsin, in which the meditator watches the stream of his consciousness without interfering with its course. In this exercise, more than in concentrated attention upon a flame, breathing, or music, he must be able to be awake to every moment in the ever-changing stream of experience; he must be able to summon up his total availability of consciousness and bring it to bear upon the now.

Essentially, the exercise is one of action-in-inaction. The river flows, the watcher sits by its bank. Swallows cross the sky, the sky remains. "The mind is like a mirror—it projects nothing, it clings to nothing." "Mind is like space. . . ."

This is an exercise in spontaneity and freedom. The river must flow on its own. You accept its course. You listen to the *dharma*. You follow the calling. Precisely because, like space, you are like nothing, you may be filled by everything. You can let everything be.

The higher synthesis of the three dimensions of meditation is something that I have presented less systematically than the convergence of techniques belonging to each dimension. For this reason I want to direct the reader once more to the relevant passages in this essay:

On the presence of the negative aspect in both the other ways, the Apollonian and the Dionysian: pp. 20, 22-23, 74, 75-76, 94-95.

On the parallel between the outer-directed and inner-directed ways: pp. 16-17, 92, 95-96, 114, 128-29.

On how the process of *letting go of anticipations* in the negative way implies the *acceptance* characteristic of the way of surrender, and vice versa: pp. 94-95.

I think that in using these three broad dimensions as the skeleton of the present essay I have been able to show the meeting point of exercises and traditions that fanatical disdain or cultural attachment tends to regard as separate or incompatible. I think that, with the occasion of "meditation," I have shown something of the common intention or original inspiration among Taoism, Buddhism, Christianity, Islam.

I hope, too, that I have been able to share some of my perception of a continuity from primitive mysticism (magic, medicine of the shaman) to the later mysticism (ritual, rules of life of religion), and to the mysticism of psychotherapy.

I have been persuading the reader that the essence of meditation is also the essence of everything else: art, philosophy, religion, life. I would probably have done the same given any other subject: art, religion, love, philosophy. Everything is the same, and everything is different. Perhaps this last statement sums up the only important thing I have to say.

PART II

The Techniques of Meditation and Their Implications for Modern Psychology

ROBERT E. ORNSTEIN

For two of life's best teachers:

Faith, who brought me along slowly
                              slowly
                                 patiently
with all her strength in reserve,
teaching by example

Alan, being and becoming himself, always

"The supreme importance of the problem for all kinds of human values, as well as scientific matters, prompts us to search ahead of the evidence from time to time as science advances for any possible new insight. Even a partial solution that would enable us to decide between very broad and general alternatives—like whether consciousness is cosmic or individual, mortal or immortal, in possession of free will or subject to causal determinism, and the like—could have profound and far-reaching ideological implications."

—Roger Sperry

Foreword

This essay is the result of a long process of learning that I didn't really know what I thought I knew. I had studied much of the Western psychological literature on consciousness until I thought I knew. As I began to look elsewhere, to Zen, to Yoga, to the Sufis, I began to understand how little progress we had made in the analysis of the nature of consciousness, and that the richness of the Eastern psychologies had much to offer us. This essay is my attempt to begin to encompass the concepts and techniques of Eastern psychologies in Western terms. What seems to result is a strange mixture of techniques, from computers and electroencephalographs to mantra and dervish dancing.

I have many to thank for different aspects of my education, but I'll mention few. My association with Joe Kamiya allowed and allows me to absorb many of the intricacies of fancy equipment and some of the enthusiasm for physiological feedback. David Galin has been a continuous source of calm yet hysterical and wise advice on many of my vague mumblings—the many times he simply said, "What could you possibly mean by *that*?" Several of the ideas in this manuscript are at least half his.

I am indebted also to Miss Beverly Timmons for her enthusiastic organization of a study group on meditation, as well as for many points of information.

The only previous attempt to consider the practices of meditation within modern psychology has been that of Arthur Deikman. Where his essay touches on similar aspects of meditation this analysis is similar to, and greatly influenced by, his work. I am in his debt as much for his conceptual analysis as for the demonstration that an attempt to bring meditation within psychology is possible and fruitful.

The interaction with Claudio Naranjo has been fruitful for me in many ways, beyond that of this book. Claudio and I have extremely different backgrounds: he is Chilean, a psychiatrist interested in therapy, psychedelics, etc.; I am an American, interested in consciousness and psychophysiology. Early in 1969 we decided that our differences in outlook could produce an interesting book on meditation, his part to discuss the experiential aspects and mine to cover the psychology and physiology. We wrote our essays geographically and temporally separated, and we found that the phenomena of the esoteric psychologies seemed to compel similar conclusions. We divided the different types of meditative exercises in basically similar ways: the concentrative form involving a restriction of attention, and an "opening up" form. Claudio's manuscript, *The Unfolding of Man*, provided me with many new inputs and ideas.

For reading and commenting on earlier versions of the manuscript I am indebted to Enoch Callaway, Charles Tart, Katie Kocel, Charles Furst, Ivan Pasternak, Roger Kramer—and to many others, thank you.

Thanks also to Majo Keleshian, Ann Skillion, and Ruby Collins for typing and retyping the manuscript, and to Faith Hornbacher for Good Stuff.

I was supported during the time of writing by a fellowship from the National Institutes of Mental Health, USPHS 2 TI MH 7082-10; by a grant from the Babcock Foundation, with special thanks to Mike Murphy and Barbara Lassiter; and a grant from Janet and Merrill Bickford.

Introduction

When we view the practices of the esoteric disciplines from the vantage point of scientific inquiry, we may put forth ideas and conceptions which to the adherents of the esoteric traditions will be minor or irrelevant. My intention is not to "reduce" totally the phenomena of the esoteric disciplines to psychological terms, but simply to begin the process of considering these aspects of the traditions which fall within the realm of a modern psychological analysis. (Several of the major tenets of these traditions remain outside this form of inquiry.) A similar point has been made by many scientists as well as by those belonging to these traditions. The physicist Robert Oppenheimer has said: "These two ways of thinking, the way of time and history, and the way of eternity and timelessness, are both parts of man's effort to comprehend the world in which he lives. Neither is comprehended in the other nor reducible to it . . . each supplementing the other, neither telling the whole story."[1]

If we consider a blind man interested in the phenomena of color, there are certain useful operations that he can perform on colored light. He might construct a machine that prints out (in Braille) the wavelength of light. He might perform certain calculations on his observations, which would enable him, for instance, to predict the wavelength of a new combination of lights, in a wide variety of conditions. We do understand, however, that his analysis in terms of the numbers obtained when a new mixture of lights is combined is in an entirely different order of knowledge from that of the direct experience of color. The Sufi Idries Shah makes the same point in discussing the meaning of the word "Sufi." He notes that many scholars have wondered about the derivation of the name, and that there exist various theories—some say the word has no etymology, some identify it with theosophy, some identify it with the Arab garment of wool. Shah says:

> But acquaintance with Sufis, let alone almost any degree of access to their practices and moral traditions, could easily have resolved any seeming contradiction between the existence of a word and its having no ready etymological derivation. The answer is that the Sufis regard *sounds* of the letters s, u, f (in Arabic, the signs for *soad, wao, fa*) as significant in the same order of use in their effect on human mentation.
>
> The Sufis, are, therefore, the people of ssssuuuufff.
>
> Having disposed of that conundrum (incidentally illustrating the difficulties of getting to grips with Sufi ideas where one thinks only along certain lines), we immediately see a fresh and characteristic problem arising to replace it. The contemporary thinker is likely to be interested in this explanation—this idea that sound influences the brain—only within the limitations imposed by himself. He may accept it as a theoretical possibility insofar as it is expressed in terms that are regarded as admissible at the time of communication.
>
> If we say "Sounds have an effect on man, making it possible, other things being equal, for him to have experiences beyond the normal," he may persuasively insist that "This is mere occultism, primitive nonsense of the order of OM-MANI-PADME-HUM abracadabra, and the rest." But (taking into account not objectivity, but simply the current phase of accepted thought) we can say to him

instead, "The human brain, as you are doubtless aware, may be likened to an electronic computer. It responds to impacts or vibrations of sight, sound, touch, etc., in certain predetermined or 'programmed' ways. It is held by some that the sounds roughly represented by the signs s-u-f are among those for reaction to which the brain is, or may be, 'programmed.' " He may be very well able to assimilate this wretched simplification of the existing pattern of thinking.[2]

We should keep Shah and Oppenheimer's comments in mind, and also remember that portions of this essay may be considered, from the viewpoint of modern psychology, in just the opposite way—as too general and as yet lacking in precise experimental verification, such as which specific brain structures are involved, etc.

This essay, however, is an attempt to begin to prepare a new middle ground between two approaches and to "translate" some of the metaphors of the esoteric traditions into those of modern psychology. The first chapter contains a consideration of the communalities of concentrative meditation exercises with an eye to the common experiences these techniques produce and their possible common effects on the nervous system. This will involve retracing part of Naranjo's path; many of the same techniques and phenomena will be considered from a slightly different viewpoint and move in a slightly different direction. The second chapter is an attempt to point out the essential similarities between the esoteric and modern psychologies of awareness and a consideration of the effects and aftereffects of the practices of meditation on awareness. The third chapter puts forth a "new" view arising within the scientific community of the capabilities of self-regulation of internal states that man possesses, and the aid that modern technology may be in implementing this extended view of our capacity. This "new" view within science is one at least thousands of years old to those of the esoteric traditions.

1 / "Turning Off" Awareness

A story that appears in Philip Kapleau's *The Three Pillars of Zen* provides us with a useful point at which to begin a psychological consideration of the practices of meditation.

The importance of single-mindedness, of bare attention, is illustrated in the following anecdote:

One day a man of the people said to the Zen master Ikkyu: "Master, will you please write for me some maxims of the highest wisdom?"

Ikkyu immediately took his brush and wrote the word "Attention."

"Is that all?" asked the man. "Will you not add something more?"

Ikkyu then wrote twice running: "Attention. Attention."

"Well," remarked the man rather irritably, "I really don't see much depth or subtlety in what you have just written."

Then Ikkyu wrote the same word three times running: "Attention. Attention. Attention."

Half-angered, the man demanded: "What does that word, 'Attention' mean anyway?" And Ikkyu answered, gently: "Attention means attention."[1]

There are many clues in other places that meditation is primarily an exercise in deployment of attention rather than in reason or concept formation. And yet the only major attempt in modern psychology to discuss the practices of meditation, using the concept of attention as the central element of analysis, has been that of Arthur Deikman.

An analysis of any experiental phenomenon in terms of science, in this case in terms of the psychology and physiology of awareness, is naturally more limited, restricted, and drier than actual descriptions of experience. When we try to bring experience within the limiting frame of reference of science, a great deal of the richness and complexity is lost in the attempt to gain a great deal of precision. We will be forced to consider only those points that are amenable to this type of analysis.

Another consideration in this analysis is that most techniques of meditation do not exist as solitary practices but are only artificially separable from an entire system of practice and belief. A given meditation exercise cannot be perfectly understood as an isolated technique but only as an integral part of a whole discipline. The entire process usually, but not always, involves many components, a belief structure, and various forms of concurrent practices. A major component is a detachment from, or even a renunciation of, world activity. Another is a concentration on an energy form, called in Yoga *kundalini*. Its activation involves special exercises said to release a form of energy through the spine; this is often combined with special breathing exercises, pranayama. Self-observation, which can be considered another form of meditation, is practiced in Zen, Yoga, and Sufism.

Since the general state of our knowledge about the various forms of meditation within science in particular, and within the West in general, is extremely low, we should perhaps first set the background and review some of the general similarities of the meditation exercises. Most involve separating the practitioner from the daily ongoing activities. He usually sits alone or with a small group in a special room set aside for meditation, or in a special place often constructed in a naturally isolated area, a quiet wood, near a waterfall, or a cave. Generally, the attempt is made to keep all external sources of stimulation to a minimum to avoid distracting the meditator from his object of meditation. This isolation is felt to be especially critical in modern cities, where random sounds or human voices can distract the person from his exercise. In most forms of Yoga and in Zen there is emphasis on maintaining a specific posture, the lotus position. This is done for the purpose of keeping bodily movements to a minimum and therefore out of awareness during the meditation period. The stiff back is said, additionally, to lessen the possibility of drowsiness in the reduced stimulation setting. Incense is often burned during meditation to provide a strong consistent background odor to keep out any small distracting changes in smells.*

Instructions for most of the meditation exercises are to attend closely and continuously to the meditation object. This is more difficult than it would seem, and most beginners lose awareness of the meditation object quite often. Each time one notices that awareness has shifted from the object of meditation, the instructions are always to return awareness back to the meditation object. In many of the traditions, each session of meditation lasts about half an hour. In most, although not all, meditation is practiced twice a day, often in the morning before the day's major work, and in the evening. Beginners usually practice for less time and work up to about a half-hour a day, and as progress is made, more and more complicated exercises are usually given.

In terms of the psychology of consciousness, there seem to be two general varieties of meditation: those exercises which involve restriction of awareness, focusing of attention on the object of meditation or the repetition of a word (which Naranjo terms "concentrative meditation"), and those which involve a deliberate attempt to "open up" awareness of the external environment.

* This suggestion was made by Dr. David Galin.

We will consider the first form, that of "concentrative" meditation, in this chapter.

In reviewing the extraordinary diversity of the actual techniques of this form of meditation, as did Naranjo earlier, one general similarity seems to come through. No matter the object of meditation or the superficial practice of meditation, the exercises seem to be attempts to restrict awareness to a single, unchanging source of stimulation for a definite period of time. In many traditions, successfully achieving this is termed "one-pointedness of mind."

If the exercise involves vision, the meditator gazes at the object of meditation continuously. If the meditation is auditory, the sound, the chant, or the prayer is repeated over and over again, either aloud or silently. If the meditation consists in physical movement, the movement is repeated again and again. In all cases, awareness is directed completely on the movement, or the visual object, or the sound.

In Zen, as a first exercise, the student is instructed to count his breaths from one to ten, and on reaching ten to return to one and repeat. When the count is lost, as it will be by beginners, the instructions are that "the count should be returned to one and begun again." After he is able to concentrate completely on his breaths, the student then begins a more advanced exercise and focuses attention on the *process* of breathing itself. He thinks about nothing but the movement of the air within himself, the air reaching his nose, going down into the lungs, remaining in the lungs, and finally the process of exhalation. This is a convenient way to begin meditating, since breathing is a natural activity, which continues whether we will it or not. This is not an attempt to control the normal breathing as in some aspects of the Yoga and Sufi traditions, but simply to be aware of the breathing and to maintain this awareness on the breathing and nothing else.

In *What the Buddha Taught*, Walpola Rahula gives these instructions:

You breathe in and out all day and night, but you are never mindful of it, you never for a second concentrate your mind on it. Now you are going to do just this. Breathe in and out as usual, without any effort or strain. Now, bring your mind to concentrate on your breathing-in and breathing-out, let your mind watch and observe your breathing in and out; let your mind be aware and vigilant of your breathing in and out. When you breathe, you sometimes take deep breaths, sometimes not. This does not matter at all. Breathe normally and naturally. The only thing is that when you take deep breaths you should be aware that they are deep breaths, and so on. In other words, your mind should be so fully concentrated on your breathing that you are aware of its movements and changes. Forget all other things, your surroundings, your environment; do not raise your eyes and look at anything. Try to do this for five or ten minutes.

At the beginning you will find it extremely difficult to bring your mind to concentrate on your breathing. You will be astonished how your mind runs away. It does not stay. You begin to think of various things. You hear sounds outside. Your mind is disturbed and distracted. You may be dismayed and disappointed. But if you continue to practice this exercise twice a day, morning and evening, for about five or ten minutes at a time, you will gradually, by and by, begin to concentrate your mind on your breathing. After a certain period you will experience just that split second when your mind is fully concentrated on your breathing, when you will not hear even sounds nearby, when no external world exists for you. This slight moment is such a tremendous experience for you, full of joy, happiness and tranquility, that you would like to continue it. But still you cannot. Yet, if you go on practicing this regularly, you may repeat the experience again and again for longer and longer periods. That is the moment, when you lose yourself completely in your mindfulness of breathing. As long as you are conscious of yourself you cannot concentrate on anything.[2]

As the student of Rinzai Zen progresses, he learns to keep himself motionless, to sit in the quite difficult lotus position, and as he learns to maintain awareness of his breath successfully, he is given a more advanced meditation exercise.

A riddle or a paradox, called a *koan*, is given him to meditate upon. Naranjo delved into the richness and subtlety of the koan method earlier.* To most other commentators, however, the koan has been the subject of much misunderstanding and confusion. The question-and-answer routine has seemed to be one for the Marx Brothers. The "question" may be, "Show me your face before your mother and father met." The "answer" may be the student's slapping the questioner in the face. The master asks the student, "Move that boat on the lake right now with your mind!," and the student stands up, runs over and hits his head against the gong, turns a somersault, and lands in front of the master. Since the student answered successfully, it is quite clear that the "answers" to the koan are not to be considered logically in the sense of their being rational problems with set answers, to be solved in the usual manner of thinking through various rational alternatives and choosing one, the way Suzuki at first tried.† We might instead consider the koan exercise in the more restricted terms of the psychology of awareness. In these terms, the koan is an extreme and compelling method of forcing intense concentration on one single thought. The first koan exercise is:

In all seriousness a monk asked Joshu, "Has the dog Buddha nature or not?"

Joshu retorted, "*Mu!*"‡

This koan is not to be taken verbally and logically, to be worked through like a problem, as Suzuki did, but as an extreme exercise in concentration. This is confirmed in instructions given in the lectures of a contemporary Zen master, Yasutani Roshi;

You must concentrate day and night, questioning yourself about Mu through every one of your 360 bones and 84,000 pores . . . what

* See pp. 41ff.
† See pp. 42ff.
‡ *Mu* is a word that has no meaning in Japanese.

this refers to is your entire being. Let all of you become one mass of doubt and questioning. Concentrate on and penetrate fully into Mu. To penetrate into *Mu* is to achieve this unity by holding to *Mu* tenaciously day and night! Do not separate yourself from it under any circumstances! Focus your mind on it constantly. Do not construe *Mu* as nothingness and do not conceive it in terms of existence or non-existence. You must not, in other words, think of *Mu* as a problem involving the existence or non-existence of Buddha-nature. Then what do you do? You stop speculating and concentrate wholly on *Mu*—just *Mu!*[3]

Later koan exercises involve other unanswerable questions, such as "What is the sound of one hand clapping?" and "What is the size of the real you?" Because no verbal logical answer to the question can be found, the koan becomes a useful and demanding focus of attention over a very long period of time. The koan becomes a meditation object, day and night, a constant and compelling focusing of awareness on a single source. The lack of a rational, logical solution forces the student to go through and to discard all his verbal associations, all his thoughts, all his "solutions"—the conceptual processing usually evoked by a question. He is then forced by the nature of the question to approach the condition known as "one-pointedness"—concentrating solely on one thing: the "unanswerable" koan.

Focusing attention is helped by the demands put on the student, by the pressures he imposes upon himself to achieve a breakthrough (to solve the koan), by the attitude of his fellow students, and by his interviews (dokusan) with the Zen master, the roshi. In the interviews the Zen student is often asked to demonstrate his level of understanding by giving an answer to the koan. Obviously, the desired answer is not verbal or logical; ideally it should be a communication of a new level of awareness brought about by the process of concentrating on the koan. The "correct" answer, which may be one of many possible ones, seems strange only on a logical level; it is intended to communicate on a different level. The koan is perhaps one of the most extreme techniques to delimit awareness.

The use of the koan is strongest in the Rinzai school of Zen, which places emphasis on sudden alterations of awareness brought about by this extreme concentration on one point over a long period of time under stress. The Soto school of Zen emphasizes another technique involving a different type of meditation exercise.

This second technique is termed "just sitting" (shikan-taza) and is an example of the form of meditation in which a deliberate attempt is made to open up awareness of the external environment. The Soto method emphasizes a much more gradual development than does the Rinzai sect, which places the emphasis on sudden flashes of expanded awareness as the aftereffect of the koan exercise. The second form of meditation, that of opening up awareness while meditating, will be considered at greater length again in the next chapter.

The practices of Yoga are much more varied than those of Zen. Concentrative meditation in Yoga is only a part of the totality of activity, and each part is considered a contributing factor to alterations of consciousness. Many Yoga practitioners devote much of their time to attempts to alter basic "involuntary" physiological processes—blood flow, heart rate, digestive activity, muscular activity, breathing, etc. There are various reports of Yoga masters being buried alive for long periods of time, of stopping their blood flow, of walking barefoot on hot coals, etc. Anand and his associates have found that some yogis can reduce oxygen consumption to levels far below that of normal.[4]

A major component of Yoga involves training in breath control (pranayama). Different cycles of breathing are used and different depths of breathing are practiced, in order to obtain some alterations (presumably) in blood oxygen content, carbon dioxide, etc., and the resulting changes in awareness. In these attempts at altering physiological processes, Yoga differs from

Zen, where there is no attempt to control breathing or heart activity. The one Zen meditation exercise that does involve breathing is one in which the student simply observes his breathing, as it occurs, rather than attempting in any way to control it. Many of the meditation exercises in Yoga are, however, quite similar to Zen.

A common form of yogic meditation practice involves the use of mantra. Mantra are often words of significance, names of the deity, but in terms of the psychology of consciousness the important element is that the technique uses a word as the focus of awareness, just as the first Zen exercises make use of breathing. The instructions are to repeat the mantram over and over again, either aloud or silently. The mantram is to be kept in awareness to the exclusion of all else. This is similar to the first Zen exercise, in that when awareness lapses from the breathing, the attention is to be returned to it. Mantra are sonorous, mellifluous words, which repeat easily. An example is OM. This mantram is chanted aloud in groups, or used individually in silent or voiced meditation. Another is OM-MANI-PADME-HUM, a smooth mellifluous chant. Similar mantra have analogous sounds such as AYN, HUM, etc., somewhat similar in sound to *Mu* in the first Zen koan. All include sonorous consonants—M's, H's, and many vowels.

Another well-known mantram is the Hare Krishna mantram. This is always chanted aloud in a group. The mantram itself involves a lot of repetition, and the entire mantram is repeated over and over.

HARE KRISHNA
HARE KRISHNA
KRISHNA KRISHNA
HARE HARE
HARE RAMA
HARE RAMA
RAMA RAMA
HARE HARE

Quite recently, a form of Mantram Yoga, "Transcendental Meditation," has become fairly well known in the West, especially in the United States. In this form of meditation, too, the practitioner is given a specific mantram and he is to repeat it silently over and over for about a half-hour twice a day, in the morning and in the evening. No special posture is required for the exercise; rather, one is instructed to assume a comfortable posture, such as sitting erect in a chair. The thoughts that arise during the meditation are considered to be of no significance, and as soon as one is aware that one is no longer focused on the mantram, attention is to be returned to it.

The specific mantra used in "Transcendental Meditation" are not given publicly, since the devotees of this technique claim that there are special effects of each one in addition to the general effects of the concentration. But it can be noted here that these mantra are also mellifluous and smooth, including many M's, Y's and vowels, similar to OM or MU in Zen. The devotees of "Transcendental Meditation" also claim that this technique involves the essence of meditation in a form suitable for Western persons. There is no doubt that Mantram Yoga, including "Transcendental Meditation," is a very convenient form of meditation. As in the breathing exercises, it is quite easy to produce and attend to a silent word, anywhere, at any time. Since there is no special posture required, the arduous training for sitting in a lotus position is unnecessary. If the essential component of meditation involves concentration on an unchanging stimulus, then "Transcendental Meditation," as well as other forms of Mantram Yoga, can be said to possess this essence.

Other forms of Yoga practice make use of visual meditation techniques. The yogin generally sits in a lotus position and views a specially constructed visual image, a mandala. Mandalas take many forms: they may be very simple, like a circle, or extremely complicated, as in the Yantra of Tantra practice.

Mandalas are used similarly to mantra. The practitioner

focuses his gaze on the mandala and restricts his awareness to the visual input. Any stray thought or association or feeling that arises is suppressed, and awareness is returned from the stray thought or association back to the mandala. Simple mandalas often employ a circular motif in which awareness is drawn to the center, as one continues to contemplate, fixing one's gaze more and more closely on the center.

Another visual meditation technique in Yoga involves a "steady gaze" (tratakam) on external objects. External objects are used in meditation to provide a focus for a fixed point of concentration, rather than for their teacher of the particular sect of Yoga, but it can be a stone, a vase, a light, a candle, etc., Rammamurti Mishra, in his manual *Fundamentals of Yoga*, gives instructions for some of these practices.

1. Exterior surface of the body

a. Nasal gaze: Keep your eyes half closed, half open, and steadily gaze at the tip of the nose. Practice regularly in the morning and in the evening; when the eyes are tired or tearing, close them fully and meditate one minute fully in that state. . . .

b. *Bhru madhya dristi* (frontal gaze): Fix your power of attention at the center between the eyebrows, turn your half-closed eyes towards the space between the eyebrows; like the nasal gaze, the frontal gaze is a powerful exercise to control wandering thoughts and mind. . . .

c. *Tratakam* on external objects: Select a picture of a perfect yogi or respected teacher, or you can select some small round object on the wall of your room if you do not know any liberated soul: a round object, a miniature, a small round point, or zero. Think of the thing selected, that is, the symbolic nature, and by gazing at the symbol you are gazing at supreme consciousness and supreme nature. Fix yourself in such a posture and position so that you may see this object easily, neither too far from it nor too near to it. Look at this object steadily, practice constantly and regularly, never gaze long enough to tire your eyes, close your eyes and mediate when you feel strained. After a few months of constant and regular practice, you will increase your power to stare at this object almost indefinitely without strain, fatigue and blinking. . . .

d. *Tratakam* on blue light: Place a bed lamp with a blue, very low voltage bulb at the head of your bed or other suitable place so that you can gaze easily; now light the lamp and recline on the bed or in an easy chair in the most comfortable posture. . . . Now gaze directly at the bulb in such a way that you do not blink your eyes but the bulb is directly overhead and you are peering intently at it; your gaze must be steady and continuous and constant; concentrate fully on the bulb. . . .[5]

The repetitive processes of the body, such as breathing and heart beats, can serve as similar foci for concentration in Yoga. These techniques are described in Mishra's manual and in many others.

Internally generated sounds (nadam) can similarly serve as the focus of meditation. Mishra gives some examples, of which the following are the most useful and frequent:

CIN NADAM: Like the hum of the honey of intoxicated bees; idling engine vibration; rainfall, whistling sounds, high frequency sounds.
CIN CIN NADAM: waterfall, roaring of an ocean
GHANTA NADAM: sound of a bell ringing
SANKHA NADAM: sound of a conch shell
TANTRI VINA: nasal sound, humming sound like that of a wire string instrument
TELA NADAM: sound of a small, tight drum
VENA NADAM: sound of a flute
MRIDAMGA NADAM: sound of a big brass drum
BHERI NADAM: echoing sound
MEGA NADAM: roll of distant thunder[6]

The sounds used in meditation can be either imagined or naturally occurring. Often the yogin sits near a natural source of repetitive sound, such as a waterfall, wind source, humming of bees, and simply listens and concentrates. When these repetitious, monotonous sounds are imagined, the technique becomes quite similar to the silent repetition of a mantram.

Creation of a meditation image can extend to visual types of meditation as well. Frederick Spiegelberg, in *Spiritual Practices of India*, describes the dharana, or fixation of consciousness procedures—the kasina exercises:

> The point of primary importance is that one should really create such a meditation-image to accompany him continuously; only as a secondary consideration does it matter what this particular image may be, that is, through which one of the kasina exercises it has been produced. Instead of contemplating a disc of earth, for example, one can meditate on an evenly ploughed field seen from a distance. In the Water Kasina, the yogi concentrates either on the circular surface of water in a jar, or on a lake seen from a mountain. So, too, the fire on the hearth, the flame of a candle, the wind that sways the crests of the trees may also be used as Kasina. The exercise of Color Kasina makes use of round colored discs, and even of bright-colored flags and flowers. In Space Kasina one meditates on a circular window opening, the attention in this case being directed primarily to the dimensional proportions of the opening.
>
> Every image that remains permanently in one's consciousness and every enduring mood can be a help to this fixation of one's consciousness. As a matter of fact, every hallucination, every unappeasable hatred, every amorous attachment provides a certain power of concentration to him who cherishes it, and helps him direct the forces of his being towards a single goal. This is of course more the case with the man who has achieved self-control and freedom from his passions, and who after having mastered his sense impulses succeeds in giving to his consciousness a definite turn of his own choosing. . . . Every activity is of equal value as a basis for a dharana exercise.[7]

The process of active construction of an image of meditation, in this particular case visual images, is elaborated in Tantra practice. In meditating on the yantra, the image is *created* piece by piece until the yogin can produce it in consciousness at will.

Many of the yantras that have been drawn out on paper from memory can be found in Mookerjee's quite beautiful book *Tantra Art*.[8] This type of active visualization also forms a portion of Tibetan Yoga practice. The practices of creating a meditation image have obvious advantages—one need not be present in any special place for meditation and one can reproduce any form at any time—so that many forms of meditation, like breathing and the verbal forms, can be done independently of the circumstance or the place.

Another variety of yogic meditation practice, mudra, involves repetitive physical movements, usually of the arms, legs, and fingers. In these exercises (which are somewhat more difficult to write about since no picture or word is involved) the movement of the limbs is performed and repeated over and over in the same way as a mantram. Awareness is continually directed toward the process of making the movements. Mudras vary in complexity; a simple one may involve touching the thumb to the other four fingers in order and repeating this procedure. The mudra may be combined with the mantram. For instance, the above fourfold repetitive *mudra* could be combined with the mantram OM-MANI-PADME-HUM, each word corresponding to the thumb's movement to a finger.

The Sufis make similar use of repetitive movements. Manuals for Sufic practice do not exist in any readily available form, as they do for Yoga and for Zen. The Sufis hold that the techniques must be administered, and the time, place, and state of the student must be taken into account. Publication of the details of their practice would lead to faulty applications of the exercises. A technique such as meditation, for instance, is held to be useful only at a specific stage of development, and persistence in any technique after the appropriate period might be a waste of time or even harmful.

There are, however, fragmentary reports available of some of the Sufi meditation exercises, which can be summarized here.

The Mevlevi (whirling dervishes) are perhaps the best known in the West. They perform a dance involving spinning and repetition of phrases. George Gurdjieff, who was trained by dervishes, explains the dance of the dervishes as an exercise for the brain based on repetition.[9] Idries Shah writes of these orders: "The so-called dancing dervishes accomplish trance and ecstatic phenomena through monotonous repetition circumambulations, and this is marked in the Maulavi order, most popular in Turkey."

The dance of the dervishes involves both the repetition of physical movements and the concurrent repetition of sounds. One of the few available first-person descriptions of this dance is found in Roy Weaver Davidson's valuable symposium, *Documents on Contemporary Dervish Communities*. It is an account by Omar Michael Berg, who traveled to a Dervish assembly in Tunisia, and participated in a dervish dance.

> Explanation of the Zikr (repetition). The Dhikr, it was explained to me, is a dance; or, more properly, a performance of a series of exercises in unison. The objective is to produce a state of ritual ecstasy and to accelerate the contact of the Sufi's mind with the world mind, of which he considers himself to be a part. . . . All dervishes and not only the followers of Maulana Rumi (as most Orientalists believe) perform a dance. The dance is defined by them as bodily movements linked to a thought and a sound or a series of sounds. The movements develop the body; the thought focuses the mind and the sound fuses the two and orientates them towards a consciousness of divine contact, which is called *Hal*, meaning "state" or "condition."
>
> Description of the *Zikr* at *Nefta*. A double circle is formed in the center of the hall. Dervishes stand while the Sheik intones the opening part of this and every similar ceremony—the calling down of the blessing upon the congregation and from the congregation upon the Masters, "past, present and future." Outside the circle stand the Sheik, drummer and flute player, together with two "callers," men who call the rhythm of the dance. The drum begins to beat, the caller begins to call a high-pitched flamenco-type air, and slowly

the concentric circles begin to revolve in opposite directions. Then the sheik calls out, *"Ya Haadi!"* (O Guide!) and the participants start to repeat this word. They concentrate on it, saying it at first slowly, then faster and faster. Their movements match the repetitions.

I noticed that the eyes of some of the dervishes took on a faraway look and they started to move jerkily as if they were puppets. The circles moved faster and faster until I (moving in the outer circle) saw only a whirl of robes and lost count of time. Now and then, with a grunt or a sharp cry, one of the dervishes would drop out of the circle and would be led away by an assistant, to lie on the ground in what seemed to be an hypnotic state. I began to be affected and found that, although I was not dizzy, my mind was functioning in a very strange and unfamiliar way. The sensation is difficult to describe and is probably a complex one. One feeling was that of a lightening; as if I had no anxieties, no problems. Another was that I was a part of this moving circle and that my individuality was gone, I was delightfully merged in something larger.

[He leaves the dance, and later] I went out into the courtyard to assess my feelings; something *had* happened. In the first place, the moon seemed immensely bright, and the little glowing lamps seemed surrounded by a whole spectrum of colors.[10]

The Sufis use other forms of concentrative meditation, some of which, in some aspects, appear quite similar to those of Zen and Yoga. Dhikrs are verbal repetition exercises. The first line of the Koran is quite often used for this purpose. Idries Shah thus describes the exercises:

Having either been given a set of Dhikrs to repeat (if he is under the direct guidance of a sheik) or having selected one himself if he is a uwaysi, working towards the goal alone, his task is to repeat it meticulously with regard for the times and frequency of its saying. If the formula is said under the breath, Dhikr Kafi, a rosary with ninety-nine beads, is used, one bead being told after each repetition; in the case of the Dhikr Jali, loud repetition, the rosary is often not used; . . . attending an actual Halka circle (meeting) the seeker goes to some quiet place or spends his contemplation time in a room set aside for the purpose.

There is, too, the exercise known as Fikr, which consists of meditation, concentration on some power that is desired or upon the immensity of the universe. When Dhikr and Fikr have been indulged in to such an extent that they become second nature, the superior form of Dhikr becomes necessary. This is the control and concentration of breath. The mind is concentrated upon a single idea, and the original Dhikr form or another is recited, this time in set rhythm corresponding to the breathing.[11]

There exist fragmentary descriptions of other exercises used by the Sufis and some of their followers. A student of George Gurdjieff writes of meditating on a series of dots on a piece of paper.[12] The dervishes repeat the phrase "Ya hud" in a way similar to the Yoga mantra and the Zen koan *Mu*, and also repeat stories over and over in their minds, as Zen Buddhists do with the koan.[13]

In conventional religions more familiar to us in the West, as well as in sects less known than Yoga, Zen, and Sufism, similar kinds of meditation practices exist. In early Christianity, for example, the exercise of contemplation performed a function similar to that of meditation in Zen, Yoga, and Sufism. Jakob Böhme, the Christian mystic, practiced fixing his gaze on a spot of sunlight on his cobbler's crystal as his object of contemplation throughout the entire day. He contemplated sunlight so much that this spot of light remained on his eyes permanently, burning part of the retina. He was then able to carry this image with him all the time, in the same way, perhaps, that the yogi can construct a yantra at will and observe it. Deikman has commented that the Christian mystics Walter Hilton and St. John of the Cross gave instructions for contemplation exercises that were strikingly similar to those of Patanjali, the author of the Yoga sutras.

In Hilton one reads, "Therefore if you desire to discover your soul, withdraw your thoughts from outward and material things, forgetting, if possible, your own body and its five senses." St. John calls for the explicit banishment of memory. "Of all these forms and manners of knowledge the soul must strip and void itself and it must strive to lose the imaginary apprehension of them, so that there may be left in it no kind of impression of knowledge, nor trace of thought whatsoever, but rather the soul must remain barren and bare, as if these forms has never passed through it, and in total oblivion and suspension. This cannot happen unless the memory can be annihilated of all its forms, if it is to be united with God. . . ." Patanjali comments, "Binding the mind stuff to a place is fixed attention, focusing the presented idea on that place is contemplation. This same contemplation shining forth in concentration. . . . The three in one are constraint . . . even these [three] are indirect aids to seedless [concentration]."[14]

Some of the current practices in the Christian Church and in Judaism have some similarities and even perhaps their origins in the practices of meditation. Prayer, in general, is a practice most similar to concentrative meditation. St. John Climacus said: "If many words are used in prayer, all sorts of distracting pictures hover in the mind but worship is lost. If little is said or only a single word pronounced, the mind remains concentrated." The "Russian Pilgrim" said: "If thou wilt that thy prayer be pure, made up of good and lovely things, thou must choose a short one consisting of a few powerful words and repeat it many times." Many of the prayers are monotonous, repetitive chants. Judaism makes use also of ritual nodding movements and intoned prayers. Hasidism and Cabalistic tradition contain many elements similar to Zen, Yoga, and Sufism. The cross and the Star of David appear as contemplation objects in traditions other than the Jewish and Christian; some of the yantras in *Tantra Art*, for instance, contain many six-pointed stars. Perhaps one reason for today's decline of interest in these more organized religions is that the stress on altering awareness has largely been muted. And, although the techniques for altering awareness still persist, the practices have become "automatic," part of a set of ritual, lacking their original purpose.

The Prayer of the Heart in the Greek Orthodox tradition, however, is much less removed from the meditative traditions considered. A similar focusing of awareness is also part of Taoist meditation. Instructions are given to sit quietly and focus awareness on the center of the body, on one point, on the abdomen. The medieval alchemists describe long and repetitive exercises —the constant redistillation of water, the prolonged grinding exercises—which were written down allegedly for the "distillation" of base metal for its transmutation into gold. These instructions can also be taken metaphorically as descriptions of attempts to alter man's awareness from his ordinary "base" level to a higher one, symbolized by the gold.[15]

Peter Freuchen, in his *Book of the Eskimos*, describes a technique for meditation in which the Eskimo sits facing a large soft stone; he takes a small hard stone and begins to carve a circle in the larger one by moving the small stone continuously around and around the larger surface. This practice, similar to the creation of a mandala, often lasts for several days at a time and is designed to produce a trance state. Many primitive peoples, such as the Bushmen of the Kalahari Desert, dance in a circle facing a fire, staring at the fire, and repetitiously chanting. Some gaze continuously at the full moon, the sun, or at a candle.

This has been a fairly quick, selective review of some of the major forms of concentrative meditation. Each of the major traditions—Zen, Yoga, Sufism—has exercises involving the different sensory modalities. A chant is repeated in each of the traditions; a word, koan, mantram, or dervish call is repeated; concentration is focused on the breath, on the heart beat, on the short prayer, longer prayer, story, or on natural sounds, such as a waterfall, or on some imagined sounds, such as the humming of bees, or on vibration. Symbols or pictures of gurus are subjected to steady gaze, and images are created only in the mind's eye of the practitioner, more like imagined sounds silently repeated. Sufi dervishes dance in a repetitive whirl; Indian yogis make continuous movements with their limbs; Taoists concentrate on the abdomen. The early Christian Fathers contemplated an object or the cross. These are all externally different forms of the same type of meditation.

The strong common element seems to lie in the actual restriction of awareness to one single, unchanging process. It does not seem to matter which actual physical practice is followed; whether one symbol or another is employed; whether the visual system is used or body movements repeated; whether awareness is focused on a limb or on a sound or on a word or on a prayer. This process might be considered in psychological terms as an attempt to recycle the same subroutine over and over again in the nervous system. The instructions for meditation are consistent with this; one is instructed always to rid awareness of any thought save the object of meditation, to shut oneself off from the main flow of ongoing external activity and attend only to the object or process of meditation. Almost any process or object seems usable and has probably been used. The specific object of meditation (for this analysis) is much less important than maintaining the object as the single focus of awareness over a long period of time.

Shah points out that some Tibetans repeat the OM-MANI-PADME-HUM mantra exactly backward, and the Sufi story quoted earlier,* of the dervish who mispronounced the call but could maintain the correct attitude, illustrates this point. The same point is made by a Russian story of three holy men *(staretzi)* who lived in complete isolation on a small island in the Arctic Sea:

> A bishop heard of them and decided to pay them a visit. On the shore of the island he found three bearded, toothless old men who bowed low before him. The bishop asked how they prayed. The old man replied: "We pray thus: 'Ye are three; we are three; have mercy on us!'" The bishop was amazed at this and began to teach them how to pray. He taught them the Lord's Prayer until they knew it by heart. They thanked him fervently for the lesson. Then he went aboard his ship with a glad heart for performing a good

* See p. 72.

deed. His ship had been sailing for a while when strange clouds formed on the horizon, and quickly approached. Suddenly the passengers realized that the clouds were the forms of three men. The three men bowed low before the bishop and told him sadly that they had forgotten the newly learnt prayer. Would he have the graciousness and patience to teach it to them again. Then the bishop crossed himself, bowed to the startsy and said: "God will hear your prayer as it is. There is nothing I can teach you. Go and pray for us sinners." The bishop prostrated himself before them. But they turned around and went over the water back to the island. And until the dawn, a light streamed forth, at the place where the pious staretzi had vanished.[16]

It seems that the mode of meditation, too, makes little difference. The primary effect can be considered as a central state evoked by the process of repetition. The stress on the communality of the techniques of meditation need not necessarily conflict with the contention of those of the esoteric traditions that certain forms of meditation may have *additional* specific effects on specific individuals. The Maharishi Mahesh Yogi, the originator of the "Transcendental Meditation" movement, feels that a specific mantram must be given to each individual. Shah "wretchedly simplifies" for Western observers and states that the letters s, u, f in the Arab pronunciation have a *specific* effect on consciousness. At a level beyond that of this analysis, the Sufis also hold that specific tales can communicate knowledge in dimensions other than the ordinary.[17]

Naranjo earlier considered the additional functions of specially chosen objects, symbols that can be used as focus and also carry significance in themselves. But, since the general level of knowledge within science about the actual practices of meditation is so scanty, the stress here is on the *major communality* of the techniques of concentrative meditation across disciplines, across sensory modalities.

These techniques are said in the traditions to lead to a "one-pointedness" or to a "clear" state of awareness. The state is generally described as "dark," or in Indian terminology, "the void," or "emptiness." It is a withdrawal of the senses, a "turning off" of perception of the external world. In yogic practice this withdrawal is most explicitly sought. In Buddhist meditation the stress is more often on an expanded rather than restricted awareness. But recall that Rahula says, in describing the breathing meditation, that "after a certain period you will have experienced just that split second when your mind is fully concentrated on your breathing, when you will not hear even sounds nearby, when no external world exists for you."* Augustine Poulain describes it as "a mysterious darkness wherein is contained the limitless Good, a void, other than solitude." St. John describes it as the "annihilation of memory."

It may be that men in different places at different times have noticed that by repeating an action or a phrase over and over again, or continuously focusing on breathing, the awareness of the external world can be shut out. Since we, the Bushmen, the Eskimos, the monks of Tibet, the Zen masters, the Yoga adepts, and the dervishes all share a common nervous system, it is not so surprising that similarities in techniques should have evolved.

These techniques have persisted for centuries. Many sensory modalities have been employed, and many different symbols or objects within any one sensory modality have been used. This may indicate that one primary effect of the concentrative meditation exercises is the state of emptiness, the non-response to the external world, evoked in the central nervous system by the continuous subroutine called up by the exercise regardless of the specific nature of the input or the sensory modality employed.

There is a whole body of work on the psychological and physiological effects of restricting awareness to an unchanging stimulus. One variety of concentrative meditation discussed involves

* See p. 146.

a "steady gaze" on either a natural object or a specially constructed one, a mandala. A very similar situation would arise if input to the eye were always the same, no matter how one moved one's eyes.

Normally, as we look at the world, our eyes move around and fixate at various points in large movements called "saccades." We hardly ever gaze steadily at any one object for a prolonged period of time. Even when we try to fix our vision on a single object, very small involuntary movements of the eye occur, called "optical nystagmus." The image on the retina is kept in constant motion by both these types of eye movements.

A group of physiological psychologists succeeded in devising a system that enables a visual image to remain constant on the retina even though the eyes are in constant motion. One apparatus for producing this "stabilized" image consists of an extremely small projector mounted on a contact lens worn by the subject. The contact lens moves with every movement of the eyeball and so does the projector. The projector faces the eyeball, and no matter how the eye is moved, the same image falls on the retina.[18] (See Figure 1)

This study of stabilized images was undertaken in psychology primarily to investigate a theory of Donald Hebb, according to which continuously varied input is needed to maintain normal awareness. It was felt that "stabilizing" the image would eliminate the continuous changes in input that normally occur as we move our eyes in space.

The effect on awareness of stabilizing the visual image is consistent: the image tends to disappear completely. The fact that it does tend to reappear periodically in some studies is most likely due to the slipping of the contact lens on the eyes. When an image is stabilized on the retina with extreme precision, using the internal structure of the eye as the stimulus, the image disappears in a few seconds and never returns.

Lehmann, Beeler, and Fender attempted to investigate the brain state evoked by the stabilized image.[19] The electroencephalo-

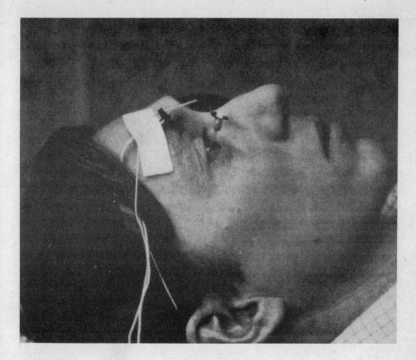

Figure 1

gram (EEG) as recorded at the scalp, consists of the tiny electrical potentials that emanate from the brain. These tiny potentials, about 5—50-millionths of a volt, are amplified and written out on paper by the electroencephalograph. The first brain rhythm was discovered by Berger in 1924, and termed the "alpha" rhythm, which consists of rhythmic activity between 8 and 12 Hz. Since Berger, other rhythms have been classified: beta, defined as 12 cycles and above; theta, 4-7; and delta, 1-4. The alpha rhythm is usually thought of as representing a state of decreased visual attention to the external environment. It is increased almost always when the eyes are closed or when the eyes are rolled up into the head —when vision is turned down.

Lehmann, Beeler, and Fender recorded the EEG from the

occipital cortex of the brain while their subject was viewing the stabilized image. They asked their subject to press a button when the stabilized image disappeared, and attempted to correlate the subjective experience of the disappearance of the image with the concurrent brain state. They found that the alpha rhythm was likely to appear at the time when the subject reported the disappearance of the image. Alpha rhythm, in this case too, seems associated with a decrease in awareness of the external world.

Another means of supplying consistent visual input provides the observer with a completely patternless visual field, called a "ganzfeld." This field can be produced in many ways. A white-washed surface can serve as a ganzfeld. Cohen, in a series of studies, produced his ganzfeld using two spheres, each 1 meter in diameter.[20] Hochberg, Triebel, and Seaman produced a homogeneous visual field more conveniently by taping halved ping-pong balls over the observer's eyes.[21] The effect on consciousness of the ganzfeld situation is similar to that of the stabilized image.

Cohen found that some observers reported an absence of any visual experience—what they called "blank-out." This was not merely the experience of seeing nothing, but that of *not seeing,* a complete disappearance of the sense of vision for short periods of time, as Cohen put it. The feeling of not seeing at all usually occurred after about twenty minutes of exposure to the ganzfeld. During blank-out the observers did not know, for instance, whether their eyes were open or not, and they could not even control their eye movements. Cohen's suggestion was that this continuous uniform stimulation resulted in the failure of any kind of image to be produced in consciousness. He also found that the periods of blank-out were associated with bursts of alpha rhythm. He suggested that the appearance of alpha during these continuous stimulation periods indicated a functional similarity between continuous stimulation and no stimulation at all. He also found that individuals with high alpha EEG's were more susceptible to the blank-out phenomenon.

Tepas performed a study on the ganzfeld similar to that of Lehmann, Beeler, and Fender's on the stabilized image.[22] His observers watched the ganzfeld for five-minute periods while EEG's were recorded. When the observer experienced the blank-out, he was asked to press a microswitch that marked the EEG record. Tepas found that the alpha activity of the brain was increased during the period of blank-out.

Both the stabilized image and the ganzfeld situation are very similar to the practices of concentrative meditation. Consider the activity of the observer in meditation and in the two precisely regulated input situations: in both an attempt is made to provide unchanging input. Analogous is the subjective experience in both situations: a loss of contact with the external world. In all these conditions the state of the brain indicates an increase in alpha rhythm. The electrophysiological studies of meditation by Bagchi and Wanger,[23] those by Anand and others in India on Yoga meditation,[24] and those by Kasamatsu and Hirai,[25] and by Akishige in Japan on Zen meditation[26] indicate that meditation also is a high alpha state. The more precisely controlled situations seem to produce, both psychologically and physiologically, effects similar to those of concentrative meditation.

The stabilized image and ganzfeld condition in themselves indicate that the phenomenon of blank-out, or disappearance of the stabilized image, or loss of contact with the external world, is due to effects on the central nervous system rather than on the characteristics of the peripheral senses. The effects of stabilized images are transferred between the eyes, indicating that the disappearance phenomenon must occur somewhere later in the visual system than in the retina. Stimulation in other sensory modalities (the sudden onset of a noise, for example) also returns the stabilized image back into consciousness.

It seems that a consequence of the structure of our central nervous system is that if awareness is restricted to one unchanging source of stimulation, a "turning off" of consciousness of the

external world follows. Common instructions for meditation all
underscore this; one is continually advised to be aware of the
object of meditation and nothing else, to continuously recycle
the same input over and over. Stabilizing a visual image or homog-
enizing visual input results in the same experience. A set of instructions by Knowles of the English mystical tradition indicates
that this blanking-out is a desired function of meditation that can
be produced by restriction of awareness.

> Forget all creatures that God ever made, and the works of them
> so that thy thought or thy desire be not directed or stretched to
> any of them, neither in general nor in special. . . . At the first time
> when thou dost it thou findest but a darkness and as it were a kind
> of unknowing, thou knowest not what, saving that thou feelest in
> thy will a naked intent unto God.[27]

The interpretations of this experience of "darkness," of "blank-
out," of the "void," of the disappearance of an image in the subject of a scientific experiment, would certainly differ: the subject
of a physiological experiment would have extremely different
expectations and ideas about his experience than a man who has
sought this experience as part of his meditative practice. But the
experiences themselves have essential similarities and are produced
simply and through quite similar procedures.

So the practices of meditation—whirling, chanting, concentrating on a nonsensical question, repeating a prayer over and over
again, picturing a cross, looking at a vase, counting breaths,
etc.—are probably not quite so exotic as those who seek the exotic
and esoteric would like, and are not properly considered as
exercises in reasoning or problem-solving,[28] but rather as exercises in restriction of attention. The somewhat bewildering superficial differences in the various practices—the koan, the mantram,
the mudra, the mandala, the kasina exercises, the dharana exercises,
the dhikr, the fhikr, the dance of the Mevlevi dervishes, the Taoist meditation on the abdomen, the "Prayer of the Heart"—all

can be understood as aids in focusing awareness on a single process, continuously recycling the same subroutine through the nervous system. When this is achieved, a common experience seems to be produced: awareness of the external environment diminishes and "turns off" for a period of time.

Psychologically, continuous repetition of the same stimulus may be considered the equivalent of no stimulation at all. The two situations, which from the psychological and physiological points of view are quite similar, insofar as they restrict awareness to that of a single source of unchanging stimulation, also seem to produce the same effects. So we can say (within our frame of reference) that concentrative meditation is a practical technique which uses an experiential knowledge of the structure of our nervous system to "turn off" awareness of the external world and produce a state of blank-out or darkness, the "void," the cloud of unknowing. The techniques of concentrative meditation are not deliberately mysterious or exotic[29] but are simply a matter of practical applied psychology.

2 / The Esoteric and Modern Psychologies of Awareness

These natural questions arise:

Why do these disciplines seem to share the common aim of "turning off" ordinary awareness of the external world for a short period of time?

What is the experience of meditators after that of "darkness"?

What are the general effects of the practice of meditation on awareness?

What is the relationship of the "turning-off" form of meditation to the "opening-up" form?

With the viewpoint adopted in this essay, we may be able to provide appropriate answers to these questions.

If we are to determine the aftereffects of concentrative meditation on awareness, it would be useful to review some aspects of the psychology and physiology of consciousness. Though we should not expect that the practice of meditation will necessarily change every aspect of ordinary consciousness, we may be able to determine more clearly the effect and aftereffect of meditation in terms of our knowledge of the psychology and physiology of consciousness.

Contemporary psychology provides several different viewpoints from which to characterize awareness. Some are completely independent of one another, some are complementary, some intersect.

We normally consider that the single function of our sensory systems is to gather information about the world: we see with our eyes, we hear with our ears. Gathering information is certainly a major function of sensation, but sensory systems also act in just the opposite way. Our ordinary awareness of the world is selective and is restricted by the characteristics of sensory systems. Many philosophers have stressed a similar view, but only recently has precise physiological evidence been available. Huxley and Broad have elaborated on Bergson's general view of the mind as a "reducing valve." In *The Doors of Perception and Heaven and Hell,* Huxley quotes Dr. D. C. Broad, the eminent Cambridge philosopher:

> The function of the brain and nervous system is to protect us from being overwhelmed and confused by this mass of largely useless and irrelevant knowledge, by shutting out most of what we should otherwise perceive and remember at any given moment, leaving only that very small and special selection that is likely to be practically useful.

And then Huxley comments:

> According to such theory each one of us is potentially Mind at Large. But insofar as we are animals our business is at all costs to survive. To make biological survival possible, Mind at Large has to be funneled through the reducing valve of the brain and nervous system. What comes out at the other end is a measly trickle of the kind of consciousness which will help us to stay alive on the surface of this particular planet. To formulate and express the contents of this reduced awareness man has invented and endlessly elaborated those symbol-systems and implicit philosophies that we call languages. Every individual is at once the beneficiary and the victim of the linguistic tradition into which he has been born—the beneficiary inasmuch as language gives access to the accumu-

lated records of other people's experience, the victim insofar as it confirms him in the belief that reduced awareness is the only awareness and as it bedevils his sense of reality, so that he is all too apt to take his concepts for data, his words for actual things. That which, in the language of religion, is called "this world" is the universe of reduced awareness expressed, and, as it were, petrified by language. The various "other worlds" with which human beings erratically make contact, are so many elements in the totality of awareness belonging to Mind at Large. Most people most of the time know only what comes through the reducing valve and is consecrated as genuinely real by their local language. Certain persons, however, seem to be born with a kind of bypass that circumvents the reducing valve. In others temporary bypasses may be acquired either spontaneously or as the result of deliberate "spiritual exercises" or through hypnosis or by means of drugs. Through these permanent or temporary bypasses there flows, not indeed the perception of everything that is happening everywhere in the universe (for the bypass does not abolish the reducing valve which still excludes the total content of Mind at Large), but something more than, and above all something different from, the carefully selected, utilitarian material which our narrow individual minds regard as a complete, or at least sufficient, picture of reality.[1]

Huxley writes more elegantly and less quantitatively than do most researchers and theorists in the fields of psychology and physiology, but much modern work in these disciplines tends to support the same general view that ordinary awareness is a personal construction. If awareness is a construction and not a "registration" of the external world, then by altering the nature of the construction process our awareness can be changed.

The normal view outside of the philosophical tradition, psychology, and the esoteric disciplines is that we experience *what exists*, that the external world is completely and perfectly reflected in our subjective experience. This idea is quite impossible to maintain even at the simplest level if we consider the many different forms of energy that impinge upon us at any moment. Sounds, electricity, light waves, magnetism, smells, chemical and electrical impulses within ourselves, thoughts, internal muscular sensations, all constantly bombard us. An appropriate question on the nature of our "ordinary" consciousness should be one that reflects a view quite different from the common one. How do we ever achieve a stable consciousness in the face of all this fantastic amount of stimulation?

There are two major ways in which we "make sense" out of the world. First, we use our sensory systems to discard and to simplify the incoming information, allowing only a few of the possible dimensions of sensation into our awareness. Second, we further sort the amount of information that does come in along a very limited number of dimensions, out of which we construct our awareness. These dimensions have been called in psychology "unconscious inferences," "personal constructs," "category systems," "efferent readinesses," or "transactions," depending on the writer's style and his level of analysis.

Quite obviously, each individual receptor is equipped physiologically to receive information only within certain limits. We wouldn't expect our eyes, for instance, to respond to the low bass note of an organ, or our ears to the taste of noodles. The eyes are "tuned" by their physiological structure to receive only a certain limited frequency range of stimulation and to send messages to the brain when energy in the appropriate frequency range reaches them—and so with the ears, the tongue, etc. That sensory receptors function to reduce the incoming information can be better understood if we study animals who are lower on the phylogenetic continuum and whose receptors discard even more information than do our own. It is difficult, otherwise, to conceive of the amount of stimulation to which we ourselves do not respond.

Perhaps the most cogent illustration of this point has been in the study of the visual system of the frog. The eye of the frog was studied by Lettvin, Maturana, McCulloch, and Pitts at the

Massachusetts Institute of Technology. They were interested, essentially, in the same point made by Huxley, that sensory systems serve mainly for data *reduction*.[2]

They devised an experiment in which visual stimulation could be offered to one of the eyes of an immobilized frog. The frog was seated so that its eye was at the center of a hemisphere with a radius of seven inches. On the inner surface of this hemisphere small objects could be placed in different positions by means of magnets or moved around in space. The investigators implanted micro-electrodes into the frog's optic nerve to measure, as they called it, "what the frog's eye tells the frog's brain"—the electrical impulses sent to the brain by the eye. Since the frog's eye is somewhat similar to our own, these investigators hoped that electrical recording from the optic nerve would show the different kinds of "messages" that the eye sends to the brain. They studied the relationship of the evoked patterns of electrical activity to the different objects displayed on the hemisphere. There are thousands, millions, of different visual patterns that one could present to a frog—colors, shapes, movements, in various combinations, the almost infinite richness of the visual world of which we are normally aware. However, in presenting a large number of different objects, colors, movements, to the frog, a remarkable phenomenon was observed: from all the different kinds of stimulation presented only four different kinds of "messages" were sent from the retina to the brain. In other words, no matter the complexity and subtle differences in the environment, the frog's eye is "wired up" to send only this extremely limited number of different messages. The frog's eye presumably evolved to discard the remainder of the information available. The structure of its eye limits the frog's awareness to only four different kinds of visual activity. Lettvin and the others termed the four related systems: sustained contrast detectors; moving edge detectors; net dimming detectors; and net convexity detectors.

The first provides the general outline of the environment; the second seems to enhance response to sudden moving shadows, like a bird of prey; the third responds to a sudden decrease in light, as when a large enemy is attacking. These are systems that have presumably evolved to abstract information relevant to survival and to discard the rest, in the manner described by Huxley.

The fourth type of "message," conveyed by the net convexity detectors, is the most obviously related to survival and the most interesting of all. The net convexity detectors do not respond to any general change in light or to contrast; they respond only when small dark objects come into the field of vision, when these objects move at a closer distance, wriggling in front of the eye. It is quite clear, then, how the frog gets its food, how it can see flying bugs in front of it even with its limited visual system. The frog has evolved its own subsystem, which is wired up to ignore all other information except that of bugs flying around close to it—a very specialized "bug-perceiving" subsystem.

So, out of the complexity and richness of the information presented to the eye, the frog extracts only images with four dimensions. Higher-level animals exhibit similarities to this kind of process but on a much more complicated level. This type of dimensional analysis has been extended to cats and monkeys by David Hubel and Torsten Weisel at Harvard University and by many other investigators, who have determined that different cells in the brain respond to different types of stimulation. They found that certain cells detect edges and corners, others respond to movement on the retina, etc. Although vision has been the sensory system generally studied, since it is much easier to record from and much easier to specify what the dimension is, one would also expect that other sensory modalities would show the same kinds of relationships.

Sensory systems by "design" reduce the amount of useless and irrelevant information. We can then say that the function of our receptors and sensory systems is not only to gather information but to *select* and discard it.

If we consider more and more complicated organisms, their capacity to "retune" their sensory systems becomes greater. If the visual world of a goldfish is turned upside down by surgically inverting its eyes, it never learns to adjust to the new situation, swimming continuously in a circle until death, or until a kind surgeon reorients its eyes. If the visual field of a human is turned around by wearing inverting lenses, he can, in a few weeks, perform actions as complicated as riding a bicycle through town. To make use of the familiar machine analogies, the sensory systems of some animals are like permanently wired-up simple machines. In a mousetrap or a pencil sharpener or even in a telephone or an automobile, a change in one part throws everything else out of adjustment, since it has no built-in capacity for self-alteration. As we consider more complicated animals, more and more advanced all the way up to man, their nervous systems seem to be more computer-like—machines, to be sure but ones that can alter the relationship between input and performance by a change in the "program." The higher mammals can be regarded as machines that are capable of "retuning" themselves in accordance with alterations in the external environment. This is not to say that there are no limits to their performance. Even the most sophisticated current computer has its physical limitations. No matter how the computer alters its own programs, it will never learn to fly. But it can alter itself within the limits of its own structure, as we can.

We can easily demonstrate this computer-like, higher-level selectivity and tuning. At a party or at a place where several people are talking at the same time, we close our eyes and listen to just one person speaking, then tune him out and listen to another person. We are able to do this, to listen to one person's speech and then suppress it as it comes into our ears and hear another person's speech that we have previously ignored. It is very easy to do. We shouldn't really be surprised since we tune ourselves continuously to suit our needs and expectations, but we are not usually aware of it. When we perspire during the summer we like the taste of foods that are more salty than usual. We don't think consciously that we need salt and we should take more salt in our foods; we *simply like* foods that at other times we would consider quite oversalted. The character in the middle of Figure 2 can be seen either as a number or as a letter depending upon the context, which governs how we tune ourselves.

Figure 2

Some examples from our everyday existence show how we become more sensitive to portions of our environment when we are in need. When we are hungry we see more restaurants, see more food, smell more aromas than when we are not. When we are awaiting someone we immediately notice anyone who resembles the other person, in his hair color, general appearance, clothes, or because he is coming out of the door through which we expect the person to arrive. When we are interested in the opposite sex, we perceive them differently than when we are not. When after a meal our need for food has diminished, so does the attractiveness of food. We are able continuously to reprogram and reconstruct our awareness, based, at least in part, on our intent.

Many contemporary psychologists have investigated this "tune-ability." Some have made use of a "tachistoscope," a visual display device that allows figures, objects, pictures, to be presented for short and measurable periods of time. One interesting series of experiments based on the tachistoscope demonstrated that we recognize familiar objects or words with less time exposure than unfamiliar ones. Our past experiences can tune input processing so that we can construct an image based on a small amount of input information. A coherent sentence, for instance, is much more easy to recognize and to remember than just a random combination of words. Again, our past experience "tunes" us to have some idea of what should follow what, and we need much less information to construct an image. Jerome Bruner calls this "going beyond the information given."[3]

A major way in which we create our awareness is by tuning out the constancies in our environment. While we are learning a new skill, like skiing, all the complex adjustments and motor movements are somewhat painfully in our awareness. As we progress, as skill becomes "automatic," the movements no longer enter consciousness. Compare the first time you tried to drive a car, especially one with a gear shift, with how it feels to drive a car now, after you've learned. When we drive to work the first time, everything appears quite new and interesting—a red house, a big tree, the road itself—but gradually, as we drive the same route over and over, we "get used" to everything on the way. We stop "seeing" the trees, the bridges, the corners, etc. We become "automatic" in our response to them. When we enter a room and a fan is turning, creating a buzzing sound, we are aware of it for the first few moments and then the sound seems to go out of awareness.

Many of the producers of the objects we buy take into account that we constantly need new stimulation, and that we adapt to and tune out the old. When we buy a new phonograph record, we play it over and over again for a period, then leave it on the shelf unplayed. We get bored, the record no longer seems "new"; it is out of our awareness—on "automatic." Most of the Market products are periodically changed slightly (automobiles, for instance), so that we begin to "see" them again, and presumably buy them.

In psychology and physiology, the phenomenon we have described is termed "habituation." The "response" in this case is one of the physiological components of the "orienting reaction" to new stimuli, the reaction that involves our registering of input. The physiological indicators of such reaction include EEG, heart rate, and skin resistance. Suppose we measure the resistance of the skin, for example, and repeat a click every five seconds. The first tone will cause a sharp drop in skin resistance. There will be less skin resistance change caused by the second tone, still less by the third, until, depending on the parameters of the particular experiment, the skin resistance no longer drops with each click. The response of the skin to this stimulus has been "habituated." When, after hearing for a while the sound of a clock ticking, we then turn the sound off, we no longer show the "orienting" or registering reaction. This does not merely involve a simple process of raising the threshold for stimuli entering into awareness and thus tuning the click out. Our computer is capable of a more sophisticated selective tuning. It is true that if we substitute a louder click, we will begin to hear it again. And if we substitute a *softer* one, the orienting reaction also returns and we will hear it again. If we change the interval between the appearances of the tone—if it appears a little bit later than we expect, or a little bit sooner, even slightly—the tone returns to our awareness, and the orienting reaction reappears.

Karl Pribram has pointed out another example of this phenomenon, which he called the "Bowery El" effect. In New York City an elevated railroad once ran along Third Avenue. At a certain time late each night a noisy train would pass through. The train line was torn down some time ago with some interesting aftereffects. People in the neighborhood called the police to report "something strange" occurring late at night—noises, thieves, burglars, etc. It was determined that these calls took place at around the time of the former late-night train. What these people were "hearing," of course, was the *absence* of the familiar noise of the train. We have a similar experience, although much simpler, when a noise that has been going on suddenly stops.[4]

If we look at the same object over and over again, we begin to look in the same way each time. We do this with the constancies of our world, our ordinary surroundings—the pictures in our house, the route we drive every day, etc. Charles Furst has studied the effect of repeated viewing of the same picture on the way we look at it.[5] He found that eye movements tend to become more and more stereotyped as the same visual stimulus is presented. When we see a new image our eyes tend to move in a new pattern around it, but as we see it again and again, like the rooms in our house, we tend to look in a fixed way at fixed portions of it and ignore or tune out the rest. The "Bowery El" effect, the "Furst" effect, and the more precise studies on habituation suggest that we tune out the recurrences of the world by making a "model" of the external world within our nervous system, and testing input against it.[6] We somehow can program and continuously revise or reprogram conception or models of the external world. If the input and our model agree, as they do most often with the constancies of the world, then the input stays out of consciousness. If there is any disagreement, if the new input is *even slightly* different, slower, softer, louder, a different form, color, or even if it is absent, we become aware of the particular input once again. This "programing" forms an additional reducing valve behind the fixed reducing valves of the senses.

Perhaps the most clear and striking trend in the psychology and physiology of perception in the past few years has been our increasing understanding of the interactive and constructive nature of our "ordinary" awareness. One of the leaders in this investigation, Jerome Bruner, has emphasized that perception involves acts of categorization.[7] As we become experienced in dealing with the world we attempt to make more and more consistent "sense" out of the mass of information arriving at our receptors. We develop stereotyped systems or categories for sorting the input that reaches us. The set of categories we develop is limited, much more limited than the richness of the input. Simple categories may be "straight," "red," or "animal." More complex ones may be "English," "rectilinear," or "in front of." In social situations categories may be personality traits. If we come to consider a person "aggressive," we then consistently tend to sort all his actions in terms of this particular category. Personality traits seem to exist mainly in the category system of the perceiver.[8]

Our previous experience with objects strengthens our category systems. We expect cars to make a certain noise, traffic lights to be a certain color, food to smell a certain way, and certain people to say certain things. But what we actually experience, according to Bruner and to others, is the *category* which is evoked by a particular stimulus, and *not* the occurrence in the external world.

Bruner and his associates conducted an extensive series of studies on the effects of category systems on awareness. In his review "On Perceptual Readiness," he suggests that "correct" perception is

. . . not so much a matter of representation as it is a matter of what I shall call model-building. In learning to perceive we are learning the relations that exist between the properties of objects and events that we encounter and learning appropriate categories and category systems. *Learning to predict and project what goes with what.* A simple example illustrates the point. I present for tachistoscopic recognition two nonsense words, one a zero-order approximation to English, constructed according to Shannon's rule, and a four-order approximation, W-R-U-L-P-Z-O-C and V-E-R-N-L-A-T, 500 ms of exposure one perceives correctly and in their place about 48 per cent of the letters in zero-order words. And about 93 per cent of the letters of the four-order words; . . . the difference in perception is a function of the fact that individuals learn the traditional probability mode, what goes with what in English writing."[9]

Bruner, Postman, and Rodrigues attempted to demonstrate the effects of our well-learned categories on the contents of awareness.[10] They used ordinary playing cards familiar to most people in our culture. Our past experience with playing cards evokes categories in which the colors and the forms of playing cards are "supposed" to fall. We expect shapes like ♣ and ♠ to be black and ♦ and ♥ to be red.

Subjects in this experiment looked at the cards one at a time. A few of the cards were "anomalous," "wrong" colors for their shapes—a red ace of spades, a black eight of diamonds, etc. Subjects tended not to see the miscolored cards as anomalous, thus "correcting" the image. They would call a red ace of spades an ace of hearts, for instance. Not until it was expressly pointed out to the subjects that the colors might not necessarily, in this situation, be those usually associated with the shapes were the anomalous cards seen for what they were. The import of these and others of Bruner's interesting demonstrations is that we expect certain correspondences of objects, colors, forms, to occur, and we tune ourselves to see them. Newspaper editors often note that numerous typographical errors go unnoticed. The reader does the "correcting" within himself, merely by selecting the category "correct English."

At about the time Bruner was studying the effects of categories, another group of psychologists, led by Adelbert Ames, was exploring a similar viewpoint on the nature of awareness. Ames characterized the nature of ordinary awareness as a "transaction" between the perceiver and the environment. In spite of the overflow of information available to our sense organs at any given time, *relevant* information is often lacking. We cannot, for instance, determine tri-dimensionality directly. We cannot tell whether a room is "really" rectangular or not, or whether a given chair is physically closer than others, since we do not possess a direct sense of distance. There are, however, perceptible dimensions usually associated with closeness of objects. If we assume constant size, an image that seems larger is closer to us. So if we are trying to determine closeness, we "bet" that the larger object is the closer. This is, again, not a conscious process of correction. We *directly experience* the larger object as closer. The Ames group set out to demonstrate the nature of the bet we make with the environment.[11]

By manipulating our "unconscious inference," as Helmbolz called it, we can become aware of the bets or, in Bruner's term, the "categories" that constitute our awareness. To give another example, normally when we see a line drawing of a room as in Figure 3, we bet that in a top view it would be shaped like Figure 4, a rectangle. But a rectangle is only one of the many possible forms that could be derived from the two-dimensional drawing. One side may not be at all parallel with the other. The top view might look like either of the drawings in Figure 5, or any of many other shapes. We bet that the room is rectangular because almost all the rooms in our experience are rectangular. But if the room is not in fact rectangular, our bet causes us to "see" objects or people in the room in a very strange way. (See Figure 6.)

George Kelly pursued a similar line of investigation, concerned more with the psychology of ordinary experience and with clinical psychology. His conception was that each man *creates* his own world by means of his "personal constructs." He considered these "constructs" as scientific hypotheses, in that they are generated on the basis of our past experience and are applied to new experiences as long as they seem to work. So, for Kelly, our experience of the world consists of our constructs, as it consists of categories for Bruner and of transactions for the Ames group. Kelly was a psychotherapist and his therapy was based on the belief that a patient's problems were in large part due to his poor construction of the situation. The treatment involved a "prescription" of new constructions that the patient could apply to his life.[12]

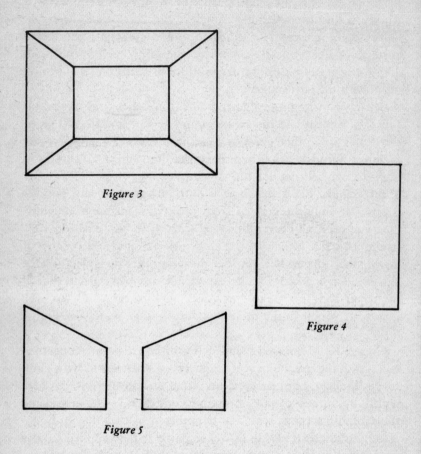

Figure 3

Figure 4

Figure 5

There have been some recent studies along these general lines. Dr. Edward Sadalla and I attempted to test the effects of different constructs on the experience of duration. The experience of duration, of time lengthening or shortening, seems to be related to the amount of information that we "remember" as required by a given situation. We tried to alter the amount of

Figure 6. The distorted room

information that a person would assume to be present in a constant situation. We made a film of a modern dancer performing several movements in a series. These movements were rather abstract to most people except modern dancers, and the interpretation could be easily altered. We trained one group of people to code the dance into two segments or constructs, another to code six segments, and a third, eleven segments. Those who were trained to code eleven segments (occurrences) perceived the dance as much longer than those who coded six, who in turn experienced the dance as longer than those who coded two.[13]

In a later study, Sadalla has shown that training to code different constructions has a basic effect on the recognition of various individual components of the dance.[14] Albert Hastorf and Hadley Cantril of the Ames group studied an even more complex effect. It is clear that we can tune ourselves on the basis of our needs and on the basis of our conception of past experience, and even on the basis of our expectations of future occurrences. Hastorf and Cantril demonstrated that people "tune" their perception on the basis of a quite complex expectation—by being "for" a team in a football game, for instance. The perception of the same events (a play in a football game, a verbal interchange) can be quite different in different people, depending upon these very general biasing factors, which can completely change the nature of the experience of a given series of events.

Since we can tune ourselves on the basis of our category systems, there must be physiological mechanisms that allow us to tune our awareness. Pribram and Spinelli have set out to demonstrate an analogue of this process on the physiological level.[15] They recorded from cells in the frontal cortex of the brain while stimulating other areas, and showed that the pattern of the receptive fields to external stimuli can be altered by the brain. The way in which stimuli are received, even as far out as on the retina itself, is "reprogrammable" on a moment-to-moment basis, and this can be demonstrated physiologically. These and other experiments demonstrate that the output system of the brain (efference) has an effect on the input (afference), the brain "selecting its input."

The investigation of the active role of the brain's output in determining the contents of awareness has been a recent major trend in the psychophysiology of perception. The work of Bruner, of the transactionists, and of Kelly demonstrate this active role on a psychological level; that of Pribram and Spinelli on the physiological. Some investigators have been explicitly concerned with the relationship between the input processing and the output systems of the brain in determining awareness. One test that we can try ourselves is that of closing one eye and pushing the other eye with a finger to a side. The visual world seems to "jump" a bit, it seems discontinuous. But if we make an eye movement in the usual manner over the same space, the world doesn't seem to jump. This difference indicates that in constructing our awareness we must also take our own movements into account and correlate them with the changes in input. If we didn't have a record somewhere of our efference, in this case our eye movements, the visual world would be constantly jumping around.

Some have gone so far as to maintain that consciousness depends *solely* upon the output of the brain, regardless of which input keys off a given output. Roger Sperry emphasized this point,[16] and after him Taylor and Festinger have provided some experimental demonstrations of this idea. Their statement that awareness depends solely on the output regardless of the input is not at all inconsistent with Bruner's contention that the category activated will determine awareness. In one case, if one is "ready" to see a black ace of spades or a red ace of hearts when a red ace of spades is shown, one will see one of the two choices one has set for himself. On the other hand, if one is "ready" to make a straight eye movement in response to a curved line, one will see the curved line as straight.

We ordinarily speak of "seeing an image" on the retina of our eyes. More properly, we do not really "see" with our eyes but, rather, with the help of our eyes. The eyes and other sense organs should be considered information selection systems. We can trick the eye, for instance, in several ways. If we press on our eyelids with our eyes closed, we "see" a white light, and yet there is no physical light energy present. What we have done is to cause the cells in the retina to fire by pressure instead of by their usual source of stimulation, light energy. The cells in the retina fire and send signals up to the brain. Messages from the retina are interpreted as light by the brain, no matter how the message was brought about, and so we are tricked into "seeing." There are times when we do not even need our eyes to "see"—for instance, when we dream at night, or in the case of hallucinations, there is no light energy reaching our eyes.

Wilder Penfield, a Canadian neurosurgeon, demonstrated the same point.[17] He performed brain surgery for patients with epilepsy and, as part of this procedure, electrically stimulated various areas of the brain. His patients would often report conscious experiences without any input at all. In addition, stimulation of the visual cortex usually leads to the experience of vision. We can understand, then, that seeing is not a process which takes place *in* our eyes but, rather, *with the help* of our eyes. It is a process that occurs in the brain and is determined by the category and output systems of the brain. Vision is a process that is fed only by the input that comes through our eyes, and our awareness is constructed from this input and from our past experience.[18]

Our eyes are also constantly in motion, in large eye movements (saccades) as well as in eye tremors (nystagmus). We blink our eyes every second, move our eyes around, move our heads, our bodies, and we follow moving objects. The view of an object is never constant, and the very receptive fields on the eyes are changing all the time. Yet our visual world remains very stable. We can walk around a horse, for instance, and although our view is constantly changing—we sometimes see the tail, sometimes the back, a side view, a three-quarter view, a straight front view— we always see the same horse. If we "saw" an "image" on our retina, the visual world would be different each second. We must then *construct* our awareness from the selected input sorted into categories and in this way achieve some stability of our awareness out of the rich and continuously changing flow of information reaching our receptors.

We might briefly review some of these general characteristics of our awareness. Our senses receive information from the external world but, for the most part, are built to discard much of the continuously changing stimulation that reaches them. We also possess the ability to restrict further and modify the information that reaches awareness, by "reprograming." The brain selects and modifies input. We build "models" or representations of the world based on our past experience. We can, therefore, tune our awareness on the basis of past experience, expectation, and needs. We use this ability to tune out the constancies of the world, the clock ticking, the route over which we normally drive, our living room, an old phonograph record. Our experience is therefore an interactive process between the external world and the continuously revised models of our categories. We can select input, tune ourselves to relevant input, categorize, and finally construct our awareness from these and from our past experiences, our associations, thoughts, and emotional state.

Similar analyses of normal awareness appear in literature. Lawrence Durrell's four novels of the *Alexandria Quartet* investigate the interactive nature of awareness. Durrell explores the same series of events as they appear to different people. For Durrell, as for Kelly, it is not important what actually happens, but what, rather, is construed to have happened. The world of Durrell's novels reflects the richness and complexity of life itself.

The current work in American academic psychology provides a useful means of understanding normal awareness as a constructive process. One dimension, though, that is lacking in the current characterization is an analysis of the continuous flow of awareness. The writers cited provide a useful series of metaphors for the frame-by-frame components of awareness, but this is a segmented analysis. There is no doubt that at any instant our awareness is a construction based on past experience, but a more general characterization of the continuing nature of our awareness is needed. A more suitable metaphor was given by William James in his *Principles of Psychology*. He considered awareness a stream, continuously flowing, continuously changing direction. James said:

> Consciousness then does not appear to itself chopped up in bits. Such words as chain or train do not describe it fitly, as it presents itself in the first instant. It is nothing joined, it flows, a river or a stream are the metaphors by which it is naturally described. In

talking of it thereafter, let us call it the stream of thought, of consciousness, or of subjective life.[19]

Our thoughts are in constant change. Awareness shifts from one aspect of the stimuli surrounding us to another, to a thought of the past, to a bodily sensation, to a plan, to a change in external stimulation, back and forth. The stream carves its own new path continuously. James would have agreed with the more recent and precise analysis that awareness is a simplification and a construction. He said:

Looking back, then, over this review, we see that the mind is at every stage a theatre of simultaneous possibilities. Consciousness consists in the comparison of these with each other, the selection of some, and the suppression of others, of the rest by the reinforcing and inhibiting agency of attention. The highest and most celebrated mental products are filtered from the data chosen by the faculty next beneath, out of the mass offered by the faculty below that, which mass was in turn sifted from a still larger amount of yet simpler material, and so on. The mind, in short, works on the data it received much as a sculptor works on his block of stone. In a sense, the statue stood there from eternity. But there were a thousand different ones beside it. The sculptor alone is to thank for having extricated this one from the rest. Just so the world of each of us, however different our several views of it may be, all lay embedded in the primordial chaos of sensations, which gave the mere matter to the thought of all of us indifferently. We may, if we like, by our reasoning unwind things back to that black and jointless continuity of space and moving clouds of swarming atoms which science calls the only real world. But all the while the world we feel and live in will be that which our ancestors and we, by slowly cumulative strokes of choice, have extricated out of this, like sculptors, by simply rejecting certain portions of the given stuff. Other sculptors, other statues from the same stone! Other minds, other worlds, from the same monotonous and inexpressive chaos! My world is but one in a million, alike embedded and alike real to those who may abstract them. How different must be the world in the consciousness of ants, cuttlefish or crab![20]

A similar characterization of awareness is offered by the Indian yogi, Vivikenanda. He more negatively compares ordinary awareness to a "drunken monkey." He calls up images of awareness moving from one random thought to another—thinking about hunger, thinking about the past, glimpsing an aspect of the present, thinking of the future, planning an action—continuously bouncing around like a monkey from one thing to another.

The esoteric traditions in general have characterized consciousness in terms similar to those of modern psychology. The Sufis are the clearest precursors of modern psychology's conceptions of awareness. Sufi teaching stories frequently focus on men who are too preoccupied to hear what is being said, or who misinterpret instructions because of their expectations, or who do not see what is in front of them, because of the limited nature of their constructs.[21] The Sufis emphasize the constantly changing biases that constitute our normal awareness. "What a piece of bread looks like depends on whether you are hungry," says a Sufi poet, Jallaudin Rumi. The Sufis quite explicitly consider the effects of our limited category system on awareness. Many of the Sufis' descriptions of awareness could have been a statement of Bruner's about category systems, or a summary by Lettvin of his research on the frog, e.g., "Offer a donkey a salad, and he will ask what kind of thistle it is." They emphasize that we can be aware of only that which we conceive to exist, and that which our senses will transmit to us.

The Sufi and other traditions contend that the selective and restricted nature of awareness is an obstacle to be overcome and that the process of meditation, among other exercises, is a way of turning down the restrictions that normally limit awareness. One specific aim in these traditions is the removal of the automaticity and selectivity of ordinary awareness. The Sufis characterize man's usual state as one of "deep sleep" or "blindness," as one of being concerned with the irrelevant dimensions of the world. Gurdjieff's image is that of man placing shock absorbers between himself and the world. "We must destroy our buffers, children have none, therefore we must become like little children."[22] In Indian thought, as we have seen, ordinary awareness is a "drunken monkey" living solely in his constructs—the world of "illusion." This same thought is the metaphorical meaning of the "fall" of man in the Christian tradition. All these metaphors, without their derogatory connotation, can be understood in terms of modern psychology as depicting our selective awareness, our model-building, our automaticity, our limited category systems.

An aim of meditation, and more generally of the disciplines involving meditation, is the removal of "blindness," or the illusion, and an "awakening" of "fresh" perception. Enlightenment or illumination are words often used for progress in these disciplines, for a breakthrough in the level of awareness—flooding a dark spot with light. The Indian tradition speaks of opening the third eye, seeing more, and from a new vantage point. *Satori*, the desired state in Zen, is considered an "awakening." The Sufis speak of growing a new organ of perception.

Reports of the experiences of practitioners of the disciplines of meditation indicate that a primary aftereffect of the concentrative meditation exercises is an "opening up" of awareness, a "deautomatization," as Deikman calls it, which may be considered as involving a reduction of the processing of input. Deikman's own subjects, who gazed at a blue vase for a half-hour at a time over a number of sessions, reported that the vase appeared "more vivid" and "more luminous."[23] Deikman quotes Augustine Poulain, who emphasized that concentrative meditation is a temporary process of withdrawal, a blank-out, in other terms, of awareness with the intent to become deautomatized or dishabituated.

It is the mysterious darkness wherein is contained the limitless Good. To such an extent are we admitted and absorbed into something that is one, simple, divine, and illuminable that we seem no longer distinguishable from it. . . . In this unity the feeling of multiplicity disappears. When afterwards these persons come to themselves again, they find themselves possessed of a more distinct knowledge of things, some luminous and more perfect than that of others.[24]

Some speak of seeing things "freshly" or as if for the first time. To William Blake, "if the doors of perception were cleansed, everything would appear to man as it is, infinite." Others, like Gurdjieff, use a loose metaphor and compare their experiences to that of a child who presumably has not yet developed many automatic ways of tuning out the world. In Zen, one speaks similarly of seeing something the five hundredth time in the same way one saw it the first time.

All of these descriptions are understandable and easily translatable into the more precise psychological terms of building a model of the environment and testing and selecting input against the model. When we see something for the five hundredth time we have developed a model for it and tune out the input.

These characterizations of consciousness represent a point of encounter between the concepts of contemporary psychology and the metaphors of the esoteric disciplines. We speak of man as controlling his input, building models, responding "automatically" to the external environment. The esoteric traditions refer to this process as man's lacking awareness of his surroundings and consider this "blindness" the barrier to his development. The practice of meditation, then, can be considered as an attempt to turn off conceptual activity temporarily, to shut off all input processing for a period of time, to get away for a while from the external environment.

A result of this "turning off" of our input selection systems is that, when we introduce the same sensory input later, we see it differently, "anew."

When we leave our normal surroundings and go on a vacation we usually return to find ourselves much more aware of the immediate environment. We play many of our old records, which we haven't "heard" in a while. We look anew at the plants in our garden, the paintings on our walls, our friends. Getting away and returning seems to have the same effect on awareness as presenting new stimuli.*

We can consider the process of meditation as similar to that of taking a vacation—leaving the situation, "turning off" our routine way of dealing with the external world for a period, later returning to find it "fresh," "new," "different," our awareness "deautomatized."

Contemporary psychology recognizes that we easily adapt to most anything new. New technology, the changes in our environment, quickly become an integral part of our lives, part of our model. The model-building process is specifically what is to be dismantled through the practice of meditation. In Zen, one is instructed to stop conceptualizing while remaining fully awake. In Yoga, the aim is to leave the "illusion"—to cease identifying the external world with our models.

The three major traditions that we've considered each speak of developing an awareness that allows every stimulus to enter into consciousness devoid of our normal selection process, devoid of normal tuning and normal input selection, model-building, and the normal category systems.

The same metaphor is used in many traditions to describe the desired state of awareness. The Sufi poet Omar Khayyám says: "I am a mirror and who looks at me, whatever good or bad he speaks, he speaks of himself." The contemporary Zen master, Suzuki Roshi says: "The perfect man employs his mind as a mirror, it grasps nothing, it refuses nothing, it receives but does not keep." Christ said in prayer: "A mirror I am to thee that perceivest me." The metaphor of consciousness as a mirror fits well with some of the psychologists' own metaphors. A mirror

* Cf, the phenomenon of "spontaneous recovery" in habituation.

allows every input to enter equally, reflects each equally, and cannot be tuned to receive a special kind of input. It does not add anything to the input and does not turn off repetitive stimuli; it does not focus on any particular aspect of input and retune back and forth, but continuously admits all inputs equally.

This metaphor leads to another consideration. Many of the traditions claim to allow men to experience the world *directly*. The Sufis speak of attaining an "objective consciousness," others of "cosmic consciousness," and the statement is often made that one can have *direct* perception of reality. Whether one can perceive "reality" directly is not yet a question for science, but some comment within the terms of psychology might be made. The ability to be a mirror, to be free of the normal restrictions, of the tuning, biasing, and filtering processes of awareness, may be part of what is indicated by "direct" perception. This state can perhaps be considered within psychology as a diminution of the interactive nature of awareness; a state in which we do not select, nor do we bet on the nature of the world, nor do we think of the past, nor do we compel awareness by random associations, nor do we think of the future, nor do we sort into restrictive categories, but a state in which all possible categories are held in awareness at once. It has been described also as living totally in the present; not thinking about the future or of the past; a state in which everything that is happening in the present moment enters into awareness.

There have been some studies of the state of awareness of practitioners in and after meditation. These studies have used the EEG to measure the response of the brain of meditators to the external stimulation.

When we enter a room and hear a clock ticking we ordinarily learn to tune it out fairly quickly. If we study this process physiologically, the normal orienting response to new stimulation would begin to disappear after a few moments and wouldn't reappear. We would have built a model to tune it out.[25] The response would have habituated. But if one's consciousness were like a mirror, then each time the clock ticked we would "reflect" the tick.

The Indian psychologists' studies on Yoga meditation showed this result. In testing the yogi's brain response to external stimuli, the current contention on the effects and aftereffects of meditation was confirmed. During the meditation and during the withdrawal there was no response in the yogi's brain to external stimuli. When the yogi was not meditating, repetition of the external stimulus showed no habituation, as it presumably would have occurred in other subjects.[26]

The Japanese neuropsychiatrists Kasumatsu and Hirai studied the habituation of the orienting response to a repeating click in ordinary people and in Zen masters. The subjects in this experiment sat in a soundproof room and listened to a click repeated each fifteen seconds while an EEG was being taken. The normal subjects showed the customary phenomenon of habituation. There was a decrease in the response of the brain's electrical activity to the click after the third or fourth click. After habituation, each time the click occurred there was no response in the brain of the subject: the click had been tuned out of awareness. When the Zen masters were exposed to this same repetitive click over a period of five minutes, they did not show the customary habituation but responded to the last click in the same way as they did to the first.[27] They did not seem therefore to make a "model" of the repetitive stimulation and tune it out.

There are important differences in intent in the particular forms of Zen and Yoga meditation, which would lead us to expect different kinds of responses to the external world during the meditation exercise and after. The early and beginning forms of Zen are similar to Yoga; the breath counting, the koan, etc., involve an attempt to restrict awareness to a single process. We remember that Rahula indicates that one will not be aware of the external world if one does the breath-counting meditation successfully. These exercises are similar to the use of the *mandala, mantra, mudra,* etc. in Yoga. In the more advanced forms of Zen in the Soto sect, once the breath-counting is mastered, the second form of meditation exercises, shikan-taza, is practiced—"just sitting." Yasutani Roshi describes this exercise as follows:

Up to now you have been concentrating on following your breaths with your mind's eye, trying to experience vividly the in-haled breath as only inhaled breath and the exhaled breath as only exhaled breath. From now on I want you to practice shikan-taza, which I will shortly describe in detail. . . .

Shikan means "nothing but" or "just," while *ta* means "to hit" and *za* "to sit." Hence shikan-taza is a practice in which the mind is intensely involved in just sitting. In this type of Za-Zen it is all too easy for the mind, which is not supported by such aids as counting the breath or by a koan, to become distracted. The correct temper of mind therefore becomes doubly important. Now, in shikan-taza the mind must be unhurried yet at the same time firmly planted or massively composed, like Mount Fuji let us say. But it also must be alert, stretched, like a taut bowstring. So shikan-taza is a heightened state of concentrated awareness wherein one is neither tense nor hurried, and certainly never slack. It is the mind of some-body facing death. Let us imagine that you are engaged in a duel of swordsmanship of the kind that used to take place in ancient Japan. As you face your opponent, you are unceasingly watchful, set, ready. Were you to relax your vigilance even momentarily, you would be cut down instantly. A crowd gathers to see the fight. Since you are not blind you see them from the corner of your eye, and since you are not deaf you hear them. But not for an in-stant is your mind captured by these sense impressions.

This state cannot be maintained for long—in fact, you ought not to do shikan-taza for more than half an hour at a sitting. After thirty minutes get up and walk around in kinhin [Zen moving meditation] and then resume your sitting. If you are truly doing shikan-taza, in half an hour you will be sweating, even in winter in an unheated room, because of the heat generated by this intense concentration. When you sit for too long, your mind loses its vigor, your body tires, and your efforts are less rewarding than if you had restricted your sitting to thirty-minute periods.[28]

We can then consider two basic types of meditation exercises —both concerned with a common effect—those which "turn off" input processing for a period of time to achieve an *after-effect* of "opening up" of awareness, and those which consist in the active practice of "opening up" during the period of the exercise.

To return for a moment to the studies of the response of Zen and Yoga meditators to external stimuli, we can expect dishabituation *during* the advanced form of Zen meditation—that is, a consistent response to a stimulus which continues—and a shutting down of awareness of external stimuli during Yoga meditation. When the yogin is not in meditation, we might expect no habituation to a repetitive stimulus (if he is advanced enough in his practice).

Active practice in opening up awareness is a part of all the traditions, but in Zen it is a specific meditation exercise. A less demanding Buddhist practice stems from one component of the Buddha's Eightfold Path and is usually termed "right-mindedness." It requires that one be "conscious" of everything one does, to attend very closely to ordinary activities, and to open up awareness to these activities while engaged in them. Rahula says:

> Another very important, practical and useful form of "meditation" (mental development) is to be aware and mindful of whatever you do, physically or verbally, during the daily routine of work in your life, private, public or professional. Whether you walk, stand, sit, lie down or sleep, whether you stretch or bend your limbs, whether you look around, whether you put on your clothes, whether you talk or keep silent, whether you eat or drink— even whether you answer the calls of nature—in these and other activities you should be fully aware and mindful of the act per-

formed at the moment, that is to say, that you should live in the present moment, in the present action. This does not mean that you should not think of the past or the future at all. On the contrary, you should think of them in relation to the present moment, to the present action, when and where this is relevant. People do not generally live in their actions in the present moment. They live in the past or the future. Though they seem to be doing something now here, they live somewhere else in their thoughts, in their problems and worries, usually in the memories of the past or in desires and speculations about the future. Therefore, they do not live in nor do they enjoy what they do at the moment, so they are unhappy and discontented with the present moment with the work at hand. Naturally, they cannot give themselves fully to what they appear to be doing.[29]

Spiegelberg gives an example of a similar practice in the Tibetan tradition. The Tibetan "Stories of the 84 Magicians" exercises, analogous to those described by Rahula, deal for the most part with the daily occupation of the meditator.

The street cleaner has to take his task of sweeping as the starting point for meditation. So, likewise, must the potter take his task of producing clay utensils on his potter's wheel and the cobbler, his handicrafts. Here, again, therefore, it is evident that one may do what he will so long as he is clearly aware of what he is doing. Every activity is of equal value as a basis for a dharana exercise.[30]

In Yoga, self-observation is called "the Witness." The attempt is to observe oneself as if one were another person. One tries to notice exactly what one is doing—to invest ordinary activtiy with attention. The witness does not judge action or initiate action. The witness simply observes.

In Zen, this practice is highly developed. Right-mindedness or attention to what one is doing can be a part of almost any activity that one performs, no matter how degrading. There is no action that cannot be used for the purposes of the alteration of one's consciousness. One simply need be mindful of what one is doing. One can be performing actions that are quite degrading to a Buddhist, such as butchering an animal, but simply by paying close attention to what one is doing, one's awareness can be developed.

In Sufism, at least in the version that is attributed to Gurdjieff, there are similar practices, one of which is called "self-remembering." As in Zen, no special constraints are put on action. There are no prohibitions as to what can be eaten or general rules of conduct. The attempt is simply to be aware of oneself. Gurdjieff's students are constantly instructed to "remember themselves" wherever they are, remember that they are present, and notice what they do. When one is "remembering oneself in Gurdjieff's terms one is considered to be "awake."[31]

A similar exercise attributed to Gurdjieff consists simply in maintaining continuous awareness on a part of one's body—an elbow, hand, leg. Another exercise of this tradition is to perform ordinary habitual actions slightly differently, such as putting shoes on in the opposite order, shaving the other side of the face first, eating with the left hand. These can be seen as attempts to return the habitual "automatic" actions into full awareness.

Recall the phenomenon of habituation. A slight change in the input is enough to "dishabituate" and to return the stimulus to awareness. Similarly, slightly altering our usual "automatic" behavior, such as tying shoes or driving cars, can return it again into awareness.

In Yoga itself there is a tradition called *Karma Yoga*. The attempt is to treat everyday activities as a sacrament and to give them full attention. This exercise performs a function similar to "right-mindedness" and "self-remembering," and is perhaps a less extreme version of *shikan-taza*.

Many schools within these traditions combine the two major awareness exercises devoting a half-hour or so twice a day to the "shutting-down" form of meditation and as much as possible of the remainder of the day to a form of self-observation.

We mentioned earlier that the other major practice which often accompanies both forms of meditation is that of a renunciation of or a non-attachment to external objects. There are several different types of these practices, involving either prohibitions on behavior or the cultivation of a psychological state that combines renunciation and non-attachment. In the Judeo-Christian tradition, these practices usually involve behavioral restrictions. For example, some churchgoers are required during Lent to abstain from eating meat. The usual result of this kind of practice is that awareness is focused on the forbidden object. Most people find themselves craving meat, thinking about it, devising substitutes (meatless meals, for instance), waiting until the period of prohibition is over.

But the practice of renunciation, according to the various esoteric traditions, is intended to create a psychological state of *cessation*, not enhancement, of desire, and it is not necessarily tied to any change in external behavior. Most of the traditions emphasize that merely abstaining in practice while desiring, planning to consume the object, is worthless—perhaps worse than not giving it up at all. Christ himself made this point, although his followers do not always seem to be mindful of it.

Renunciation is the process, it is said, of conquering desire, of not requiring or needing anything. The Indian practices emphasize the cultivation of a psychological state of non-attachment as well as prohibitions on actual behavior. Most yogis are vegetarian, chaste, and live in poverty. Often yogic practice involves a withdrawal from society and its "temptations" into an *ashram*, in which one lives as a monk on a simple diet. Christian monasteries also emphasize psychological non-attachment as well as the actual cessation of certain "impure" behavior—the vows of poverty, chastity, solitude—a separation from the culture in order to "purify" oneself.

In the Zen and Sufi traditions the emphasis is solely on the psychological state of non-attachment and not on prohibitions in actual practice. Both Zen and Sufism emphasize, as they do in the exercise of self-awareness, that one can do whatever one wants as long as one is not attached to it.

The difference between the Sufis and Zen on the one hand, and much of Yoga and Christian tradition on the other, is illustrated in some advice given to Rafael Lefort, who traveled to the Mideast in search of the teachers of Gurdjieff—the Sufis—and was asked:

"Are you prepared to leave the world as you know it and live in a mountain retreat on a very basic diet?" I signified that I was.

"You see," he nodded his head regretfully, "you still feel that to find knowledge you must seek a solitary life away from impure things. This is a primitive attitude and one satisfactory for savages. . . . Can you comprehend the uselessness of abandoning the world for the sake of your selfish development?

"You may need a course," he went on," at a Sarmoun Centre, but that will not mean total abandonment of your mundane worldly activity provided you do not allow it, nay invite it, to corrupt you. If you have enough skill you can actually harness the negative forces to serve you . . . but you must have enough skill."[32]

Zen also points out that "worldly" activity can be a perfect vehicle for development as long as one is free from attachment. Worldly activity and pleasures are legitimate in Zen as long as one is not in their service. The Sufis admonition is: "Be *in* the world but not *of* the world." The attempt is to isolate the important aspect of renunciation, the psychological state of non-attachment, from the external behavior. This is illustrated by a student's experience with Gurdjieff, when she felt that she was a "slave" to her habit of cigarette smoking. Gurdjieff, who stressed that men were often the slaves of their habits, instructed her to give up smoking. On returning to him a year later, she told Gurdjieff triumphantly that she had given up smoking and was no longer a slave to her cigarette habit. Gurdjieff smiled and immediately offered her a very expensive Turkish cigarette, indicating that it was not her behavior but the fact that she had been slave to her cigarette habit that was important. Only when she no longer needed to smoke was it permissible to smoke again.[33] Gurdjieff himself kept a quite well-known larder stocked with delicacies from all parts of the world.

But why is non-attachment to "worldly" pleasures a major part of the meditative disciplines? One answer can be given in terms of our analysis of ordinary consciousness. Recall that normal consciousness is constructed from our past experience, our expectations, and our needs. When we are hungry we are likely to search out food, or to *create* food images or smells, or to enhance food images that are present, or to think about food. A Sufi tale illustrates this general point:

> Two men were sitting in a cafe and a camel walked past.
> "What does that make you think of?" said one.
> "Food," said the other.
> "Since when are camels used for food?" said the first.
> "No, you see, everything makes me think of food."[34]

The meditative traditions consider that one major barrier to the development of expanded awareness is that we continuously tune out those portions of the external environment that do not suit our needs at the moment. If we are hungry we would be very unlikely to notice the river around us or the people whom we see. We are concerned solely with food and construct our world around food.

In its effect on awareness, the practice of non-attachment can be considered as an additional way to remove the normal restrictions on input. If there are no desires, there is less of a bias at any one moment to "tune" perception. Our awareness of the external environment becomes less restricted, less of an interaction, less solely a function of our desire at the moment, and more like a mirror.

There is another function of non-attachment. If, for instance, one *needs* nothing from another person or from the external environment—prestige, sex, food, love—one can exist "for them" as a mirror, as do Omar Khayyám, Suzuki Roshi, and Christ. We sometimes reach this state when our needs are satisfied. We all have observed that the world appears different when we are in love or are a success.

It is also commonplace to observe, however, that the sensualist is often the one who becomes the renunciant, a "worldly" man who gives up all for his religion—a Thomas à Becket.

In many ways the aims of the disciplines of meditation— total attention to the moment, "dishabituation," "extended" awareness—are the same ones we seek in many of our "ordinary" activities. We buy new products, new clothes, new records; we slightly change our surroundings to attempt to return them to awareness. Dangerous sports, for example, engage our awareness and bring us into the present moment in which we think of nothing else but the activity in which we are engaged. We arrange the conditions so that it is *absolutely necessary* for us to pay full attention to what is taking place at that moment. When we race a sports car or motorcycle, or ski or ride a toboggan down a slope, or sky-dive, anything less than complete awareness to the moment may lead to injury or to death. The necessity of opening up our awareness is perhaps one of the reasons people are willing to risk injury or even their lives in dangerous sports. A particularly good example is the sort of rock climbing that requires intense concentration over a prolonged period of time. Doug Robinson writes in *Ascent*, the journal of the Sierra Club:*

. . . to take a familiar example, it would be hard to look at Van Gogh's "The Starry Night" without seeing the visionary quality in the way the artist sees the world. He has not painted anything that is not in the original scene, yet others would have trouble recognizing what he has depicted. The difference lies in the intensity

* I would like to thank Dr. E. K. Sadalla for pointing this example out to me.

of his perception, at the heart of his visionary experience, he is painting from a higher state of consciousness. Climbers too have their "starry nights." Consider the following from an account by Alan Steck of the Hummingbird Ridge Club on Mount Logan. "I turned for a moment and was completely lost in silent appraisal of the beautifully sensuous simplicity of windblown snow. The beauty of that moment, the form and motion of the blowing snow was such a powerful impression, and so wonderfully sufficient that the climber was lost in it. It is said to be only a moment and yet by virtue of total absorption he is lost in it and the winds of eternity blow through it!"

A second example comes from an account of the 7th day and the 8th day of the first ascent under trying conditions on El Capitan's Muir Wall. Yvon Chouinard relates, in the 1966 *American Alpine Journal*: ". . . with our more receptive senses we now appreciated everything around us. Each individual crystal in the granite stood out in bold relief. The varied shape of the clouds never ceased to attract our attention. For the first time we noticed tiny bugs that were all over the walls, so tiny they were barely noticeable. While belaying, I stared at one for fifteen minutes, watching him move and admiring his brilliant red color. How could one ever be bored with so many good things to see and feel? This unity with our joyous surroundings, this ultra penetrating perception gave us a feeling of contentment that we had not had for years."

In these passages the quality that makes up the climber's visionary experience are apparent: the overwhelming beauty of most ordinary objects—as clouds, granite, and snow—of his experience, the sense of the slowing down of time to the point of disappearing, and the "feeling of contentment" and an oceanic feeling of supreme sufficiency of the present, and while delicate in substance these feelings are still strong enough to intrude firmly into the middle of dangerous circumstances, and remain there temporarily superceding even apprehension and the drive for achievement."[35]

Much of Western art is similarly an attempt to "cleanse" perception, to return our awareness to things that are seen automatically. One critic considers the function of art to "make strange" ordinary objects, to allow us to see our usual surroundings as if they were "strange"—as if for the first time. The recent trend in Pop Art is an example. There is an important difference in the way we look at a Warhol sculpture of a Campbell's soup can in a gallery and at the same object at home. By presenting ordinary objects in a context that demands that we attend to them, we "see" them in a new way. We do not immediately call up our customary category of "soup can," in which we ignore everything but the particular label ("is it vegetable or noodle?"). We now "look" at the shape, the lettering, the way the light falls on the surface of the can. We are brought out of our ordinary responses of ignoring the object. Looking at a common object in a gallery is a means of deautomizing our awareness of it.

We could give many more examples from the fields of art, music, and literature. There are many essayists and poets who have written directly about meditative experiences and traditions; among them, William Blake, Herman Hesse, Aldous Huxley, T. S. Eliot; but it would be useful here to consider a writer whose work is quite different and who is not usually associated with this subject.

The sensualist Henry Miller would seem to share little with Huxley, Hesse, Eliot, the traditions of meditation, the rock climber, or the visual artist. But, in a volume of *The Rosy Crucifixion* (*Sexus*), Miller states the aim of his work and life in terms almost identical to those of the esoteric traditions, namely, that men are "blind" and have first to acquire "vision."

> . . . the world is not to be put in order: the world *is* order incarnate. It is for us to put ourselves in unison with this order, to know what is the world order and in contradistinction to the wishful thinking orders that we seek to impose on one another. The power which we long to possess in order to establish the good, the true and the beautiful would prove to be, if we could have it,

but the means of destroying one another. It is fortunate that we are powerless. We have first to acquire vision, then discipline and forbearance until we have the humility to acknowledge a vision beyond our own, and until we have faith and trust in superior powers, the blind must lead the blind. Men who believe that work and brains will accomplish must ever be deceived by the quixotic and every unforeseen turn of events.[36]

In the *World of Sex*, Miller makes the point, which could have been made by a Zen monk, that any ordinary activity, if one is mindful (in the Zen sense), can lead to a breakthrough. He also recalls Spiegelberg's comments that "every hallucination, every unappeasable hatred, every amorous attachment provides a certain power of concentration to him who cherishes it and helps to direct the forces of his being to a similar goal."

Life moves on whether we act as cowards or heroes. Life has no other discipline to impose, if we could but realize it, but to accept life unquestioningly. Everything we shut our eyes to, everything we run away from, everything we deny, denigrate or despise, serves to defeat us in the end. What seems nasty, painful, evil can become a source of beauty, joy, and strength if faced with an open mind. Every moment is a golden one for him who has the vision to recognize it as such. Life is now, every moment, no matter if the world be full of death. Death triumphs only in the service of life.[37]

In *"Creative Death"* Miller writes:

Strange as it may seem today to say, the aim of life is to live, and to live is to be aware, joyously, drunkenly, divinely, serenely aware. In this state of godlike awareness one sings, and in this realm the world exists as poem, no why or wherefore, no direction, no goal, no striving, no revolving. Like the enigmatic Chinaman, one is rapt by the ever-changing spectacle of changing phenomenon; this is the sublime, the amoral state of the artist, he who lives only in the moment, the visionary moment of utter far-seeing lucidity. Such clear icy sanity that it seems like madness.* [38]

Although many of our endeavors are directed toward achieving a meditation-like state of awareness, these means are held to be inefficient by the esoteric traditions. If we actually do achieve states of total awareness to the moment by ordinary means, this achievement does not last for long, does not carry with it a permanence. Our success fades, our love ends, we must come down from the mountain.

Noting the common aim of many of our interests and that of the disciplines of meditation, another function of detachment becomes more clear. The practice can be seen as an attempt to separate the subjective state produced by sports, sex, love, music, art, etc., from that of its usual object, and to detach the effect—the resultant internal state—from the usual cause, the stimulus object. The person works then within himself to attempt to generate the internal state directly. "What need have I of an external woman when I have an internal woman," says a practitioner of *Tantra*. The "worldly" sensualist perhaps

---

* I was beginning to wonder whether the contention that much of our endeavors are directed to the same end as that of the disciplines of meditation is exaggerated. Perhaps I was forcing some of these into a mold. Then I happened to pick up two of the most popular magazines in this country, *Life* and *Look*, and read them at about the same time as this chapter was being prepared. In *Life* we read, in the introduction to a photographic essay; "Imprisoned in the narrowness of our human scale, we are blind to the vast reaches of reality. Mysteries lie all around us, even within us, waiting to be revealed by a new way of seeing." Then, in *Look* magazine: "Up, quick if you can it's long past time to do. You've stayed so long you've lost yourself and now exist cut off from all that is around you, from all of you that's human, you're civilized beyond your senses: out of touch, narcotized, mechanized, Westernized, with bleached out eyes that yearn for natural light. The intellects turn tyrant on us all and make our daily lives neatly laid-out, over-intellectualized, over-technological exercises in sinister lunacy. . . . We are severed from ourselves and alien to our sensibilities, fragmented, specialized, dissected, pidgeonholed into smothering." In popular music, a friend recalled the Beatles' song "Tomorrow Never Knows," which begins, "Turn off your mind, relax and float downstream,/it is not dying,/lay down all thoughts, surrender to the void/that you may see the meaning of within/it is shining."

sees the same possibility—to achieve a result that is similar to what he seeks in sensual activity, but one more permanent and under his control. He then gives up the outward manifestations of what he is seeking. The process involves a detachment from the usual triggers to this state—sex, love, prestige, power, money, food, etc.—and an attempt to concentrate upon internal "centers," which are held to give rise to these and to "higher" experiences. The energy force is called *kundalini* in Yoga, and these centers termed *chakras* in Yoga and *lataif* in the Sufi tradition. There are some differences in the two systems but these two centers are for this consideration analogous.*[39]

In the terms of this essay, detachment and concentration on these internal centers can be considered as an attempt to stimulate internally the structures that are usually associated with the experiences of dishabituation, pleasure, etc. We can consider the process as learning to stimulate the "reward" circuits of the brain.

Physiologists working with animals have implanted electrodes in those parts of the brain in which stimulation seems to serve as a reward, and they have had interesting results. In a situation where animals can continue the stimulation of these systems themselves, they will do so at the expense of everything else. Some actually worked to stimulate these circuits until they died, even though food and drink were available freely. They had no need of external stimulation because they could do it internally.[40]

The second function of renunciation and the concomitant concentration on various parts of the body can then be considered as a functional training technique in self-stimulation of the centers of the nervous system.[41]

These first two sections of this essay have covered a lot of ground, so it should be of some use to recall briefly some of their major points.

* This energy system is not at all understood in science. The exercises are almost always given a secret and little is ever written of them.

If we ignore our preconceptions about the function of meditation and overcome both attraction and repulsion toward the
exotic and esoteric, it is clear that the practices of meditation can
be analyzed in terms of modern psychology. The repetitive or
concentrative form of meditation can be seen as an exercise in
"turning off" awareness of the external environment, inducing
a central state in the nervous system equivalent to that of no
external stimulation. In the traditions we are considering, this
state is known as the "void" or the "darkness." If restriction of
awareness is accomplished by other means, such as that of a
ganzfeld, there is a similar result—the "blank-out" of experience
of the external environment.

The production of a state in which one is insulated from the
external world has some consistent aftereffects on awareness. Many
meditators report seeing the world "anew," "fresh," seeing
everything "glowing," illuminated, enlightened. A metaphor
used in most traditions for this state is that of a "mirror."

It is interesting to note the similarities between the esoteric
and the modern psychologies of consciousness. Both stress that
our awareness of the environment is a process of selection and
categorization, that our sensory systems serve the purpose of
discarding much of the information that reaches us, and that
we finally construct our awareness from this heavily filtered
input. The "shutting-down" form of meditation can be compared
to taking a vacation. We often leave a situation to "get out of
our rut." When we return we see things differently.

The meditation exercises can be seen as attempts to alter the
selective and limited nature of our awareness, to change the
habitual way in which we respond to the external world. In
physiological terms it might involve a reduction in the efferent
modification of input and in the "models" that we usually make
of the external world.

Another form of these meditation exercises consists in the
active practice of "opening-up" awareness. *Shikan-taza* in Zen

is one of the most difficult of these exercises. Sufi, Zen, and Yoga followers emphasize the process of self-observation. In some of the traditions specific exercises are performed for the purpose of returning awareness to actions that usually occur "automatically," a practice analogous to "dishabituation."

The third major technique in these systems involves renunciation and detachment from "worldly" pleasures. Detachment can affect awareness by removing one of the components that serve to tune awareness: our needs and desires. By removing our needs with their biasing function, our awareness can be more like a mirror.

The second function of renunciation involves the consideration that many of our ordinary pursuits are attempts to reach a state similar to that produced by the practice of meditation. Dangerous sports, sex, food, art, etc., at their best moments, produce a state in which we exist just then, totally in the moment, devoid of our automatic way of responding. This has been termed a state of increased receptivity or expanded awareness.*

The problem of reaching this state in the usual way, say the spokesmen of the disciplines of meditation, is that ordinary means are inefficient, that men usually concern themselves with irrelevant dimensions, that the subjective state desired is not often produced by the ordinary means themselves, and that, if produced, its aftereffects do not persist.

Detachment can be seen, then, as an attempt to reach a similar state *within* by separating the state itself from the stimuli that

---

* Within psychology this state is not well defined as yet. It is hardly clear whether "being like a mirror" involves an actual increase in the amount of information that reaches awareness, or whether it involves a leveling of the normal filtering processes—letting no more information into awareness, but simply letting the same amount in with less bias. The only evidence on this question so far is that relating to the brain response of meditators to quite simple stimulation. It will be necessary to extend these studies to get a measure of the "channel capacity" within and across sensory modalities, before, during, and after meditation, and, perhaps, to follow practitioners longitudinally as they progress in meditation training.

usually trigger it, and by the conjoint practice of concentrating on the parts of the nervous system that produce this experience. These exercises, the centers upon which one concentrates, the *chakra* and the *lataif* in the Yoga and Sufi traditions, can be considered as techniques for inducing a state in the nervous system similar to that which may be transiently produced by external means.

The attempt in these two chapters has been to begin the process of extracting the psychological aspects of these Eastern meditative disciplines. No attempt has been made to provide an airtight case sealed by relevant experiments at each point. But we may begin most usefully by the simple process of translating the metaphors of the esoteric traditions into those of contemporary psychology and physiology, and noting the overlap.

3 / An Extended Concept
of Human Capacities

In this Chapter we shall shift our focus on the relation of concentrative meditation to other aspects of the esoteric disciplines. In accounts of the esoteric psychologies we read of "fantastic" examples of alteration in the activities of the "involuntary" nervous system. Yoga masters, for instance, are said to stop or at least to drastically lower their breathing rate and oxygen consumption, to stop blood flowing from a cut, to raise body heat even on cold nights high up in the mountains of Tibet.

We tend not to investigate these "fantastic" and at this point scientifically unstudied claims because they involve that portion of our nervous system which we generally consider to be beyond volition. The philosophical line of thought from Plato to Descartes has emphasized a split of human nature into two distinct parts, mind and body. The "mind," through reason, will, thought, has been interpreted as involving volition—consideration of an alternate course of action, movement of the skeletal muscles, etc. The "body" has been considered as an "automaton," going on about its processes, making adjustments automatically. If the name of a process is "autonomic," we obviously do not expect it to be subject to high-level control or alteration. These very terms given to the "lower" nervous systems—"autonomic," "involuntary," "vegetative"—have essentially ruled out inquiry into any possible conscious alteration. So, for instance, the claims of yogis seem so far beyond the realm of possibility, since they involve what we consider to be involuntary processes, that we do not even bother to investigate them.[1]

And yet there are strong indications that Western man's distinctions between voluntary and involuntary components of his constitution are not at all valid. There are other metaphors for considering concentrative meditation that may provide some insight into the relationship of the practices of meditation to the voluntary alteration of physiological processes.

Meditation has been described as a process of calming the ripples on a lake; when calm, the bottom, usually invisible, can be seen. In another metaphor meditation is likened to the night: stars cannot be seen during the day, their faint points of light overwhelmed by the brilliance of the sun. In this image, meditation is the process of "turning off" the overwhelming competing activity that is the light of the sun, until, late at night, the stars can be seen quite clearly. To one who is limited in his observation of the stars to the daytime the idea that many faint distinct points of light exist and can be seen is obvious nonsense.

That concentrative meditation involves a "turning off" of competing activity does seem quite clear. We recall in Anand's study of Yoga meditation that while in meditation the EEG of the yogins did not show any response to the external world. We also recall that the repetitive stimulation of the ganzfeld and the situation of the stabilized image lead to a state equivalent to that of no external stimulation at all. The repetitive form of meditation is a technique to turn off awareness of the external enviroment, to enter a state of "darkness" or "void," to turn off the bright light of the sun.

We are generally unaware of many of our internal physiological processes. Our attention is deployed outward, usually for good reasons, for the same reasons that we automatically respond to much of our external environment. It would be quite difficult to behave appropriately if we were continuously aware of every single internal process. We tune out these signals in favor of those impinging upon us from the external environment, which may require immediate action related to survival. Tuning out internal signals is presumably quite an easy process since the signals themselves are more or less constant, and we are quite capable of tuning out the much more irregular familiar signals of the external environment.

The Russian physiologist Bykov, who has extensively studied the relationship between the cerebral cortex (generally considered to process information about the external environment) and the subcortical structures (more involved in internal environment "introception"), makes a similar point: "Thanks to the active state of the cerebral cortex, there constantly arises a functional focus of adaptation which negatively induces the subcortex. As a result of this introception, impulses normally do not reach the sphere of our sensation, remaining presensory."[2]

To return to the daylight and star image, it may be that another function of the repetitive form of meditation is to turn off awareness of the external world, to produce a state of "darkness," to turn down the bright lights of day, this allowing the faint signals to enter into awareness. Our general view of the relationship between the voluntary processes (reason, concept formation, will) and the involuntary processes (emotion, digestion, blood pressure) may be based on a limited observation of the states of the nervous systems, somewhat like watching for the appearance of stars at noon only.

There is no doubt that the "higher" activities occupy our awareness and are under our control most of the time, and that the "autonomic" processes are almost never in awareness and under control. This does not, however, rule out the possibility of bringing the involuntary processes under self-regulation—by bringing the autonomic processes into awareness, making unconscious processes conscious. Perhaps the Yoga claim that what we call the autonomic or involuntary system is capable of alteration is not so "fantastic" after all. Careful physiological study of meditators may indicate the dimensions of mastery that we are capable of gaining over our nervous systems.

A review of the physiological studies on meditation and a review of the work of the Russians, especially Bykov, and of the recent, quite precise, and elegant work of Miller, DiCara, and associates, indicates that there is much more voluntary control over our involuntary activity than we had thought possible.

The "trick" discussed in Chapter 1 of controlling awareness by repetitive stimulation and by shutting off external awareness is a well-studied aspect of the control over our nervous system's activity. In the stabilized image situation and the ganzfeld, the appearance of alpha rhythm is found, and awareness of the external environment ceases. In Zen and in yogic meditation, researchers have found similar results: there is an increase in the alpha activity of the brain during meditation. Kas-matsu and Hirai's study on Zen meditation disclosed that the more advanced the practitioner, the more alpha was produced in the meditation exercise. As the meditation of more expert practitioners continued, the frequency of the alpha rhythm slowed down, its amplitude increased, and the alpha began to move from its customary focus in the occipital cortex to the central part of the brain and finally to the frontal area.

Perhaps the most extensive series of studies yet conducted on Zen meditation have been those of the Psychological Institute of Kiyushu University headed by Yoshiharu Akishige.[3] These studies, too, show that physiological changes occurring during Zen meditation include an increase in the alpha rhythm. They also indicate that it is the "mental attitude" of Zen meditation that correlates with the EEG changes and not the posture or the setting. When the subject assumed the posture of Zen without the "attitude," there was no rise in alpha activity. When the "attitude was set for Za-Zen," alpha rhythm appeared in both ordinary postures—sitting in a chair and in *Za-Zen*.

The series of investigations that Bykov and his co-workers began in Russia in 1924 provide evidence that the autonomic nervous system is only *relatively* autonomic and is subject to voluntary control if the situation is set up appropriately. Bykov and his associates used Pavlov's method of the conditioned response. A bell sounds, and this carries with it no special significance to a hungry dog; but if sounding the bell always precedes feeding, the dog will begin to salivate each time the bell sounds. This method of conditioning is often maligned within psychology, since it has led to many analyses of human behavior *exclusively* modeled on the process of conditioning. The unwarranted extension of this method should not, however, deter us from making use of the information available in studies about conditioning. Bykov's studies indicated that, if a process can be conditioned, then it is a modifiable process and, if autonomic processes can be conditioned, they are not really autonomic at all.[4]

Several investigators working in Bylov's laboratory demonstrated that many involuntary processes could be conditioned. Animals could slightly change the level of their body heat as well as the heat in their limbs by changing the blood flow to the limbs, and they could alter their heart rhythms, removing blocks in the electrocardiogram introduced by morphine. The pancreatic secretion could be altered, and the action of the kidneys—urine excretion—raised or lowered. The volume of the blood in the spleen could be changed, the secretion of bile altered, etc. These processes had been considered unalterable. After all, they were part of the "automaton," the body.

The work of the Russians clearly indicates that there is a far greater degree of modifiability of the heart, liver, spleen, kidneys, blood flow, etc. than we normally suppose. It also indicates that the division some have made between mind and body—mind as a process of reason and will and body as an automaton à la Descartes—is foolish and false. As Bykov and Gantt put it: "The gap between the two disconnected worlds of psyche and soma is being bridged."[5]

There are and have been other sources of evidence on this question. The original explorations of Freud and Breuer on hysteria point in the same direction. Their first, quite well-known case cites a woman whose hand was paralyzed. Her paralysis took the shape of a glove, which Freud considered "anatomical nonsense" since the muscles that would have been affected by a "real" paralysis did not stop at the line marked by the glove. Freud's insight was that this paralysis was under the voluntary, although in his terms "unconscious," control of the woman. From this woman's problem and from those of many other of Freud's patients, the concept of psychosomatic medicine was born—a discipline whose very name links the worlds of the mind and the body. Freud's theory was that the woman's paralysis could be cured by bringing this "unconscious control" into her awareness.

So far the work in the discipline of psychosomatic medicine has been limited to removal of misapplications of the latent power that we possess. But there is an important theoretical point for our consideration here. The fact that one can voluntarily bring about a hysterical paralysis in the shape of a glove makes it clear that one can achieve precise control of the blood flow and musculature in quite specific areas of the hand. The yogi's claim to controllability of blood flow and related matters seems much less fantastic. Since Yoga masters spend many years attending to these processes after meditating with the purpose of attempting to alter them, it seems reasonable that, in view of Bykov's work and that of psychosomatic medicine, these alterations can be accomplished.

Certainly the most sophisticated and the most theoretically relevant of recent research in voluntary alteration of physiological processes has been that of Neal Miller and Leo DiCara of Rockefeller University.[6] Their research has been designed explicitly to investigate the possibility that learning may take place in the autonomic nervous system without any involvement of the skeletal musculature. Bykov's work had been limited to classical (involuntary) conditioning, which learning theorists consider an inferior type of learning if compared with that subject to voluntary control (operant conditioning). Bykov's work, as he himself stated, was intended to show that the activity of the autonomic nervous system could always be modified by the central nervous system.

Miller and DiCara's work indicates that the alterations in blood flow, in the activity of internal organs, and with the glands, can be brought about on an operant basis through the type of learning that some psychologists consider to be somewhat "higher." Most important, their research demonstrates that learning can take place within the autonomic nervous system* without involvement of the voluntary skeletal musculature. In most cases, when we try to discover the possibilities of human self-regulation, these academic distinctions may not be very important. Most often it will be of no practical concern whether an action, such as slowing the heart rate, may be accomplished with the involvement of the skeletal muscles or without, but the distinctions are theoretically of great significance because they rule out any possible conception of an autonomic nervous system existing alone.

Miller, DiCara, and their associates studied experimental animals, rats for the most part, in which they could implant electrodes, thermistors, or photocells at specific sites in the stomach, kidney, parts of the cardiovascular system, and the brain. Information about the selected activity in these sites (say, in one instance, blood flow) was converted into electrical stimulation of "rewarding" areas of the brain. (Stimulation of certain areas of the

---

* It is almost impossible to rule out central nervous activity *completely* even in these quite careful experiments.

brain has been found to be a reward to most animals.) In order to increase the rate of the electrical brain stimulations the animals were required to alter an aspect of their "autonomic activity" —in this example, blood flow. Miller and DiCara eliminated the possibility of the involvement of the skeletal muscles in this "autonomic" learning by administering to the animals the drug curare, which selectively paralyzes the musculature and allows no central nervous system commands to reach the muscles.

With sensors implanted in specific sites to pick up the signal and information given to the brain in terms of direct brain reward, the animals could learn very easily to alter their blood flow, blood pressure, stomach blood flow, kidney functioning, and the electrical activity of their brain. Miller and DiCara required that differential control over each process be demonstrated—for instance, the raising and lowering of blood flow, the altering of the kidney functions, etc. It would seem that once the information is available to consciousness and the signals can be perceived, many involuntary processes are quite modifiable. The processes controlled can be surprisingly specific. In one experiment sensors were implanted in both ears of a rat and reward was given only when there was a difference in the blood flow of one ear as compared with the other. The rat could not, in this instance, produce the desired results by altering a *general* process, such as an increase in blood flow or an alteration in heart rate. The rat learned to control its blood flow to each ear *differentially*, raising it in one and then in the other.

Another result of the studies of Miller and Dicara relates directly to the aspect of meditation as a process of turning off competing activity, or, in the words of the metaphor, turning off the light of day. When Miller first administered curare to his animals he feared it might slow down their rate of learning to control physiological processes. The reverse turned out to be true. The animals that were paralyzed by curare could learn much more quickly to alter their heart rate, blood flow, kidney functions, etc. Recall that curare is a drug that halts all ordinary movements and the proprioceptive impulses that would normally enter awareness. It may be, then, that curare in these experimental animals performed a function similar to that of meditation in people. Both are means of reducing irrelevant activity, and both may make the detection of faint signals much more easy.

There is perhaps a way in which our sophisticated technology can help many in our culture to alter voluntarily their nervous system's activity without undertaking a pilgrimage to India. We believe that the practice of meditation turns off irrelevant activity so that faint signals can enter awareness. We may also look at this operation as making conscious unconscious processes. It may be that the old distinctions between mind and body were drawn on the basis of a mere inability to attend to the relevant information.

Keeping our sunlight and stars image in mind, let us consider how we might use technology to amplify the faint signals *themselves* so that they could be "seen" even in the daytime. If we study meditation physiologically, we can obtain an idea of the limits of voluntary alteration that humans can achieve. Once we decide that it seems desirable to alter a certain process in humans, we can attempt to bring this dimension into awareness through amplification and determine whether it is alterable voluntarily.

For example, one effect of meditation on brain activity is that the alpha rhythm of the EEG is increased. One could build a machine to detect the alpha rhythm and to signal us when we produce it. Such a machine would bring the faint signal (the alpha rhythm) into awareness through a circuitous route. The faint signal would be detected on the top of the skull; the amplified and filtered signal could be converted into a tone, which could then bring the information into awareness. With amplification of faint signals we can be made aware of the periods in which we are producing the alpha rhythm. And since alpha is associated with progress in meditation, this may be a way of receiving information about one of the physiological changes brought about by meditation.

Joe Kamiya of the Langley Porter Neuropsychiatric Institute in San Francisco has shown, with a system that converts the alpha rhythm into sound, that ordinary people can learn quite quickly to alter their brain waves in order to enhance or suppress their alpha rhythm at will.[7] A similar finding has been reported in animals by Miller and by Sterman.[8] These investigators rewarded their animals when they were producing high voltage, low frequency EEG's, similar perhaps to the human alpha, and found that augmentation of the alpha rhythm could be learned. The animals became quiescent and relaxed. Miller reports that the cats sat like sphinxes.

Those who have tried alpha training themselves report a relaxed yet somewhat alert state with attention directed more inward than usual. Subjects in experiments conducted by Nowlis, MacDonald, Kamiya, and my own study in Kamiya's laboratory, tend to describe the state as more "dark," "back in the head," "relaxed," "floating" (compared with non-alpha), all terms that sound somewhat similar to the state of meditation.[9]

Learning to alter the alpha rhythm of the brain seems surprisingly easy. All sixteen of Nowlis's and Kamiya's subjects were able to show some voluntary alteration of their alpha rhythm within fifteen minutes, and twenty-eight of thirty-two of Nowlis's and McDonald's subjects within only seven minutes. My own study has yielded less striking results—eight of eleven were able to learn a significant differential control in eight hours. The process of physiological feedback, as this training is usually termed, consists of creating a connection that did not exist before, amplifying faint signals that are present in the nervous system and bringing them into awareness. Following Kamiya's lead, Joseph Hart of the University of California at Irvine, Charles Tart of the University of California at Davis, B. Brown, and many others have confirmed and extended the work on the voluntary alteration of the brain's electrical activity. Other aspects of the EEG—the beta and theta activity—can also be altered. Once the relevant information is brought into consciousness by technological means, once the stars are made bright, it seems quite easy for us to learn to modify this activity of our brain.*

Out of the increased interest in human consciousness during the past few years a new group of investigators have coalesced around the techniques of physiological feedback. The group consists of psychologists, physiologists, physicists, computer scientists, and many others who joined to form the Bio-feedback Society. Their main purpose is to explore the implications of our "new" (old to those of the older meditation traditions) view of our nervous systems, to determine the range of physiological processes that can be voluntarily altered, and to find the most efficient methods of training these alterations, including different varieties of feedback, hypnosis, meditation, etc. Their hope is to bring this extended and more Eastern view of our capabilities into the culture at large. Our technology has been mostly concerned with more and more efficient manipulation of the external environment. That we have been remarkably successful in the past hun-

---

* Two notes on physiological feedback training:

1. In a sense, the process of physiological feedback can be compared to the use of a bathroom scale, itself a feedback device. If one tries to lose weight, it may not be clear visually whether one is doing the correct thing. It is hard to look at oneself in a mirror and tell whether one weighs 200 or 199 pounds. But the scale can give a more precise indication. If the weight was 200 pounds and is now 199, one should continue doing the same thing and the weight will continue to decrease. In the same way the tone and the scores of physiological feedback devices provide a sensitive indication of quite small alterations, which can be continued and summed up to produce greater changes in physiological processes—*e.g.*, "shaping the behavior."

2. Within psychology the relations between mind and brain have been a major problem. One primary difficulty has been that observations on the physiological end have been restricted to naturally occurring combinations of activity. If we obtain some experimental control over the system at a high level (such as training a specific brain state), we might be able to determine more clearly the relationships between physiology and conscious experience.

dred years is beyond doubt. Many of the problems that once plagued man have been solved. Only political considerations, for instance, stop us from feeding and clothing the entire world. We have, however, neglected to turn our technological sophistication inward. We have in general ignored the possibilities of voluntary alteration, which lie within. Our view of our capabilities is now changed largely because of the influence of the disciplines of meditation and the recent quite precise work within science. With this new view of our nervous system we can explore the dimensions of self-regulation that have been the province of a few working in the esoteric traditions, which have not neglected (or forgotten) the possibilities that lie within each of us.

As we have seen, then, our heart's activity can be brought under control; experimental animals can do this, yogis report the ability to do this, and so could ordinary people if they were provided with the proper information. Elmer Green of the Menninger Foundation has presented preliminary data on a yogin who can quite dramatically accelerate or decelerate his heart rate as well as alter his skin temperature.[10] Bernard Engel of the National Institutes of Mental Health has been the first to show that heart rate can be altered voluntarily in normal subjects. He has been able to treat cardiac arrhythmia by the feedback method. Cardiac arrhythmia is a condition in which, as the name implies, the heart beats irregularly. If the patient can simply listen to the irregularity, he can often voluntarily make the heart beat more regularly.[11] David Shapiro and his associates at Harvard University have shown that humans, as well as rats, can alter their blood pressure, given the proper information.[12] If those with high blood pressure could learn to lower it at will, we would have a tremendous reduction in heart disease.

Similarly, Green has shown that a yogi can dramatically alter the temperature in his hand—raising the temperature in one spot while lowering that of another spot a few inches away, producing a separation of $11°$ F quite quickly.[13] When normal subjects are given information on skin temperature, similar, though not so dramatic, control is possible. (Comparing this with physiological feedback training, if one were to claim control over heart rate, for instance, and demonstrate a rise in heart rate by running up and down a flight of stairs, few would be interested. To take a less extreme example, if one were to speed up heart rate by imagining a stressful situation, or by producing anger, this too would not be of great import.) But what seems to occur is a more *direct* kind of learning—learning to alter the heart rate as one learns to flex a muscle—without mediation.*[14]

The proper kind of physiological feedback training, if the discipline develops the appropriate range of techniques, could simply be prescribed as a drug is today. The advantages are obvious. "Psychologically," the patient would feel that he himself is actively participating in his own improvement. If the patient learns to alter voluntarily the process giving him trouble, then he can, under the doctor's guidance, keep his condition within tolerable limits, and drugs might not be needed. The advantage of physiological feedback as a therapeutic tool as compared with drugs is obvious. Drugs often do the job that is needed, but their effects persist far longer than necessary, and they often have unwanted side-effects as well. The major alterations brought about by feedback would cease when the training period was terminated and side-effects would be minimized. We should not think, however, that physiological feedback training will be without *some* aftereffects. If any process of the nervous system is altered, there are bound to be compensatory alterations in other processes. The alterations caused by feedback training, though, are likely to be less severe than those caused by drugs. This training would be much more preferable to drugs if it were found that substantial alterations in brain and cardiovascular and muscular activity could be permanently learned.

* Subjects in Engel's experiments have reported these experiences.

We know little about feedback training at present. The limits of our voluntary alteration, as well as the aftereffects, are still items for speculation and for further empirical research. However, we do know that, in addition to the brain and heart rate, the galvanic skin response, the muscular tension of certain groups, (the frontalis muscles on the forehead) and the skin temperature are alterable in people. Stoyva and Budzynski at the University of Colorado Medical Center have been investigating the possibility of "deconditioning" or " desensitizing" by feedback. In behavioral psychotherapy, many psychological problems—such as phobias, headaches, and anxiety—are thought of simply as faulty learning.[15] According to this view, a person is simply responding in an inappropriate manner, becoming anxious and increasing muscle tension in a situation that does not call for it. The therapy consists in training a person to relax, instead of tensing, in response to the "threatening" stimulus. Stoyva and Budzynski have used the electromyogram (EMG), which measures muscular tension level, as an indication of relaxation in response to previously threatening stimuli. Their preliminary findings indicate that the process of learning to relax in a situation that previously had elicited anxiety can be greatly speeded up by the use of physiological feedback techniques. If a person can "hear" his own muscle tension and his brain's electrical activity, he can monitor them continuously and keep them more precisely in the desired state. These examples built around current research are an exciting and useful development of science's new view of the nervous system. The focus is still traditional—on removing misapplication of control or correcting problems, functional or organic.

We might also briefly consider some possibilities, more in line with the aims of the disciplines of meditation, of extending the "normal" capacities of man. The implications of the voluntary alteration of physiological processes may lead to an extended conception of the function of education. We might be able, for instance, to learn more precise control over the deployment of our attention. First, simply and obviously, the great increase in the number of students, in larger and larger classes, means less and less individual attention for each student. Computer-assisted instruction is held to be the answer to this problem, but this technique does not take the individual much into account, save perhaps to remember the pace and level of each student. The application of computing machines to teaching has primarily been directed toward the development of very fast capable drill and practice machines. This type of instruction has never tried to take the "state" of the learner into account. While reading, for instance, we have all experienced those times when our attention lapsed and we were "looking" at the pages and nothing was registering in our awareness. At other times we may have been too tense or too preoccupied to "pay attention" to what was presented to us. Physiological feedback training may be of aid here. Suppose that research could delineate certain physiological processes that are associated with, say, efficient verbal information processing. We would then connect the student's nervous system as well as his hands and eyes to the computer teacher, which would make the presentation only if and when the student produces an appropriate pattern of physiological activity. So, in order to see the text, the student would necessarily need to be in a state in which he could read efficiently. If his attention lapsed (and if we could find a pattern of activity that correlated with this) the material would disappear and the student would be made aware immediately that he needed to change his state.

We do not really know at this point whether it is actually possible to determine patterns of physiological activity which unequivocally indicate efficient attention and memory, but this general aim is certainly worth investigating. We have little firm evidence to go on as yet, save the obvious step of working with students who are motivated to learn but who are so tense that they cannot. These students might be trained to produce low levels of muscular tension before they can see the information presented. Allowing a computer-tutor to monitor the physiology of the learner could be one of the possible solutions, and an extremely valuable one to the existing problem of overcrowded schools. It may be possible to train different modes of conceptualization—verbal, logical, spatial, etc.—based on different patterns of brain activity, perhaps taking the brain's lateralization of function into account. The larger import of the newer view of our voluntary capabilities is that the definition of education itself may be broadened. Our teaching is currently limited to the intellectual verbal skills. But if there were objective, easily monitorable, physiological feedback devices generally available, we could include as part of everyone's basic learning experience a training of the ability voluntarily to alter one's own physiological state. We might then learn to relax, to alter our heart's activity, our muscles, and our brains at will. We could, if we wished, alter our awareness, shut it down for a period. The capacities that the meditative disciplines have held to lie within ourselves could become available to many of us.

If the work proceeds at a reasonable rate, this type of training could become a part of every schoolchild's education. He could learn to alter his own physiology as he now learns to manipulate the external environment and receive external information. It is also possible that children who learn at a young age how to alter voluntarily their physiological processes may develop a greater capacity for it than those who learn it at a later age.

These possibilities are still quite remote. All that is known at this moment is that the capacity for voluntary alteration exists and can be exercised using feedback. There is little current knowledge about the long-term effects of this training—whether the physiological definitions of a state of awareness can be consistent enough for enough people to make the techniques useful, and whether the training procedures themselves can have significant long-term effects on the individual. It is far from clear that any of the techniques we discussed before—lowering blood pressure, slowing heart rate, altering the gastrointestinal reactions—can actually be applied in therapeutic situations. But it is known for the first time within the scientific community that such therapy may be feasible. And we have, for the first time, developed technological means to make this type of training possible. It should be worth the effort to discover the potential usefulness of these techniques.

To conclude briefly, "forgotten" esoteric disciplines are rich sources of information for contemporary psychology, and a new and extended view of the human capacity is emerging from the blend of contemporary and older psychologies.

Theoretically these older psychologies were the precursors of the modern analyses of the interactive nature of awareness. They also offer alternative conceptual models for human behavior (cf. Gurdjieff's division of man into several "centers"—motion, intellectual, emotional, and the "higher" ones).[16] Their centuries-old non-dualistic approach to mind and body has only recently been accepted by science. They describe an extended set of variables that affect human behavior, which generally are not investigated as part of modern science. These psychologies also offer techniques for altering awareness and the "involuntary" aspects of nervous and glandular activity, which Western science has for a long time ignored. The study of accomplished practitioners of these disciplines may yield a glimpse of the scope of the mastery that may be achieved over these processes.

For the future, once the rich vein has been opened, three major lines of research remain to be fully explored.

1. In the scientific study of meditation and other techniques of the esoteric psychologies, the physiological data gathered so far are quite scanty and the brain changes have been reported in very general terms by individual investigators. We do not know, at this point, how consistent the changes in alpha rhythm are within a session of meditation and across subjects. To say that meditation is "high alpha" is like saying that someone is in New

York City. Some information is conveyed, but a large number of questions remain unanswered. We do not know how continuous the alpha is in meditation, or whether there are differences between persons with different EEG's as they practice meditation. Now that computer analysis of EEG signals is possible, we may be able to approach the problem from a quantitative angle. Subtle differences between the patterns of Zen and Yoga meditators may be described and quantified. If people are to be trained to match the EEG patterns of meditators, more quantitative assessments of these patterns are needed.

Studies need be done on the long-term effects of meditation, on metabolism, on sleep cycles, and on patterns of daily activity. Many of the associated exercises of these disciplines should be investigated physiologically. So far there have been only a few studies on the physiological effects of the Yoga breathing exercises and the asanas. Behannon reports that some subjects show increased oxygen consumption in certain exercises, but again, as in the case of brain activity, more modern techniques may allow a quantitative look at basal metabolic rate, carbon dioxide output, and oxygen consumption. One interesting line of investigation may be that of breathing techniques that may differentially innervate each hemisphere of the brain. One Yoga exercise involves breathing in and out of one nostril or the other. Since the olfactory nerve enters directly and bilaterally into the brain, this technique may have its effects on separate halves of the brain.* In split-brain patients, Sperry has shown differential effects to the hemispheres of olfactory stimulation, and some of the Yoga breath manipulations may be regarded as attempts to stimulate asymmetrical activity of the brain.

As mentioned in the previous chapter, our knowledge of the effects on awareness of the meditation exercises is still imprecise. Some studies of information-processing during and after medita-

---

* This research in progress is primarily that of David Galin of LPNI, with me as a sounding-board and spear carrier.

tion exercises would be of great interest, and so would studies of the effects of the recent increase of interest in meditation in Western culture. Thus we might be able to determine the type of person likely to adopt meditation and the type of person likely to benefit from it. One possible "use" of meditation may be in the "treatment" of drug abuse. Many of the conventional therapies do not take into account that a reason for the use of drugs is in many the search for extended experiences, and the substitutes for the drug experiences are often turned down as uninteresting by the addict. The practice of meditation may be an effective substitute, since it involves a discipline that strives for altered experiences and does not have the harmful aftereffects of drugs. Benson, for instance, proposes a similar idea, and a project of the University of California at Berkeley, headed by Dr. William Soskin, is working along these lines.[17]

The Sufis make use of healing techniques that have not yet been investigated by scientific methods, if they are indeed approachable by science.[18] Studies of these kinds of techniques may yield an extended view of the potential of certain medical therapies.

2. In this chapter we've discussed at length physiological feedback. It is a blend of an older conception of the capabilities of man and of technical innovations to allow some of these capabilities to be exercised quickly by many within our own culture, and perhaps to speed up training in these "ineffable" non-verbal learning situations. Feedback training draws on the older traditions of meditation as well as on the rich literature of autogenic training and hypnosis. Further research will determine the most efficient methods of training in self-regulation, the suitability of different training procedures for different individuals, and their most useful application to therapy, education, and the culture at large.

3. The older traditions hold that man is subject to influences from sources other than those which are usually considered within

science at present. But there are sketchy indications within science that are beginning to show man's sensitivity to other orders of variables. The rotation of the earth and of other celestial bodies has influence on physiological processes (usually called "biological clocks") in animals and in man.[19] Electromagnetic energy in the visible spectrum has been found in the brain of mammals.[20] The ionization of the air has effect on the ciliary action and is reported to affect sinus activity and healing.[21] Perhaps it might be profitable to devote serious attention to these sources of stimulation (and others, such as radioactivity and earth magnetic field) and their effects on human physiology and behavior.

A Closing Note

Man's search for knowledge about himself has been carried out in two modes, the empirical-experiental in the East, and the empirical-experimental in the West. For the first time a blend of the two great traditions of human inquiry may be possible. Some of the new techniques may enable the latent capacities of man to be developed more efficiently and by many more people in the two worlds.

We should note, however, that Western science, as yet, has little or no understanding of the conditions under which these capacities are to be exercised. The techniques and experiments discussed in this book merely serve to modify and—hopefully—to extend our idea of the limits of the capacities of man. Beyond these lie much more radical possibilities, which these traditions also hold to exist—on the physical or non-physical nature of consciousness, on the possibility of "extra," "quasi," or "neo" sensory perception, for example. These capacities are held to be an integral part of an entire body of knowledge (or elements of a higher technology). Many of the writers of the esoteric traditions stress that the use of these capacities must be restricted to the proper time and place. Perhaps these matters should first be explored with those of the traditions themselves in order to gain the particular kind of knowledge that would enable us to put the techniques and methods of science to more efficient use.

Notes

PART I

INTRODUCTION

1. For my discussion of this point, see *The One Quest* (to be published).
2. I have done this to some extent in the article "Contributions of Gestalt Therapy," in *Ways of Growth* (New York: The Viking Press, 1969).

CHAPTER 1.

1. Richard of St. Victor, *De Gratia Contemplationis seu Benjamin Major*, I, 3, in *Selected Writings on Contemplation*, tr. Claire Kirchberger (London: 1957).
2. Philip Kapleau, ed., *The Three Pillars of Zen: Teaching, Practice and Enlightenment* (Boston: Beacon Press, 1965).

CHAPTER 2.

1. Ramana Maharshi, *Collected Works*, ed. Arthur Osborne (London: Rider & Co., 1959).
2. Quoted in Wilhelm Fraenger, *The Millennium of Hieronymus*

Bosch: Outlines of a New Interpretation, trs. Eithne Wilkins and Ernst Kaiser (Chicago: University of Chicago Press, 1951).

3. Paul Reps, ed., *Zen Flesh, Zen Bones: A Collection of Zen and Pre-Zen Writings* (New York: Doubleday & Co., 1961).

4. Thomas Merton, *The Way of Chuang Tzu* (New York: New Directions, 1965).

5. *Ibid.*

6. Swami Prabhavananda and Christopher Isherwood, trs., *The Song of God, Bhagavad-Gita*, with an introduction by Aldous Huxley (Hollywood: Marcel Rodd Co., 1944).

7. *Ibid.*

8. Dante, *The Divine Comedy, Paradiso*, XXXIII, 143-45, tr. Dorothy L. Sayers.

9. Douglas E. Harding, *The Hierarchy of Heaven and Earth: A New Diagram of Man in the Universe* (New York: Harper & Brothers, 1957).

10. Arthur J. Arberry, *Tales from the Masnavi*, Unesco Collection of Representative Works: Persian Series (London: George Allen & Unwin, 1961.

11. Idries Shah, *Tales of the Dervishes: Teaching Stories of the Sufi Masters over the Past Thousand Years* (London: Jonathan Cape, 1967).

12. Anagarika Govinda, *Foundations of Tibetan Mysticism* (London: Rider & Co., 1969).

13. Farid al-din Attar, *The Conference of the Birds: A Sufi Allegory Being an Abridged Version of Farid-uddin Attar's Mantiq-ut-Tayr*, tr. R. P. Masani (London: H. Milford, 1924).

14. Quoted in Karlfried Graf von Durkheim, *The Japanese Cult of Tranquility* (London: Rider & Co., 1960). This passage echoes the same idea in a very different language.

15. Quoted in Evelyn Underhill, *Practical Mysticism* (London: Jonathan Cape, 1914).

16. Ajit Mookerjee, *Tantra Art: Its Philosophy and Physics* (New Dehli: Ravi Kumar, 1966).

17. Aleister Crowley, *Magick in Theory and Practice by the Master Therion (Aleister Crowley)* (New York: Castle Books, 1960).

18. Daisetz T. Suzuki, Erich Fromm, and R. de Martino, *Zen Buddhism and Psychoanalysis* (New York: Grove Press, 1963).

19. John Heider (Ph.D. diss., Duke University, 1968).
20. Arthur Deikman, "Deautomatization of the Mystic Experience," *Psychiatry* 29 (1966): 324-38.
21. Daisetz T. Suzuki, *The Training of the Buddhist Zen Monk* (Kyoto: The Eastern Buddhist Society, 1934).
22. Isshu Miura and Ruth Fuller Sasaki, *The Zen Koan* (New York: Harcourt, Brace & World, 1965).
23. Daisetz T. Suzuki, *The Field of Zen*, ed. Christmas Humphreys (London, The Buddhist Society, 1969).
24. Idries Shah, *The Sufis* (Garden City, N.Y.: Doubleday & Co., 1964).
25. R. Simac, "In a Naqshbandi Circle," *New Research on Current Philosophical Systems* (New York: Octagon Books, 1968).
26. Martin Lings, *A Moslem Saint of the Twentieth Century* (London: George Allen & Unwin, 1961).
27. Cyprian Rice, *The Persian Sufis* (London: George Allen & Unwin, 1964).
28. *Ibid.*
29. Israel Regardie, *The Tree of Life: A Study in Magic* (New York: Samuel Weiser, 1969).
30. *Ibid.*
31. Quoted in David Krech, Richard S. Crutchfield, and Norman Livson, *Elements of Psychology* (New York: Alfred A. Knopf, 1969).
32. Quoted in Regardie, *op. cit.*
33. Shah, *supra*, note 24.
34. *Writings from Philokalia, on the Prayer of The Heart*, trs. E. Kadloubovsky and G. E. H. Palmer (London: Faber & Faber, 1951).
35. *Ibid.*
36. Durkheim, *op. cit.*
37. William H. Sheldon, *The Varieties of Temperament: A Psychology of Constitutional Differences* (New York: Hafner, 1969).
38. Govinda, *op. cit.*
39. *Ibid.*
40. Erwin Rousselle, "Spiritual Guidance in Contemporary Taoism," *Papers from the Eranos Yearbooks: Spiritual Disciplines*, Bollingen Series XXX No. 4 (New York: Pantheon Books, 1960).

41. Govinda, *op. cit.*
42. *Ibid.*
43. *Ibid.*
44. Edward Conze, *Buddhist Meditation*, Ethical and Religious Classics of East and West, No. 13 (London: George Allen & Unwin, 1956).
45. *Ibid.*
46. *Ibid.*
47. Mircea Eliade, ed., *From Primitives to Zen: A Thematic Sourcebook in the History of Religions* (New York: Harper & Row, 1967).
48. Rouselle, *op. cit.*
49. Dante, *op. cit., Inferno*, I, 16-18.
50. Regardie, *op. cit.*
51. Shah, *supra*, note 11.
52. Friedrich Heiler, "Contemplation in Christian Mysticism," *Papers from the Eranos Yearbooks: Spiritual Disciplines*, Bollingen Series XXX No. 4 (New York: Pantheon Books, 1960).

CHAPTER 3.

1. I. K. Taimni, *The Science of Yoga* (Adyara, Madras: Theosophical Publishing House, 1965).
2. In Trevor P. Legget, *The Tiger's Cave* (London: Rider & Co.).
3. Friedrich W. Nietzche, *Thus Spoke Zarathustra* (Chicago: Henry Regnery Co., 1957).
4. Gama Chen Chi Chang, *The Practice of Zen* (New York: Harper & Brothers, 1959).
5. Shrinyu Suzuki Roshi, a lecture in *Wind-Bell*, Vol. V, No. 3 (1966).
6. Suzuki, *loc. cit.*, Vol. VII, No. 3-4 (1968).
7. Perhaps the best exposition of this is by Sayadow's disciple, Nyaponika Thera, *The Heart of Buddhist Meditation* (London: Rider & Co., 1969). Other good sources are Mahasi Sayadaw, *The Progress of Insight* (Kandy, Ceylon: Buddhist Publishing Society); and Nanomoly Thera, *Mindfulness of Breathing* (Kandy, Ceylon: Buddhist Publishing Society, 1964).
8. Nyaponika Thera, *op. cit.*

9. *Ibid.*
10. The interested reader may find more of its rationale and application in Claudio Naranjo, *The Attitude and Practice of Gestalt Therapy* (to be published by Science and Behavior Books); and in Joen Fagan and Irura L. Sheperd, eds., *Gestalt Therapy Now* (Palo Alto, Calif.: Science and Behavior Books, 1969).

CHAPTER 4.

1. Haridas Chaudhuri, *The Philosophy of Meditation* (New York: Philosophical Library, 1965).
2. Chang, *op. cit.*
3. Kapleau, *op. cit.*
4. Quoted *ibid.*
5. Mircea Eliade, *op. cit.*
6. Quoted *ibid.*
7. Quoted in *Encyclopedia of Religion and Ethics*, ed. James Hastings, *s.v.* "Possession" (New York: Charles Scribner's Sons, 1908-1927).
8. Carl T. Jung and C. Kerenyi, *Essays on a Science of Mythology*, rev. ed. (Princeton: Princeton University Press, 1963).
9. Andreas Lommel, *Shamanism: The Beginning of Art* (New York: McGraw-Hill, 1967).
10. Shah, *Tales of the Dervishes.*
11. Julian Silverman, "Shamanism and Acute Schizophrenia," manuscript in preparation.
12. See Aubin, *Cruel Effets de la Vengeance du Cardinal Richelieu, ou Histoire des Diables de Loudun* (Amsterdam: 1716), quoted in T. K. Oesterreich, *Possession, Demoniacal & Other, Among Primitive Races in Antiquity, the Middle Ages, and Modern Times* (New Hyde Park, N.Y.: University Books, 1966).
13. Mentioned in *Trance and Possession States*, ed. R. Prince (R. M. Burke Memorial Society).
14. Henry Corbin, *Creative Imagination in the Sufism of Ibn" Arabi*, tr. R. Manheim (Princeton: Princeton University Press, 1969).
15. See my discussion of this point in *The One Quest*, Chapter IV: "The Question of Identity."
16. References to the techniques are widely scattered through Jung's

work. The interested reader might consult the thematic indexes to Jung's work.

17. Robert Desoille, *The Directed Daydream*, tr. Frank Haronian, P.R.F. Issue No. 18 (New York: Psychosynthesis Research Foundation, 1966). This was a series of lectures delivered by Desoille at the Sorbonne and published originally in the Bulletin of La Société des Recherches Psychothérapiques de Langue Française (1965).

18. Claudio Naranjo, "Psychotherapeutic Possibilities of Fantasy-Enhancing Drugs," manuscript in preparation.

19. Harold A. Abramson, ed., *International Conference on the Use of LSD in Psychotherapy and Alcoholism* (Indianapolis: Bobbs-Merrill Co., 1966).

20. Alan Watts, *Psychotherapy East and West* (New York: Pantheon Books, 1961). Watts has devoted his book to the parallels between the modern and traditional ways of liberation.

21. Idries Shah, *The Way of the Sufi* (London: Jonathan Cape, 1968).

22. Anita M. Muhl, *Automatic Writing* (New York: Garrett Press, 1964).

23. The essay appeared in the 1910 volume of *Annalem der Naturphilosophie* and was published as a book in 1912.

24. Heinrich Zimmer, "On the Significance of the Indian Tantric Yoga," *Papers from the Eranos Yearbooks: Spiritual Disciplines*, Bollingen Series XXX No. 4 (New York: Pantheon Books, 1960).

25. Quoted in Oesterreich, *supra*, note 12.

26. *Ibid.*

27. Zimmer, *op. cit.*

28. Signe Tokskvig, *Swedenborg, Scientist and Mystic* (New Haven: Yale University Press, 1948).

29. *Ibid.*

30. *Ibid.*

PART II

1. The quotation on p. 136: Roger Sperry, "A Revised Concept of Consciousness," *Psychological Review*, 76 (1969): 532-36.

INTRODUCTION

1. This quotation and several others of interest are contained in an article by Lawrence Le Shan, "Physicists and Mysticism: Similarities in World View," *Journal of Transpersonal Psychology*, Fall 1969.
2. Idries Shah, *The Way of the Sufi* (London: Jonathan Cape, 1968).

CHAPTER 1.

1. Philip Kapleau, ed., *The Three Pillars of Zen: Teaching, Practice and Enlightenment* (Boston: Beacon Press, 1965).
2. Walpola Rahula, *What the Buddha Taught* (New York: Grove Press, 1959).
3. Quoted in Kapleau, *op. cit.*
4. B. Anand, G. Chhina, and B. Singh, "Some Aspects of Electroencephalographic Studies in Yogis," *Electroencephalography and Clinical Neurophysiology*, 13 (1961): 452-456. Reprinted in C. Tart, *Altered States of Consciousness* (New York: John Wiley & Sons, 1969).
5. Rammamurti Mishra, *Fundamentals of Yoga* (New York: Julian Press, 1959).
6. *Ibid.*
7. Frederick Spiegelberg, *Spiritual Practices of India* (New York: Citadel Press, 1962).
8. Ajit Mookerjee, *Tantra Art: Its Philosophy and Physics* (New Delhi: Ravi Kumar; 1966).
9. P. D. Ouspensky, *In Search of the Miraculous* (New York: Harcourt, Brace & World, 1949).
10. Roy W. Davidson, *Documents on Contemporary Dervish Communities* (London: Hoopoe Ltd., 1966). The address of the publisher is: 12 Baker Street, London W1.
11. Idries Shah, *Oriental Magic* (London: Octagon Press, 1968).
12. T. Pauwels, *Gurdjieff* (London: Times Press, 1964).
13. See Idries Shah, *The Exploits of the Incomparable Mulla Nasrudin* (New York: Simon & Schuster, 1966).
14. Arthur Deikman, "Deautomatization and the Mystic Experience," *Psychiatry*, 29 (1966): 324-38. Reprinted in Tart, *supra* note 4.

15. See Idries Shah, *The Sufis* (Garden City, N.Y.: Doubleday & Co., 1964).

16. Vladimir Lindenberg, *Meditation and Mankind* (London: Rider & Co., 1959).

17. Cf. Idries Shah, *Caravan of Dreams* (London: Octagon Press, 1968). See the Introduction to "The Magic Horse."

18. R. M. Pritchard, "Stabilized Images on the Retina," *Scientific American*, June 1961.

19. D. Lehmann, G. W. Beeler, and D. H. Fender, "EEG Responses During the Observation of Stabilized and Normal Retinal Images," *Electroencephalography and Clinical Neurophysiology*, 22 (1967): 136-42.

20. W. Cohn, "Spatial and Textural Characteristics of the Ganzfeld," *American Journal of Psychology*, 70 (1957): 403-410; W. Cohen and T. C. Cadwallader, "Cessation of Visual Experience under Prolonged Uniform Visual Stimulation," *American Psychologist*, 13 (1958): 410 (abstract).

21. J. E. Hochberg, W. Triebel, and G. Seaman, "Color Adaptation under Conditions of Homogeneous Visual Stimulation (Ganzfeld)," *Journal of Experimental Psychology*, 41 (1951): 153-59.

22. D. T. Tepas, "The Electrophysiological Correlates of Vision in a Uniform Field," M. A. Whitcomb, ed., *Visual Problems of the Armed Forces* (Washington: National Academy of Science, National Research Council, 1962), pp. 21-25.

23. B. Bagchi and M. Wenger, "Electrophysiological Correlates on Some Yogi Exercises," *Electroencephalography and Clinical Neurophysiology*, Suppl. No. 7 (1957): 132-49.

24. Anand, Chhina, and Singh, *op. cit.* Also their "Studies on Shri Ramanada Yogi during His Stay in an Airtight Box," *Indian Journal of Medical Research*, 49 (1961): 82-89.

25. A. Kasamatsu and T. Hirai, "An Electroencephalographic Study Zen Meditation (Za-Zen)," *Folia Psychiatria et Neurologia Japonica*, 20 (1966): 315-36. Reprinted in Tart, *supra*, note 4.

26. Yoshiharu Akishige, *Psychological Studies on Zen*, Bulletin of the Faculty of Literature of Kyushu University, Japan, No. V (1968). Dr. Akishige can be written to c/o The Zen Institute, Komazawa University, Komazawa 1, Setagaya-Ku, Tokyo, Japan.

27. Quoted in Deikman, *op. cit.*
28. *See* Arthur Koestler, *The Lotus and the Robot* (New York: Harper & Row, 1960).
29. A. Dalal and T. Barber, "Yoga, Yoga Feasts, and Hypnosis in the Light of Empirical Research," *American Journal of Clinical Hypnosis,* 11 (1969): 155-66.

CHAPTER 2.

1. Aldous Huxley, *The Doors of Perception and Heaven and Hell* (New York: Harper & Row, 1954).
2. J. Y. Lettvin, H. R. Maturana, W. S. McCulloch, and W. H. Pitts, "What the Frog's Eye Tells the Frog's Brain," *Proceedings of the Institute of Radio Engineers,* 47 (1959): 1940-51.
3. Jerome Bruner, "On Perceptual Readiness," *Psychological Review,* 64 (1957): 123-52.
4. Karl H. Pribram, "The Neurophysiology of Remembering," *Scientific American,* January 1969, pp. 73-86.
5. Charles Furst, "Automatization of Visual Attention," *Perception and Psychophysics* (1971).
6. For a development of this idea, see Y. N. Sokolov, *Perception and the Conditioned Reflex* (London: Pergamon, 1960).
7. Bruner, *op. cit.*
8. See Walter Mischel, *Personality & Assessment* (New York: John Wiley & Sons, 1968).
9. Bruner, *op. cit.*
10. *Ibid.*
11. W. H. Ittleson and F. P. Kilpatrick, "Experiments in Perception," *Scientific American,* August 1951.
12. George Kelly, *The Psychology of Personal Constructs,* Vols. 1 and 2 (New York: Norton, 1955).
13. Robert E. Ornstein, *On the Experience of Time* (New York: Penguin Books, 1969).
14. E. K. Sadalla, (Ph.D. diss., Stanford University, 1970).
15. D. N. Spinelli and K. H. Pribram, "Changes in Visual Recovery Functions and Unit Activity Produced by Frontal and Temporal

Cortex Stimulation," *Electroencephalography and Clinical Neurophysiology*, 22 (1967): 143-49.

16. Roger W. Sperry, "Neurology and the Mind-Brain Problem," *American Scientist*, 40 (1951): 291-312.

17. W. Penfield and L. Roberts, *Speech and Brain Mechanism* (Princeton University Press, 1959).

18. For current psychology's most sophisticated account on the "constructive" nature of awareness, see Ulric Neisser, *Cognitive Psychology* (New York: Appleton-Century-Crofts, 1967).

19. William James, *The Principles of Psychology* (New York: Dover Publications, 1950).

20. *Ibid.*

21. See Shah, *The Way of the Sufi, Caravan of Dreams,* and *The Exploits of the Incomparable Mulla Nasrudin.*

22. K. Walker, *A Study of Gurdjieff's Teachings* (London: Jonathan Cape, 1957).

23. Arthur Deikman, "Experimental Meditation," *Journal of Nervous and Mental Disease*, 136 (1963) 329-43. Reprinted in Tart, Supra, Ch. 2, note 4. Also, A. Deikman, "Implications of Experimentally Produced Contemplative Meditation," *Journal of Nervous and Mental Disease*, 142 (1966): 101-116.

24. Quoted in Deikman, "Deautomatization and the Mystic Experience."

25. Y. N. Sokolov, *Perception and the Conditioned Reflex* (New York: Macmillan Co., 1963).

26. Anand, Chhina, and Singh, *op. cit.*

27. Kasamatsu and Hirai, *op. cit.*

28. Quoted in Kapleau, *op. cit.*

29. Rahula, *op. cit.*

30. Spielberg, *op. cit.*

31. Walker, *op. cit.*

32. Rafael Lefort, *The Teachers of Gurdjieff* (London: Gollancz, 1966).

33. K. Hulme, *Undiscovered Country* (Boston: Atlantic–Little, Brown, 1966).

34. Shah, *The Way of the Sufi.*

35. Doug Robinson, "The Climber as Visionary," *Ascent, The Sierra Club Mountaineering Journal*, Vol. 64, No. 3, May 1969.

36 Henry Miller, *Sexus* (Paris: Obelisk Press, 1949); also, Lawrence Durrell, ed., *The Henry Miller Reader* (New York: New Directions, 1959).

37. Henry Miller, *The World of Sex*, rev. ed. (Paris: Olympia Press, 1957); also, Durrell, *op. cit.*

38. Henry Miller, "Creative Death: An Essay," *The Henry Miller Reader*, ed. Lawrence Durrell.

39. See Shah, *The Sufis.*

40. For a full discussion of the science of electrical brain stimulation, see Jose Delgado, *Physical Control of the Mind: Toward a Psychocivilized Society* (New York: Harper & Row, 1969).

41. For experiments related to these considerations, *see* W. Wyrwicka and M. B. Sterman, "Instrumental Conditioning of Sensorimotor Cortex EEG Spradles in the Walking Cat," *Physiology and Behavior*, 3, (1968): 703-707.

CHAPTER 3.

1. Dalal and Barber, *op. cit.*
2. K. M. Bykov and W. H. Gantt, *The Cerebral Cortex and the Internal Organs* (New York: Chemical Publishing Co., 1957).
3. Akishige, *op. cit.*
4. Bykov and Gantt, *op. cit.*
5. *Ibid.*
6. Neal Miller, "Learning of Visceral and Glandular Responses," *Science*, 163 (1969): 434-45. Leo DiCara, "Learning in the Autonomic Nervous System," *Scientific American*, January 1970, pp. 30-39.
7. J. Kamiya, "Conscious Control of Brain Waves," *Psychology Today*, 1 (1968): 57-60.
8. Miller, *op. cit.*; Wyrwicka and Sterman, *op. cit.*
9. D. P. Nowlis and J. Kamiya, "The Control of Electroencephalographic Alpha Rhythms through Auditory Feedback and the Associated Mental Activity," *Psychophysiology*, Vol. 6, No. 4, (1970), pp. 476-84; D. P. Nowlis and H. MacDonald, "Rapidly Developed Control of EEG Alpha Rhythms Through Feedback Training with Reports of Associated Mental Activities" (Stanford, Calif.: Stanford University Press, 1970).

10. Elmer Green, Reported at the Conference on Voluntary Control of Consciousness, Council Grove, 1970.

11. B. T. Engel and S. P. Hansen, "Operant Conditioning of Heart Rate Slowing," *Psychophysiology*, 3 (1966): 176-87.

12. D. Shapiro, B. Tursky, E. Gershon, and M. Stein, "Effects of Feedback Reinforcement on the Control of Human Systolic Blood Pressure," *Science* 163 (1969): 588-90.

13. Green, *op. cit.*

14. B. T. Engel, Presentation at the Society for Psychophysiology Research, Monterey, Calif., 1969.

15. Thomas H. Budzynski, Johann Stoyva, and Charles Adler, Feedback-Induced Muscle Relaxation: Application to Tension Headaches," *Journal of Behavioral Therapy and Experimental Psychiatry*, 1 (1970): 205-211.

16. Walker, *op. cit.*

17. H. Benson, "Yoga for Drug Abuse," *The New England Journal of Medicine*, 281 (1969): 1133.

18. A brief description is: Hallaj, "Hypnotherapeutic Techniques in a Central European Community," in R. W. Davidson, *Documents on Contemporary Dervish Communities* (London: Hoopoe Ltd., 1966).

19. K. C. Hamner, "Experimental Evidence for the Biological Clock," in J. T. Fraser, ed., *The Voices of Time* (New York: George Braziller, 1966).

20. E. E. Von Bount, M. D. Shepherd, J. R. Wall, W. F. Ganong, and M. T. Clegg, "Penetration of Light into the Brain of Mammals," *Annals of the New York Academy of Sciences*, 117 (1964): 217-24.

21. A. H. Frey, "Behavioral Biophysics," *Psychological Bulletin*, 63 (1965): 322-37.

22. *Ibid.*

Bibliography

This is a selected bibliography of introductory reading on some of the matters discussed in this book.

Behanan, Koovor T. *Yoga: A Scientific Evaluation*. New York: Dover Publications, 1939.

Journal of Transpersonal Psychology (P.O. Box 4437, Stanford, Calif. 94305) carries very good articles on the psychology of mysticism, meditation, physiological feedback, and related matters. The Spring 1970 issue contains an excellent bibliography on meditation, compiled by Beverly Timmons.

Kapleau, Philip, ed. *The Three Pillars of Zen: Teaching, Practice, Enlightenment*. Boston: Beacon Press, 1965.

Lefort, Raphael. *The Teachers of Gurdjieff*. London: Gollancz, 1966.

Luce, Gay. *Time in The Body*. New York: Pantheon Books, 1971.

Ouspensky, P. D. *In Search of the Miraculous*. New York: Harcourt, Brace & World, 1949.

Rahula, Walpola. *What the Buddha Taught*. New York: Grove Press, 1959.

Shah, Idries. *The Sufis*. Garden City, N.Y.: Doubleday & Company, 1964.

————. *Tales of the Dervishes: Teaching Stories of the Sufi Masters over the Past Thousand Years*. London: Jonathan Cape, 1967.

Spiegelberg, Frederic. *Spiritual Practices of India*. New York: Citadel Press, 1962.

Taimni, I. K. *The Science of Yoga*. Adyar, Madras: Theosophical Publishing House, 1965.

Tart, Charles. *Altered States of Consciousness*. New York: John Wiley & Sons, 1969. (Many of the articles referred to in the Notes are reprinted in this book. An excellent source book.)

Underhill, Evelyne. *Practical Mysticism*. London: J. M. Dent & Sons, 1914.

Walker, Kenneth. *A Study of Gurdjieff's Teaching*. London: Jonathan Cape, 1957.